Notes from the deep end:

Nurturing courage in an often shallow world

Nancy Boxer

PSĪpress

Perfectly Scientific Press
www.perfscipress.com

Perfectly Scientific Press
3754 SE Knight St.
Portland, OR 97202

First Perfectly Scientific Press paperback edition: October 2011.
Perfectly Scientific Press paperback ISBN: 978-1-935638-16-2

Cover art by Julia Canright.

Cover image by Lukasz Drapiewski.

Visit our website at www.psipress.com

Printed in the United States of America.
9 8 7 6 5 4 3 2 1 0

Contents

Part 1: Stories and musings

Chapter 1: Definition of courage

Stranded on a mountaintop

↓

Heroes on the therapist's couch

↓

Courage eludes the wordsmiths

↓

Pinning down courage in order to get tenure

↓

Blushingly modest heroes

Eighteen of us stood together on a high meadow in the remote Marble Mountains of Northern California. We were camping at a site many miles from the nearest town. If anyone needed tampons, chocolate, or emergency medical care, it would be a long downhill trek to our cars, followed by two and a half hours spent bumping over rutted dirt roads to civilization. We were enjoying mild July weather during the day, but at night the temperatures plunged into the 30s at our elevation. The lake we swam in—those who were hearty or foolish enough to attempt it—was bone-cracking cold, fed by snowmelt and so frigid that when you jumped in, you thought your heart might stop beating. After five days of camping with no showers, of hiking and fishing and foraging for dinner, we were tired, stronger than ever, exhilarated. All of us smelled alike, man or woman, child or adult.

We had come for a week of camping and to pick up some wilderness survival skills. All of us were physically fit, but this experience pushed us up against our boundaries every day. We were city folks or suburbanites, here for an adventure which, the brochure promised, would absolutely change our lives. We had already learned to build fires without matches, stalk wild animals without them noticing us, set up emergency shelters, and feast on edible plants. Now they were leading us at dusk up the mountain. Tim, our leader, a solid rock of a man, made us take off our shoes and tie them to our belts. He and his helpers blindfolded us, turned us around several times to disorient us, and told us to find our way down the mountain, back to camp.

"See ya down there," he said casually, a sharp note of glee in his voice. Our only clue homeward would be the occasional thump of a hand drum from another helper stationed by the campfire, tending the stew we'd get to feast on, assuming we managed to find the way back.

None of us was prepared for this. If we could see, we'd be looking at each other searching for clues. "What the...?" a man complained, incredulous. "Oh my God," someone moaned. "I don't know if I can do it. I might fall off this damn mountain and break a leg or something."

"You'll come get us if we get lost?" a girl worried.

One of the helpers goaded us. "You'll never make it," he cackled. I recognized his voice; he was the scrawny, pimple-faced teen, the one usually sent off to chop wood, haul water, or scrub the pots. "Ha, ha! You'll be stuck up here all night with just the bears for company!"

Bears. We had seen their traces—scat underneath a berry bush, claw marks on trees. A flash of fear zipped through me, raising every hair along my arms and neck. What did I get myself into? I could get mauled or eaten. I could fall off a cliff and break a lot of bones; I could freeze to death in the night if I didn't make it back to camp. My sleeping bag, laid out on a patch of bumpy ground which only that morning I'd been complaining about, suddenly seemed like an immense luxury.

My son was there with me, but for once I wasn't worrying about him. He'd probably do fine in his usual competent fashion. He, after all, had earned brown belts in two different styles of karate; in spite of his thinness and his glasses, other kids in the schoolyard always looked to him for help when one of the class bullies came their way. At 14 he already had a physical presence that was resilient and strong. Unlike me, who tended to bump into things, or drop and break them. A klutz, my mother had long ago termed me, and I never managed to outgrow that designation.

It is a mother's nature to worry, of course, but my oldest son was always saying, with equal parts affection and exasperation, "Mom, I'm fine. You worry about yourself."

Usually I worried anyway, but this one time I thought maybe I'd take his advice.

I was in this particular kind of trouble because of him, after all. The week was part of my program for raising my sons to be modern American men: capable and sensitive as well as strong. Their father was a loner by nature, a workaholic with pale skin and a chronic, asthmatic cough. His idea of manhood was to throw himself for long hours at his computer projects and eventually astonish everyone with his results.

This was fine and good, but I wanted my sons to have a wider set of roles to choose from for the time they became men themselves. Maybe including some level of physical prowess, carpentry, sports, or the ability to hang out with friends and bond with people. So we tried various boy-friendly activities— softball and soccer, martial arts, a bow-and-arrow making workshop. My younger son took up piano with a noted jazz musician. My older son started going camping, sometimes with family, sometimes with friends.

That's how we found ourselves blindfolded on this mountain. And yes, he was having the time of his young life, though this was not exactly my ideal vacation. A nice walk on the beach somewhere, a quiet place to curl up with a book, a visit with my girlfriends. . . I sighed. I could have been getting a nice massage somewhere. Yet there are things a mother will do for her kids that she would do for no one else, not for herself or her spouse, not for her sister or best friend. Sometimes a mom's got to do what a mom's got to do. I wanted this week to be a growth experience for him; as for me, mostly I was hoping not to embarrass either one of us.

This new challenge had been sprung on us unexpectedly—a good thing too, or several of us might have chickened out, discovering a sudden generous urge to help Dave the cook set up tomorrow's breakfast. I spent several moments wondering if it was too late to volunteer. I could be setting out the cereal bowls right now. I could be gathering wild blackberries for our pancakes.

But, no, that would be entirely too obvious. And with the outsized sensitivity of a young teen, my son would feel horribly embarrassed. I would have to tough it out somehow. If I died in the process, at least it would not be a shameful death.

Oh, shut up, that's enough melodrama, I scolded myself. Just set yourself going, one foot before the other.

"You can do it," I encouraged the worried kid. And if she could do it, I'd probably manage too, even if it took all night to find my way.

Making the trek barefoot turned out to be a good idea, though tough on the soles of the feet. Without shoes, you could pick up a lot of useful information. You could sense the slope of the mountain more easily without shoes, and each time the slope changed, it would tell you something else. The mountain should trend generally downhill to the campsite, but there was a plateau before that, with a river running through it, then a slight uphill stretch, a flattish meadow, and then the campfire area. So as the angle of the ground changed, I could keep track on my internal map of the progress made.

With bare feet, you could feel the soil texture too—the ground was rocky with a lot of brushy groundcover here, but there would be trees, plants and more brush all the way to the river. Near the river, the texture would change— colder, damper, sandier, followed by wet silt along the river bottom, then more hilly scree until we came to the grassy knoll of the campground.

Use your feet to feel the way, I reminded myself. They taught us how to feel for stones before putting weight on each foot, something we'd been practicing all week. That was how you stalked animals and walked silently through the forest; that way you wouldn't lose your balance and go sprawling, and barefoot now, it would keep you from cutting your feet too badly. Use your arms to feel the way before you, pushing aside branches before they whip you in the face. A blindfold is not much protection; you don't want to lose an eye.

But most of all, keep listening. Hone in on that sound beacon. Sometimes it seems like you're going the right way but you could easily get turned around. Only that drum beat is there to call you home.

Firmly suppressing my own doubts, I set forward. I had cheated, slightly, keeping approximate track of where north was while they turned me three and a half times around. I turned back to what I thought was north and set off gingerly, wincing as a sharp stone cut into my foot. Most of the others sounded like they were going off to my right, though I heard a few to the left. The group was largely younger than me and older than my son, mostly in their twenties or early thirties, and they quickly left me behind. I didn't mind coming nearly last on almost every adventure we took. Coming back at all was a plus, I figured.

I kept going forward now, though the slope seemed gentler than it should be. Suddenly I couldn't hear the drum where I thought it should be. Oh well. Tracking more to the right, I corrected my direction, listening again for that beacon. Several times I stopped altogether, waiting for the beat. What were they teaching us with this exercise anyway, patience? Endurance? They would probably say, "You'll never panic again, even if you're lost and it's too dark to see." Or, "Nothing like having your sight snatched away to open up all your other senses."

Thwap! My arms were tired, and I'd let them slip downward, no longer protecting my face. I'd have one painful bruise, and dozens of small red scratches. Ouch. I was caught in a patch of brambles and they hooked, painfully, into my clothing and skin. Going forward would lock me in even worse. I'd have to backtrack and find some way around this prickly mass. Afterward I'd have to listen and reposition myself, orienting toward the drum as best I could. My feet were cold and aching, bearing all my weight against rock and small stones without any cushion. But there was no choice; I had to keep moving forward. That, or stay all night, cold and miserable, in one spot, and be rescued tomorrow.

Probably. If they had any mercy at all.

Eventually I reached the cold running stream, which washed the aches away. Or pushed them to a new level of frozen agony; you could probably think of it either way. Still, there was progress. I felt a small thrill of satisfaction. I could do this; it wasn't actually all that hard!

The feeling lasted for all of maybe 20 seconds, until I stumbled, another of my fellow campers falling on me from above. It was one of the guys, though I couldn't tell which one by voice alone. He apparently lost his balance on the crest of the riverbank and reached out to steady himself, finding my arm and dragging me down with him. Fortunately the stream was only a foot deep at that point, a blessing because it was cold enough to shock us. Any deeper at that temperature and we might have been overwhelmed. He used my shoulder to pull himself up before apologizing and scrambling ahead of me.

By now the beat of the drum was stronger. Still I got confused and tracked too far left, blushing when I heard a muffled giggle from one of the campers who'd already made it. They were supposed to watch silently until we found our way back and someone came to remove the blindfold from our eyes. Yet I'd made it, safe and sound. Surprisingly, I was not the last. Two others were still out there somewhere, and I could relax and watch them the rest of the way.

Holding a warm cup of tea between my hands, letting its steam revive my frozen face, I had the privilege of seeing my son bring up the rear, completely unconcerned with speed. He gracefully placed one foot down, using the other to feel his way, cocking his head to listen for the calling sound, making his way up the bank towards warmth.

After dinner, the young man who'd tumbled both of us into the river, approached me gingerly, almost in tears.

"I feel so bad," he said, shame-faced. "I knocked you down and then blasted ahead. I could have waited for you. I could have reached out and given you a hand after I climbed up the bank. I am such a jerk!"

"You could have done that," I agreed, but decided to let him off the hook. He was young, after all, in his early twenties. Certainly when I was his age I needed all the mercy and forgiveness I could find. "That's okay," I assured him. "I did fine on my own. I'm actually pretty proud that I did it all by myself."

"Oh, in that case," he mumbled. But he lingered. Apparently something was still missing. A benediction, perhaps, or some other note of grace.

"Isn't it great how everyone did something they never thought they could?" I asked him. "We were all pretty brave."

"Yeah, I guess," he said . "That was amazing."

We smiled and nodded companionably, both feeling satisfied. A star winked overhead. The fire crackled, and sparks shot upward into the inky sky. The moon shone brightly while a gentle breeze ruffled through the pine and cedar boughs, and an owl hooted somewhere off in the distance.

⋆   ⋆   ⋆

This book tells a series of stories about courage and other aspects of something we might call depth of character. Some are about people who did things they never thought they could manage; others are about people trained to do the tough work most of us prefer not to. A few are about people who were tempted away from their purpose and didn't manage to stay the course. Many of these stories and musings emerged from my research into the convoluted subject of courage. Some have come from my own life, or the lives of clients in my former therapy practice (with names and other identifying information obscured to preserve their privacy).

I do not regard myself as particularly brave. In signing up for the wilderness experience, my son and I set ourselves up for something more challenging than a week in Hawaii, but less than a trek up Everest. Intrepid, perhaps, but a little short of outright heroism. I have my moments, but they are more often in the realm of emotional courage; beyond that there are plenty of things that give me pause. Yet I've been fortunate to have the most amazing life, one which has offered many opportunities to study and appreciate the depths in others.

My career has swung wildly from one high point to another. I've been a state bureaucrat and a wily entrepreneur, a Harvard-trained economist and a meditation teacher leading groups into the redwood forests for rites of passage or personal growth. I have rocked newborns to soothe their post-birth distress, sung hymns and rubbed the feet of the dying to sweeten their passage beyond. I've raised some great kids and loved many wonderful people, and taught every level of student from pre-school through college and beyond. I have worked in high-rise offices and on chaotic construction sites, sat cross-legged with kindergartners and negotiated nose-to-nose with Fortune 500 executives. I've been moderately rich, deeply broke, and everything in between. With so much experience to draw on, I am a lucky woman indeed.

For many years I was a therapist, and clients came to my quiet corner office, mired in emotional quicksand. Their job was to take a deep breath and relate what was bothering them. My job was to ask questions, to help them understand why those things bothered them and how they might change things so they no longer did. In their ongoing struggles there would often be a sticking point. They might understand what was going on, but couldn't imagine how to shift things. They lacked, at least for the moment, both vision and courage—two things, as we shall see later in this book, that often go hand in hand.

At some point, understanding a bad situation creates so much discomfort that change becomes inevitable. Who can look upon an obvious mess and not roll up their sleeves to begin straightening it out? It is easier to ignore chaos when it stays tidily behind a fog of misunderstanding or denial. For the most part, the more my clients began to understand their entanglements, the more clearly they could see how their values conflicted with them, and the more their natural frustration and indignation would begin to fuel their engines to pull them out of the mire. At that point my job sometimes shifted; I might have to steady them, slow them down long enough so they could plan their new direction, find allies, or plot a course through the minefields to some safer zone ahead.

Over time I began to see these processes as personal journeys of courage, with a beginning, middle and an end. The beginning was a long prelude of trouble, of trial and error, sometimes featuring a bumbling series of attempts at change. The middle period would be quieter, a time of contemplation—some of it in my office, some on their own. This was a time when they could take a step back. They were beginning to realize the shape, weight, depth, and texture of the problem, gathering the courage to tackle it, reaching out for resources or support. Then finally the endings, where they went on the offensive, often requiring more than one foray against whatever held them back.

No matter what the outcome, these efforts brought them into a new stage of life. My clients were courageous in their personal battles. Their bravery may have lasted only a brief time, or may have lit up the rest of their lives. Either way they deserve to be celebrated, for they righted some wrong and made the world a better place, even if only a tiny bit better.

After the attack on the World Trade Center, I began reading accounts of heroes on another stage altogether. The varieties of heroism were astonishing and inspiring, but most interesting to me were parallels between the firefighters on September 11 and my own clients. It was fascinating to see how many types of courage there were in the world—and yet how much they had in common.

Most people, I began to see, want to make the world a better place, but many are afraid to confront the people or forces making it worse. Or they let themselves turn their gaze away, focused on their own problems and pursuits. This is not a phenomenon restricted to those troubled enough to seek therapy; it is widespread. It doesn't matter whether the confrontation comes in the form of a physical threat, an emotional tangle, or a moral wrong of some kind; it is uncomfortably common for people to stand on the sidelines or walk away.

And yet some brave souls persist, shoving their fears and pleasures aside and moving courageously forward in spite of it all. What kind of people are these, I wanted to know. How can I be more like them myself? Why is courage the rarest of traits, so out of the ordinary that when we see it, like spotting a member of an endangered species, it is noteworthy enough to remember for years, to broadcast it in magazines and around the internet? How can we make it more common so that it's less like an asteroid strike and more like a cherished family recipe that you can pull out and cook up whenever you want? Are there teachable skills, creatable conditions involved so that more of us can learn to be as good, as enduring, as stout-hearted, generous, and brave?

Because if there are, it seems worth it to figure out how.

⋆   ⋆   ⋆

One of the things I soon discovered in my research is that courage may indeed be a capacity that can be encouraged, though not many parents, teachers, or mentors in our culture seem to do so intentionally.[1] Conditions that reward or stimulate brave or enduring, stick-your-neck-out behavior can be amped up; conditions that interfere can be redirected or changed. People can teach themselves, or be taught, to deepen their being even in a world that more often encourages shallow behavior. In recent years, research from many fields—social psychology, biology and neuroscience, among others—is beginning to grapple with the question of what courage is, why some display it and others don't, and how we can systematically promote it. This book is an effort to synthesize those findings in a way that is accessible, helpful, and inspiring.

In the process of writing, I came to realize how little we prepare ourselves and our children to hang in there in tough times, to fight through bad situations to make things better for all. In the modern world, we train people largely in two dimensions. Parents, for example, train their children to reach high—to grow, to move up in the world, to aim for high incomes and high status, to do well in their careers and their own parenting, to set up better lives than the parents managed for themselves. This dimension of height allows us to mature and attain some level of status in the world.

In contrast, schools, the media, and our peers encourage us to broaden our understandings, to learn about the greater world around us, and to understand the things that may not affect us directly, but touch on our lives indirectly. This gives us our breadth, the second dimension, which creates some degree of context and comfort for us within the world as it is.

But depth is a dimension we are rarely trained in. Each of us is born with a certain propensity for deepness and some develop it further. Often in our culture, though, we are encouraged to "shallow up" instead of deepening. There is an ambivalence towards heroes, who often make us feel uncomfortable, and toward any form of intense passion or commitment beyond their most shallow forms. "Be cool," people say, backing away from the intensity, and

---

[1]The Johnny Cash song *A Boy Named Sue* was a particularly notable exception, even in the fantasy land of song lyrics. The song describes a father who knew he wouldn't be around to toughen up his son, so he gave him a girl's name to force him to learn to fight and defend his honor.

when they are far enough away they start looking for the flaw that makes the hero human again, or the reason why the commitment should not involve them. "Take it easy," we are warned if we seem too driven to others. "Lighten up," perhaps, when the depth of our focus makes friends or family uneasy. Be shallow and let things lie as they are. Come to terms with the situation. Stay unattached. Learn from the circumstance if you want to, and adjust your expectations downward.

Courage often takes the opposite approach. Perhaps it is rare in our world because it cuts against the grain of a pervasive philosophy of adjusting and accepting what is. To have courage is to be deeper than most, to hang in there through tough times, to fight the wrongs and not let things lie as they are. Depth, the third dimension, is what allows us whatever staying power we have. Depth allows us to create and leave behind a legacy when we are gone. Courage, tenaciousness, endurance, generosity, love and connection to others in a meaningful way—all these are aspects of depth.

This, then, is a book largely about courage, about how to find or encourage it, and about making and honoring deep connections. Courage is not the only aspect of depth, but it is a major one, and touches on many other, related areas; it often coexists with love, connection, endurance, and so on. Thus whatever I figure out about how courage works might apply to these other areas too. I have chosen to explore this third dimension through the lens of courage; it is the part of the map that intrigues me the most. Other voyagers may explore the other aspects more fully.

And so this book is filled with stories of people who decided, implicitly or explicitly, to care deeply, who chose to put themselves at risk for some cause or community that mattered more to them than keeping their cool. Often I come back to the same few contexts—the firefighters on September 11, the civil rights activists of the early 1960s, the people who risked their lives to hide Jews from the Nazis during World War II—because they are so full of instructive moments, so accessible, so stirring to the soul. Their stories, along with others presented here, will help uncover what courage means, and what circumstances support or limit it. We examine how people act even when they are scared, what if feels like to be in the middle of a courageous moment, and what it means to do the right thing even if it isn't easy. Some of the examples are physical acts of bravery, others are emotional, psychological, or moral. All are illustrations that anyone can consider for guidance and his or her own understanding.

The last section sets out a series of exercises and challenges to build up and expand your own third dimension, allowing you to deepen, to be braver and more focused, and to hang in longer than you might have managed on your own.

This book is not designed to help shed pervasive anxiety or phobias, though people with such conditions may find a few useful and interesting ideas here. It is, instead, designed to inspire you to your own acts of bravery, to encourage you to find a passage towards them, arouse you to support others who are on their own paths.

You who are reading this book come to it looking for many different things. Some to be inspired, some to expand your universe, and some for instruction on how to proceed with the tasks ahead of you. There are several blank pages at the very end. I invite you to pick up a pen and keep it by your side. As you read along, take note of every idea that may be helpful for your own purposes, and jot it down on these pages. When you are done, you will have created your own action plan, a personalized instruction set for the future. Don't be shy; no one will be grading you. It is only yourself that you need to impress. Don't just sit there. Go get that pen—right now!

⋆   ⋆   ⋆

Courage, as Mark Twain wrote in one of his more somber moments, is not the absence of fear, but it may be a resistance to fear, or some sort of mastery over fear.

Fear, or its weaker cousins—anxiety, faint-heartedness, dithering, a tendency to back down—are old acquaintances for anyone who has ever been called on to step out and be brave. In a wry nod to this hard-won bit of experience, British politician Harold Wilson once described courage as the art of being the only one who knows you're scared to death.

Courage is a hard thing to pin down. To define it is a slippery effort, like trying to catch ice cubes in the rain. Supreme Court Justice Potter Stewart once sidestepped a similar dilemma when he refused to try defining the elusive concept of pornography. In his famous 1964 opinion in the obscenity case *Jacobellis v. Ohio*, he wrote that hardcore pornography was tough to define, but "I know it when I see it."

Courage is much the same. We admire it and cheer it on, though we don't always recognize it right away. Sometimes it appears to us as foolhardy or bull-headed until time has passed and a different perspective arrives. Most of us would love to consider ourselves brave when the circumstances call for it. Yet secretly we may suspect we might fall short. Who are the truly courageous among us? The boy defending his younger brother against a bully? The pedestrian who stops a litterbug from tossing a paper cup over his shoulder? The nurse who says she is merely doing her job when she walks into the contagious ward? The train engineer who stops doing his job if the train he drives is hauling innocent victims to a concentration camp?

While there is no single right answer, most would probably include the examples above. Still we have trouble defining courage, and any attempt to mold it into some easily definable shape leads to other related questions. What does it take to be a hero? What conditions support courage, and which ones discourage it? What is the relationship between courage, bravery and heroism?

Throughout this book we will use the words "courage" and "bravery" almost interchangeably. Psychologists Cynthia Pury and Cooper Woodard have defined courage as the intentional pursuit of a worthy goal, despite the perception of personal threat or risk, and despite an uncertain outcome. In other words, the person's intention is important, the goal must be non-trivial, there must be some risk involved that the brave will ignore or work around, and the person acts even if their actions may come to nothing in the end.

Most definitions of either bravery or courage describe character (states of being), instead of action (states of doing). There are heroes who are not courageous—sports heroes, for example, may not be—but for most purposes throughout this book we will assume that a hero is a person who demonstrates courage. Heroism itself refers to actual behavior, courageous behavior.

$$\star \qquad \star \qquad \star$$

What does it take to be a hero? Lt. E. F. Andrews of the U.S. Navy described the demolition experts under his command during World War II, a team that often had to painstakingly disconnect land mines and clear away obstacles while enemy bullets and mortars were exploding all around them. The men who stuck it out had a great deal of skill, courage, perseverance, dedication, and a substantial tolerance for discomfort and pain. They liked the challenge of their assignment. They were willing to dedicate themselves to a mission, even as they recognized and accepted its dangers. They knew it was no game they were playing, but a serious and risky endeavor. And still they were willing to do it. The sense of working with others on the same team may have helped. Andrews thought of his guys as hero material, almost to a man. Apparently the military establishment agreed with him, for his team won a host of medals for their contributions during the war. Most people who have thought about what it takes to be a hero describe some combination of these necessary conditions, shared by most of Andrews' demolition crew:

- **Bravery or courage**, which can be physical (as with the firefighters entering a blazing inferno) or moral (embodied by people such as civil rights leaders Diane Nash and her friends, Dr. Martin Luther King, Jr., Gandhi). To have courage does not mean a person is fearless; many brave acts are committed by people who afterward confess they were deeply frightened, but acted regardless of their fears.

- A **moral commitment to some larger purpose**, and the willingness to live with the costs associated with that commitment. This commitment might be to justice, freedom, fairness, saving children, helping the poor or the needy, to a religion promising eternal salvation, or to a set of laws uniting people under fair and just conditions. Such a sense of dedication lends patience, perseverance, and endurance to the person's efforts to help advance that purpose.

- **Love or commitment to some larger community**—a spouse, a family, a team of colleagues, or a nation that the person will go to great lengths to protect or help, a community of people that they are loath to let down. Gandhi worked to free India; Dr. King worked to secure respect and civil rights for African Americans. The patriots who fought in the American Revolution exemplify this, as did the doctors and nurses who risked their lives treating patients during the highly contagious flu epidemic of 1918–1919.

- **A history of reaching out to help others**. Those who help others tend to do so again and again in life. Those who don't help others can be encouraged to emerge from the shell they live in, and learn to respond more generously and bravely.

- **Faith or a strong commitment to some set of ethics** that the person tries to live by.

- **Willingness to take responsibility**, including the risks or costs associated with it, even if the person is reluctant to do so at first.

- **Generosity, character, or greatness of soul** demonstrated by acting on behalf of a cause or a community larger than the person's immediate circle, and at some cost—emotional, economic, loss of status, risk to safety, and so on. Beyond this, heroes tend not to complain, brag about their efforts, or look for credit or some other form of payback. It is common to see the deeper heroes modestly claim they were doing what anyone else would do, if they only had the opportunity to do so.

- **Confidence in the expertise, the training, or the allies** they gather while heading into danger. Often people persisting through a tough project will need to lean on someone or something; these aids can be an enormous boost to any major effort. The tougher the effort, the more essential the training and the allies are to fall back upon.

- A sense that there is **little to lose**—that something needs to be done, and they may as well do it because otherwise some terrible fate is impending. This situational bottom line has been reported by civil rights leaders, by slaves escaping to freedom, and people active during World War II at the Warsaw Ghetto uprisings and the few concentration camps (Treblinka, Sobibor and Auschwitz) where the victims managed to pull off a mass revolt.

- **Extraordinary achievement**—they have succeeded at something that most people wouldn't try. This is not a characteristic of the heroes themselves, but of the situations we deem heroic, after the fact. Had these particular people tried and failed, they might be regarded as well-meaning but misguided, maybe even foolish—though the thoughtful among us may call those idealists heroes, even if they did not succeed, because of the effort they made.

These are the most frequently cited characteristics, and the more of these qualities someone has, the more likely they will be known as a hero to others. Do all of these need to be present? Not necessarily. Remember the 1992 movie

Hero? Dustin Hoffman played a small time criminal, almost an anti-hero, a weaseling, complaining con man who could not be depended upon to help even his own family. And yet there he was, on the spot, when a plane crashed. Against type he rescued all the passengers before the plane exploded. He had this single heroic moment in spite of a lifetime of avoiding helping anyone but himself. Another man, seemingly more the heroic type, stepped forward to claim the role, and for a while the world believed him because he looked and sounded believably heroic. This other character, played by Andy Garcia, appeared to have the character, the largeness of soul expected of a hero. But he was not the man at the scene, and if he were, who knew whether he would have had the courage to walk into the wreck and pull people out? Perhaps Garcia's character would have called 911, still a good deed, but not in the same category as risking his life to actually save them.

$\star$ $\star$ $\star$

Success deserves its own lengthy discussion, of which this is a bare beginning. We do not hear of the many efforts which do not succeed; what we hear about are the rare successes. Courageous attempts of any sort are infrequent enough, and the vast majority of them fail, usually through bad luck, insufficient strength, poorly thought out plans of attack, insufficient resources, or insufficient endurance to overcome what may be a well-entrenched or overwhelming danger. Our own minds may offer rationales to quit the effort—family responsibilities, a task that is outside our domain, the lack of time or training. Friends offer temptations ("Don't be such a bore, come have a drink with us") or solace ("At least you tried"). The question is not "Who is brave," since most of us have that capacity to some extent or another. Better we should ask, "What sustains the brave impulse, and how can we help it succeed in the hard tasks it sets up for us?"

Bravery is a good thing and deserves recognition and honor in its own right. But for obvious reasons the biggest honors go to those who manage to pull together some necessary combination of vision, nerve, endurance, strategy, logistics, and whatever else is necessary to right the wrong, to snatch the child from the jaws of the wolf, to stand up to bullies and put a stop to their abuse. Most of this book is devoted to investigating the components of that necessary combination, all so we can help ourselves and each other cover the distance between the spot we stand on and that shimmering goal in the distance. Swimming lessons, you might say, for time spent moving in and out of the deep end.

⋆   ⋆   ⋆

Other traits are not necessarily part of heroism, yet they often seem to coincide.

Honesty, for example. People with moral courage and strong commitments to larger causes tend to be deeply honest people. Any deviation from honesty (or any perception that they have been dishonest) tends to draw away from their heroic image. Indeed, their original deep honesty in the face of the dishonest behavior, the justifications and hypocrisies of the social or legal structure that the hero fought against, or the justifications of others who would not risk themselves in the face of danger, may be part of what allowed or even forced the hero to act heroically in the first place.

It is interesting to probe why lying makes us uneasy in the context of heroism. Honoring the truth and sticking to it, two traits we associate with honest people—neither of these has any obvious connection with the ability to shut out the fears and chaos of the world in order to go forth into an inferno to save some hapless soul. And yet somehow they are connected.

When we catch someone in an outright lie, it casts doubt on everything they are, and everything they've done. Their being and their behavior both, and every word we've ever heard them say, all become quicksand instead of the solid foundation we have been grasping for, to support whatever comes along next. Lies erode the integrity of whatever we thought we knew about them, like finding termites eating away at the floor joists, and no one knows how deep they've gone.

Courage, in contrast, seems almost the opposite. In the presence of courage, what is superficial or false is stripped away. Gone, the justifications; fallen by the wayside, any excuse or hesitation. Courage walks us into the deep heart of what should be. It rights the wrongs, and in doing so, helps us restore children to their parents, and brings people safely back to the lives they were bound for. Courage restores dignity to the abused. With courage we can align the world that is with the world as it ought to be.

Lies have no place there. Lies are part of what get burned away in the process. Thus, to hear lies told—lies about the awesome event where courage came on stage and took a bow—feels like an abomination. Lies told by anyone make us curl a lip and turn away in disgust. But lies told by a person whom we admire for their bravery—even lies told about something else altogether—raise doubts that the speaker is the same one who actually did that amazing deed.

Lies make us uneasy when planted anywhere near hallowed ground.

Of course any categorical statement made will have its exceptions. Battalion Commander Richard Picciotto, one of the firefighters at the World Trade Center on September 11, 2001, reports an ethical dilemma that snagged his mission to clear the North Tower of people on that fateful day.

Picciotto had to beg and plead to get assigned to the towers in the chaos of the first plane's impact. When he finally arrived, even the most experienced of firefighters were overwhelmed by the scope of this unprecedented disaster. Nobody knew how to take charge, and though the Fire Department of New York had schooled him well in following the hierarchy of command, the guys in charge were standing around looking at each other, completely baffled. Nothing of this scope had ever happened before, no building this large had experienced such a calamity, overwhelming their their equipment; none of the usual procedures were appropriate.

Picciotto finally assigned himself a job he knew would be useful and necessary, told the commander what he was up to, and started up the tower. He ran up the stairs, organizing efforts on each floor to clear the civilians out of the possible danger zones and point them in the direction of safety. The firefighters could at least do that, even if they couldn't contain the fire. But as he was banging on doors and directing people toward the stairway exits, he kept running into well-intentioned people waiting for their friends or associates, hoping to ensure they got out safely too. They didn't want to leave behind the handicapped, the older office workers, the people with asthma, choking to catch their breath. Others were rescue workers like him, who had been commanded to wait for a partner or a battalion leader, yet the people they were waiting for might have been called away to face a bigger emergency on another floor. Rescue workers waiting around were rescue workers who weren't doing anyone any good; civilians who were waiting around tended to get in the way of everyone else.

Either way, he was increasingly certain that everyone who could go down was already gone. There may have been a few holdouts who were unwilling to leave their desks, or people who were unconscious, yet the rescuers had already taken extensive steps to clear the building, and by that point the building looked like it might collapse. Yes, his mission was to save lives, and those waiting might be of some help, but the balancing concern was, at what cost? Did it make sense to linger, looking for one or two possible strays if it cost dozens of additional lives?

No, it did not, Picciotto decided, but he didn't have time to argue the point with each and every one of those good-hearted people. Instead he resorted to a series of quick lies. He asked each one to describe who they were waiting for, and then pretended to remember seeing them go down a different stairway a few minutes earlier. Under normal conditions, lying may be questionable from an ethical point of view, but in retrospect he felt no qualms about misleading them; his deceit probably saved several dozen lives. His mission, after all, was to save as many as he could.

⋆   ⋆   ⋆

Kindness, compassion and empathy are other traits that often go together with heroic behavior. A stereotype of the hero might include someone with a lot of musculature, like a strong man barreling into an inferno to save a small child, for example. Yet surely some basic warm feeling for the welfare of those who cannot save themselves is part of what motivates such behavior. And if that same brave man or woman were to turn around and do something nasty or underhanded, it would be hard for others to keep holding them in high esteem. General George Patton was a military hero who liberated dozens of communities across Europe during World War II, but when he publicly slapped one of his soldiers in the face, he lost face himself. No more top ten for him; this one ugly incident slid him off the charts. Few babies were named after him; almost nobody afterwards wanted their kids to be like him.

Charisma, leadership, and the ability to command respect or love and affection from others also go along with heroism. For without some measure of these, we would have no movements, only the isolated actions of individuals, and social change would come about only through a kind of random, Brownian-motion phenomenon.

Intelligence is to some extent a prerequisite for courageous action, though it may come in the form of emotional or moral intelligence as well as intellectual intelligence. Indeed, in Nechama Tec's study of 189 Christians who risked their lives to rescue Jews in Nazi-occupied Poland, she found that members of the intellectual class of society (defined primarily as professionals and artists) were more likely than any other to hide victims from their persecutors.

Psychologists Kowalski and Pury found that courageous actions call for other significant character strengths, particularly **hope or optimism** (why risk yourself if you see it as a fool's errand?), **kindness towards others**, **persistence** to continue in the face of obstacles, **integrity** (being true to one's own values), and bravery.

Independent thinking may be another such trait. For most people, a clear-headed assessment of the personal risks resulting from acting in the face of danger will outweigh the personal benefits of such actions, and they are therefore likely to avoid risking themselves. This is one key reason why courage is such a rare thing: the conscious or unconscious weighing makes most of us too cautious to react unless we or our loved ones are directly threatened. We pick our battles carefully and often that means we don't enter into battle at all.

Yet some people are more willing to put themselves at risk. Thinking for themselves, they may assess the risks and rewards differently and come up with another set of answers. Some of these people may be risk-takers by nature. They may be less afraid of risk, pain, or loss. They may be younger and thus less experienced with weighing their options rationally. Others may have less at stake—younger people, the poor, outsiders—either because they have few responsibilities, or have established little position or status as yet. Some may feel they are less important than the ones they defend. Bodyguards, Secret Service agents, and other such professionals may be good examples of this form of motivation, as well as people with low self-esteem, or those with strong family hierarchies (younger siblings, younger generations, or the parents of young children may sacrifice themselves more readily for the others).

Bravery may have additional motives that deserve some consideration here. Some people may be ambitious and eager to make a name for themselves. Others may be more morally sensitive and thus more easily offended by injustice. There may be some who are more emotionally open to bonds connecting them with larger groups of people; some with higher levels of empathy may feel more strongly the pain of others. Others may feel guilty about their own past actions or privileged status, and hope their efforts will exonerate them.

Diversity, they say, is a strength for a society. Diverse ways of calculating risk is one of the ways it is strengthened.

⋆   ⋆   ⋆

Some researchers distinguish between various kinds of heroes. One common categorization separates those who exhibit **physical courage**, risking life and limb in a crisis, from those with a more **moral courage**. Physically courageous people include firefighters, policemen, military, and the people who run out to grab the kid who chased a ball into the street and fearlessly step in front of a moving vehicle. Morally courageous people fight injustice, dishonesty, wrongdoings in many forms, and, although they may occasionally face physical threats, their targets are not the fires and guns but the institutions that hold others prisoner. Clearly some brave souls blur the line, fitting into both categories.

A third type of courage is what we might call **psychological courage**, when a person does something they are scared to do, like killing a spider themselves instead of asking someone else to take care of it. We might term these moments of triumph 'personal growth.' Such instances of psychological courage do not necessarily make the world a better place, but for the person who has just succeeded in such a moment, their internal world has definitely improved. And some instances of psychological courage may prepare a person to take on bigger moments of physical or moral courage.

Other types of courage are sometimes distinguished. Social psychologists in Germany, for example, speak of **civil courage**, brave behavior accompanied by anger and indignation that intends to enforce or redefine societal and ethical norms without worrying about the social costs. Scolding, for example, when you see someone jaywalking, or intervening when you see a big man hitting a small woman. In Brazil and Germany, civil courage is enforced by law; if a crime is committed either in public or privately, bystanders are obliged to act by alerting the authorities or directly stepping in to stop the conflict. Such nationwide expectations are designed to empower the timid and strengthen the social contract for people to watch out for each other.

Another common categorization separates the **one-time** courageous from the people who put themselves at risk on an **ongoing basis**. Often heroism is an almost instantaneous reaction to a situation. When a self-described "average guy" named Dale Sayler pulled an unconscious driver from a vehicle which was about to be hit by an oncoming train, he felt it was a high point in an otherwise bland life.

Alternatively, courage might be displayed through a well-thought-out series of actions taking place over days, months, or years. The former slave Harriet Tubman is an example from the 1800s. She stood up against her owner on numerous occasions before escaping into a precarious freedom. Having left her master behind, she set up her base in Philadelphia, in a state where slaveholding had long been illegal. However, the law of the land said that escaped slaves had to be returned to their masters, even if they'd made it to a free territory; anyone who harbored them was committing a felony.

Thus she lived always with the risk of being caught as a fugitive and turned over to the bounty hunters to be returned to slavery. Yet she could not be content with merely having secured her own independence. She carried her defiance several steps further, saving her money and darting off on expeditions to steal away additional slaves, transporting them across state lines to freedom.

The one-shot wonders are heroes for a moment, and, bless their hearts, we are all better off for their efforts. But the continuing determination of a Dr. Martin Luther King, a Harriet Tubman, or a Gandhi is almost unfathomable to most of us: admirable, and yet a little bit frightening at the same time. Imagine what it might be like to devote so much of your time, your money, your energy, and your heart to such a cause; imagine too what it might be like to be married to, or a child of, someone so fiercely on the trail of a goal only barely related to you and your own welfare.

Consider the exhaustion, the moral resolve, the unstinting sacrifices made by such people. Then, when you hear of their imperfections, stack those tiny weeds on the scale against the fruit of their other efforts before deciding how to judge them.

★   ★   ★

A third categorization is suggested by Dr. Frank Farley, who distinguishes longitudinally between the long-term, **cause-based heroes** such as King, Nelson Mandela, or Gandhi; the **career heroes** who take employment in risky sectors, the police force, the fire department, the military, emergency workers of many kinds; and those "**situational heroes**" who rise from a more everyday life to respond to a particular crisis.

Situational heroes, like the man who rushes into a burning building to save a baby, the mother who lifts up the car which is crushing her child, or the person who swims out to grab a struggling swimmer—these people tend to respond without thought to a crisis. They seem to go into some sort of meditative trance, acting on autopilot in the heat of the moment. Intensely focused on the target, they function in the crisis by blocking out all outside distractions, seeing only the next step ahead of them and possibly the next one after that. Fueled by adrenaline, they do what is needed until the crisis is over. They may be bewildered afterwards as to how they managed it.

Some people run away from danger, but the ones who can rise to the occasion are different. There is some evidence that a small segment of the population tends to run towards danger instead of away. Often these people were raised with a strong emphasis on helping others. They may have firm religious beliefs or some of the other traits discussed above; they may additionally have a tendency toward impulsive behavior. Also they may have previous training or experience—first aid, military training or other emergency response experience—which lends a sense of confidence they can draw on in times of crisis, as well as a sense of "of course I have to volunteer; this is what I am."

Canadian Stephen Knight has twice won Canada's Medal of Bravery for heroism, once for diving into a frigid river to save a suicidal teenage girl after she jumped from a bridge, the other for intervening at a nightclub when a bouncer was surrounded by three rowdy patrons and repeatedly stabbed. True, Knight is a trained career policeman, but he was off-duty at the nightclub, and could have called for help or considered some safer option. But, he says modestly, "It's who I am, the kind of person who gets involved." Not only is he someone who gets involved, he's the kind of guy who reflexively gets involved without thinking twice about it.

He was alerted to the girl jumping off the bridge when a passerby called the emergency line for help. Several police cars were dispatched but there was some confusion about which bridge she'd jumped from. By the time Knight's car arrived, her coat was all that was visible under the rapidly-forming ice on the surface of the river. So he jumped out of the car, ran across the street, slid down the snowy embankment, and plunged into the water, not even bothering to shed his gun, body armor, or his heavy coat and shoes. He was up to his neck in freezing water, but he held her securely with one hand, holding onto a rock with the other until three more policemen arrived to pull them out. Afterwards, he was happy to pass the credit to his fellow officers. "What they did was amazing," he said.

Career heroes rarely think of themselves as heroic, though some may enjoy the perks of being seen that way by the rest of the world. More often they are fueled by a general desire to help people, or by the inclination to help those who cannot help themselves. But when they talk with trusted friends and colleagues, they generally regard what they do more modestly as "just doing my job."

Outside the realm of their bravery, heroes are everyday people. They struggle with their checkbooks, their personal lives, and the little or big temptations and crises that define life for all of us. Yet if they make mistakes and falter, there may be an excruciating level of attention drawn to it, an unfortunate irony which punishes those who have already done so much for the rest of us.

Yet even in this ironic, post-industrial world, we continue to need our heroes. We may even need them more than ever before.

We need them to help us escape the dilemmas we've created for ourselves, in an increasingly confined world, a world where we are eager to point the blame anywhere but on ourselves, and sue or punish people for even small omissions or bad judgment calls. We need our heroes so we can measure ourselves against them, and use their examples to pull ourselves higher. We need to believe in them so that we can have hope for ourselves going forward, and the world we will someday give to our children.

We need to believe. Oh, how we need to believe.

Chapter 2: Physical and moral courage

"Prayer indeed is good, but while calling on the gods, a man should himself lend a hand."—Hippocrates

Nashville gnashes its teeth at little Diane Nash

↓

Who's got the edge, men or women?

↓

The teen that saved Denmark's dignity

↓

Talking down the terrorists

A flash of pure terror burned a shadow across her heart. If she could have snuck away, if she could have left without anyone seeing her, she might have done it. If she could disappear in a puff of smoke without causing shame to herself or letting down the others... But she was bound to stick with the plan they decided on, bound to, after spending months together with all her friends, male and female, working towards this very moment. Loyalty kept her striding forward, her back straight, an intent frown on her face, into the nameless but palpable danger that would descend on them at any moment. It seemed crazy, but the others, though they were older and stronger, were all looking to her, meek little Diane Nash of politely middle-class Chicago. Somehow they'd gotten the idea that she was fearless and could lead them, she whose hands were damp with sweat, whose heart just skipped another beat. She who was clenching her jaw so that no one would see her trembling.

Yet to go ahead and do the terrifying thing was exactly what she and her friends decided they had to do. Sitting on the stool and asking the waitress to bring them lunch at a whites-only lunch counter; boarding and riding a bus through the segregated South—these mundane actions were four-alarm dangers for black Americans in 1959. People had gotten beaten or lynched for less.

But it was exactly because they were unsafe that it was the right thing for these young college students to do. It was all very simple, when you looked at it that way. They would test the unwritten rules of racism, push at them *en masse* until they broke. They would take on this task and do it gladly, while they were young and strong, so that the older, the weaker, and the children would be able to follow in safety, and never face these unfair and humiliating restrictions again.

Diane Nash was one of the most beautiful women on campus, a mere freshman with curly hair, pale skin, and unusual blue eyes. Many wondered why she bothered herself with the struggle for black rights in the South. She could easily pass for white; she could have readily enjoyed a carefree sorority life at her prestigious college, snagged a wealthy husband and enjoyed an upper-class black lifestyle in the easier North. But that was not the life Nash chose. She was a deep person by nature, looking to lead a deeper life.

Growing up in the 1940s and 50s in an urban Northern city, she took for granted a certain level of civility, so when she arrived in Nashville, the more overt racism there was an unexpected shock. A date took her to the Tennessee State Fair one day, and when she went to wash her hands and the women's room door had a sign saying "Whites Only," it felt like she'd been slapped in the face. The man she was with didn't even flinch. "Over there," someone indicated, and the smaller, dirtier room with the "Colored" on the door hit her as a deep insult. All the more perturbing was that no one else even seemed surprised. That's what they expected, living in the American South in the era of Eisenhower and Elvis; it was one small part of the ongoing stream of casual insults against black Americans.

Suddenly she began to notice discrimination everywhere. Downtown, black people carried bagged lunches to eat, sitting outside on the grass because no restaurant, not even the department stores they shopped at, would serve them food at their lunch counters, as if whites might be soiled if they sat too near. When her dates took her to the movies, they couldn't casually walk inside; people of color had to use a rickety side staircase to a separate balcony over the main audience, where you couldn't get up close to see. Her friends moved to the edge of the sidewalk if a white person was passing. She was warned: "call them sir or ma'am; don't ever look them in the face; they'll take it as an insult and swear at you or hit you. And certainly don't expect the white police force or the legal system to back you up, no matter the merits of your complaint." There was no telling how strongly they'd react, but you could bet good money the outcome would not favor the black person registering a grievance.

The system was more than she could stomach, and when she began to hear about the on-campus workshops on Gandhi-style nonviolent protest being led by a graduate student named James Lawson, she began attending immediately.

The workshops, beginning in the fall of 1959, provoked plenty of discussion among her new friends, and they began looking for ways to put their new ideas into practice somewhere. They came up with a number of ideas, but where, Lawson asked, would the black citizens of Nashville welcome their help? It turned out that the women in the community hated being barred from eating while they were shopping at the stores downtown. They hated having to shop while hungry in order to get all their errands done. They hated having to pretend to their young children that the food was no good there, or that they had better food at home, or that they weren't really hungry, rather than be humiliatingly turned away.

Lawson's students didn't know what they would encounter, but they had their first real-world target now. They would aim themselves at integrating the lunch counters of Nashville.

As they began discussing ways and means, the students began to feel the first flutters of fear. Who knew if they'd be beaten, even thrown into jail? Who knew if they would disappear from the jail in the middle of the night, never to be heard from again? It had happened in Southern towns before. They weren't merely walking into danger, they knew; they were planning to do something even harder. They would walk into danger and refuse to protect themselves against it. That would violate their new but strongly felt principles. Christian love, some called it; others spoke of Gandhi's teachings on non-violence. They wouldn't raise a hand to deflect the blows, and they certainly would not raise a fist to fight back. They trained themselves to fall down and assume a fetal position, or to use their bodies to shield others under attack. That was as far as they could go and still stay true to the teachings they held. But Gandhi, for all his greatness, might not keep them safe. They would surely be hurt, and some might die, though many of them were not even legally adults yet.

Their numbers might have been small, but their ideas were not. Their teacher, James Lawson, knew in his heart that if his group of activists took a stand, the authorities would react against them, and the world would begin to take notice.

People would begin to recognize that they were acting on behalf of those who needed help, and it would be harder and harder for those others to sit on the sidelines. Some would feel moved enough, or guilty enough, to join in. This was the power of action, in a time and place where the laws and customs were unjust. Jesus and Gandhi had both followed this route, letting the forces of unjust authority become their unwitting recruiting agents for the cause.

These young students were the advance guard and might pay the heaviest price. But Lawson believed that others would pick up the cause in their wake and help carry it forward. Their work would, without question, make a difference. If not today, then tomorrow; if not tomorrow, then next week or next month or next year.

He turned out to be right.

★   ★   ★

Physical courage—the image that comes to mind is a muscular guy, quick-thinking and decisive, staunch in emergencies. Are most of our brave heroes male? The tendency to take physical risks seems to be stronger among men than women. The Carnegie Hero Fund[2], for example, has given out more than nine thousand medals since 1904, recognizing people who voluntarily risk their lives to save the life of another. The kind of courage they reward is primarily physical courage, and about 90% of their honors have been awarded to men. One might argue that institutional prejudices toward men have skewed these awards, or that cultural influence once kept women from being strong or brave, but the tendency for men to dominate these awards still exists, even in recent times.

Yet women are well-represented in the ranks of heroes when it comes to other forms of courage. Living organ donors, for example: people who donate one of their kidneys to a family member or even a stranger, risking themselves not only during the operation itself, but for the rest of their lives in the event that disease or accidents might degrade the functioning of their sole remaining kidney, are approximately 60% female. And those who helped save Jews during the Holocaust, according to some studies, were more often women than men.

Heroes can come from either sex, from any social group, income level, or walk of life. This is true no matter whether we are speaking of physical, moral,

---

[2]See online at www.carnegiehero.org.

psychological, or civic courage, regardless of whether we look at one-time, career, or long-term heroes, cause-based or situational. Heroism casts its brand on very few of us, but apart from these gross generalizations, it leaves no easily discerned pattern. What this means is that you cannot predict in advance who is likely to be brave and who is not. Any of us is a possible candidate, at least once in our lives.

17-year-old Arne Sejr lived in a small town in Denmark when the German Army invaded during World War II. He was outraged, watching his fellow townsmen greeting the invaders in a friendly manner, and he determined not to join them. Instead he went home to type up 25 copies of a bold call to non-violent resistance:

"TEN COMMANDMENTS FOR DANES

1. You must not go to work in Germany and Norway.
2. You shall do a bad job for the Germans.
3. You shall work slowly for the Germans.
4. You shall destroy important machines and tools.
5. You shall destroy everything that may be of benefit to the Germans.
6. You shall delay all transport.
7. You shall boycott German and Italian films and papers.
8. You must not shop at Nazis' stores.
9. You shall treat traitors for what they are worth.
10. You shall protect anyone chased by the Germans.

Join the struggle for the freedom of Denmark!"

Sejr took his list around and stuffed it into the mailboxes of the most prominent people in town. Not all of them agreed, but at least some did. The manifesto was recopied and passed from hand to hand to people all around the country. For a country too small to resist the military might of its aggressive neighbor, Denmark managed to retain its dignity through the war. Granted more lenient terms than most occupied countries, the democratically elected officials who were allowed to stay in place discouraged violent resistance because they feared a backlash from German authorities. But many individual Danes continued acting on their own.

In contrast to other occupied countries, the Danes managed to save more than 90% of their small Jewish population by ferrying them to safety in neutral Sweden, and small cadres of resisters around the country set up various effective underground publications, spy networks, and acts of sabotage. One group of teenage schoolboys in the town of Aalborg, calling themselves the Churchill Club, managed to commit 25 acts of sabotage before their arrest; eventually they escaped and continued to resist.

"The hottest places in hell are reserved for those who in a period of moral crisis maintain their neutrality," President John F. Kennedy once said. The Rev. Dr. Martin Luther King, Jr. liked the statement so much that he picked it up and repeated it. It's a pithy statement, inspiring enough that others picked it up, quoting either Kennedy or King, and used it for encouragement, especially when calling people to assert themselves on some tough but important moral issue.

Statements and maxims can be useful in pulling people off the fence. Testimonies from close personal associates are also helpful. References to deeply held beliefs work well too.

Not surprisingly, one of the highest participation rates of any group defying the Nazis during World War II occurred among the small groups of Quakers living in occupied Germany and Holland. A typical Sunday Sabbath service in the Quaker Meetinghouse is light on singing, but heavy on prayerful, meditative silence. At their service, members of the Society of Friends invite divine inspiration to touch them directly; sometimes people stand up and share with the congregation whatever words or visions come to them. It is by allowing this sacred space and time, some argue, where your mind is quiet, where any moral failings can creep in and tap you on the shoulder, reminding you of what you ought to be doing. This regular prayerful practice keeps modern Quakers in the forefront of many movements of conscience. Modern Quakers consider all people equal in God's eyes, and minister to any they see in need.

Almost every single wartime member of the Berlin-based Society of Friends hid or sheltered threatened Jews. Some took on additional hazardous responsibilities such as sending food packages to internees, scavenging identity papers for refugees, or running a day school for non-Aryan children who were otherwise banned from schools. The tiny Quaker community in Holland, only 43 members at its peak, also actively sheltered Jews, educated Jewish children at the Friends' school in Eerde, and fed Jewish children in hiding. Rescue work at both centers were greatly aided by fundraising, lobbying and other efforts of the Philadelphia- and London-based Friends Societies before, during, and after the war.

Too bad there were so few of them; too bad so many others were willing to maintain their neutrality.

★   ★   ★

George Mitchell, the former senator from Maine, was drafted by President Clinton in 1995 as his Special Envoy to Northern Ireland, where he headed negotiations putting an end to decades of violence. Plenty of others had tried to establish peace before him, but it took a special combination of physical and moral courage, leadership, craftiness, stubbornness, and persistence to get the job done. Not that he deserves all the credit; as we discuss below, it should rightly be shared among him and a small group of sometimes fearful, sometimes vainglorious politicians and activists on both sides of the conflict.

Senator Mitchell had only a tenuous connection to Ireland. Descended from Irish ancestors on his father's side, his immediate family felt little allegiance to the old country. His father had been adopted as an infant by a Lebanese couple and raised with no sense of Irish culture. Yet Mitchell accepted the challenge and began to feel a growing tie as he labored through protracted negotiations for the sake of peace.

There were many periods when the peace process threatened to break down, turning the Emerald Isle bloody red. Mitchell had to make a number of personal sacrifices: he lived with the constant fear that someone might bomb them for their temerity in working towards peace, in addition to the strains and stresses and long, often thankless hours. He was forced to forgo visiting his dying brother back in the States, and even missed the funeral; he couldn't comfort his wife when she miscarried their child for fear the negotiations would break down without his calming presence.

Called "the most sainted man to visit Ulster since St. Patrick himself," Mitchell spent months wrestling with ten fractious parties over the rules of negotiating and the agenda for the talks. One of the problems dogging their progress was that many of the people involved had more motivation to posture and storm out of meetings than to do the hard work of setting aside their grievances and learning to respect each other. They were, after all, politicians, and most of them had been voted to high positions in their parties promising to take a strong stance against their long-hated enemies.

At one point, after hours of wrangling over such deeply significant issues as to whether the chairman should have "due regard" for the parties' views or just "regard," Mitchell wryly confessed, "I didn't know the answer before... and I didn't know it after." Yet he hung in there, crafting the Mitchell Principles in 1996, six ground rules on which all parties had to agree on in order to participate in the talks, primarily requiring them to put down their weapons and abide by a peaceful resolution of their disagreements. It took another two years to work out the peace agreement itself. Finally, on Good Friday, 1998, all the major parties were ready to sit down and sign the historic Belfast Agreement, which was overwhelmingly approved by voters a month later.

The three-year process called on incredible reserves of tact, intelligence, and patience, though there were times when Mitchell's steel came through and he had to make tough demands on each of the parties at the table. Asked later to reflect on the process, he concluded, "This sounds corny, but it's not. If you really believe what you're doing, you can tolerate almost anything in order to achieve it."

In wrapping up the agreement that put an end to the decades of guerrilla warfare and terrorism, including the murder of 3,600 people from both sides, Mitchell praised the other participants in the talks. Many of them had been terrorists themselves. The father of one of the participants was shot and killed while planning to murder another man; the intended victim survived and was now negotiating from the other side of the table. Indeed, the hatred and rivalries were so entrenched and incestuous that it was hard to believe at the start of the talks that there was any hope for peace.

Still, they eventually agreed to terms, and some even apologized to the victims and their families in the process. Overall the Belfast Agreement benefitted all sides, though each had some difficulty persuading their constituents.

And that, ultimately, is what counted. They were willing to give up the private and secret use of arms, and instead used the public forums of debate and compromise. Let us wish Mitchell another success as he negotiates between the Israelis and the Palestinians for peace in the Middle East.

"It doesn't take courage to shoot a policeman in the back of the head," Mitchell often told the warring parties, "or to murder an unarmed taxi driver. What takes courage is to compete in the arena of democracy, where the tools are persuasion, fairness, and common decency."

Where you might not always get your own way, and you have to be gracious enough to let someone else occasionally get theirs.

Chapter 3: Vision and values

"In whatever arena of life one may meet the challenge of courage, whatever may be the sacrifices he faces if he follows his conscience— the loss of his friends, his fortune, his contentment, even the esteem of his fellow men—each man must decide for himself the course he will follow. The stories of past courage can define that ingredient— they can teach, they can offer hope, they can provide inspiration. But they cannot supply courage itself. For this, each man must look into his own soul."—John F. Kennedy, *Profiles in Courage.*

Donning Superman's cape

↓

Bugs Bunny's carrot vision

↓

The value of values

↓

Even Joisey produces heroes

Vision, which can come in the form of a heroic imagination, is an important ingredient for setting out into scary territory. A person who cannot see himself acting bravely under any circumstance is unlikely to step beyond his normal capacities in a time of danger or challenge. Conversely, a person reared on heroic sagas, stories of martyrs, folk tales and myths, or true life adventures may identify enough with these heroes to offer themselves up in a crisis. An ancient Greek raised on stories from the Odyssey might have faced danger and thought "What would Ulysses do," following whatever inspiration came into his head from that. A modern child might say to himself, "I'll be like Spiderman, swinging into action." Others might ask, "What would Jesus do," "How would Mother Teresa handle this," or, among the Communist Chinese of the 1960s, "Learn from Comrade Feng."

Those who live with such heroic universes inside their heads may occasionally dream about facing physical or social risks, and wrestle in their own minds with hypothetical crises and decide how they would handle them. They may consider the risks and costs to themselves and decide they would be willing (at least in theory!) to shoulder them if necessary. Thus when a threat arises, they may be more prepared than most. They may be secretly delighted to have a chance to square their shoulders, roll up their sleeves and don their (metaphorical) Superman capes. To some extent they model themselves on these heroic prototypes and strive towards those higher standards of behavior and achievement. They may not entirely succeed, but they are more likely to at least give it a shot, in spite of personal risk or cost.

We might call these people idealists, for they live with ideals well-entrenched in their minds. They may be more likely than most to be brave when called on. But they are not the only ones capable of courage.

$\star$ $\star$ $\star$

Most of us have an inner sense of the range of activities we are willing or able to pursue—what kind of physical activities we will or won't do, when we will be completely truthful and when we might shade the truth or outright lie, for whom we will go out of the way and to what extent, and so on. This range grows out of our personal histories and is often restricted to what we have actually done, with perhaps a small margin beyond that. A runner who has run a mile in 4 minutes and twenty seconds sees themselves as capable of doing it again, given the right conditions; perhaps they might think they could run a 4:10 minute mile if they push it. Yet in an emergency, a runner who grew up on comic books or cartoons might place an image of Speedy Gonzales or The Flash in the forefront of his or her mind, kind of like Bugs Bunny's vision of a carrot perpetually dangling in front of his eyes, and do even better than a four minute mile. Or they may just run full out, hoping or praying for speed, or dropping any thought beyond, "Go, go, go!"

For some, the sense of their own range may be smaller than their actual history allows. Sometimes people feel that their capabilities have diminished. They may think, "I could do that then, but I could never do it now." They may even block out the memory of earlier successes if those memories contradict who they think they have become.

Yet a larger range of possibilities may come to people through inspirational stories. Reading about Mother Teresa feeding the poor may inspire someone to donate to a food bank or help out at a soup kitchen for the first time. Vision may also come through more abstract forms—a general commitment to helping the poor, a sense that God is directing your movements—or in a narrower form—an immediate, one-time image of the thing that needs to be done.

Vision can be as simple as a mental picture—a kindly smile, a helping hand pulling a drowning man out of the mire, an older brother or grandmother who was always there in times of trouble. Inspiration may come from observing somebody else's example—a parent, a community leader—or through a benign form of peer pressure, for example when a group of people set out to do community service work, perhaps a congregation, a group from work, or a volunteer organization. Children collecting funds for some good cause often inspire their parents to reach out and help in places they otherwise wouldn't.

Inspiration sometimes derives from a story, a metaphor, an ideal, a biography which influences a person to become more like the hero. It may come in the form of an inner voice, an intuition that you should follow some particular path opening up ahead. "Follow your curiosity," advised author/activist Frances Moore Lappé. Her own willingness to pursue answers to the questions she began asking led her to write *Diet for a Small Planet*, the ground-breaking book that sparked a small but committed movement to eat lower on the food chain, and to start a number of pro-democracy agricultural initiatives around the world. Intuition, role models, positive ideals—any of these can offer vision where others, lacking such inspiration, might not know what to do.

27-year-old Tony Gouverneur, a long-haul truck driver from Texas, was driving his rig through the desert of San Bernardino County, California in March of 2002 when he came upon an auto accident, the car already engulfed in flames. He'd been thinking all day about his grandfather, who'd just been hospitalized, a man he loved and admired for his quiet generosity towards others. Tony pulled over and shut off the engine. Other motorists had already stopped, but no one was brave enough to try to help.

But Tony was different. He came from a family with a history of reaching out to help others. His parents served refreshments to rescue workers at a fire across the street from their house; his grandfather regularly helped people till their gardens if they were too old or weak to do it themselves. His own life was saved when his twin brother donated a kidney to him.

With the image of his grandfather in the back of his mind, he walked over to the burning vehicle. The driver was already dead, but he could see a shadow moving in the passenger seat of the other car. He hurried over and found a woman still buckled in, dazed from the crash. Tony broke the window, reaching in to open the door. He pulled her out to safety, suffering minor burns himself.

Tony's vision was a personal one. James Lawson, the theological student who established workshops to train civil rights activists for the sit-ins and lunch-counter integration actions in the early 1960s, had a more universal vision driving him:

> "When you are a child of God, you try to imitate Jesus, in the midst of evil. That means if someone slaps you on the one cheek, you turn the other cheek, which is an act of resistance. It means that you do not only love your neighbor, but you recognize that even the enemy has a spark of God in them, has been made in the image of God and therefore needs to be treated as you, yourself, want to be treated."

Mohandas Gandhi, possibly one of the deepest men of the last century, wrote in his autobiography that he based all his work on a kind of search for truth.

> "My experiments in the spiritual field [are where] I have derived such power as I possess for working in the political field. What I have been striving and pining to achieve is self-realization, to see God face to face, to attain *Moksha*[3]. All my ventures in the political field are directed to this same end, for only truth is the sovereign principle. Truth must be my beacon, my shield and buckler. Though this path is straight and narrow and sharp as the razor's edge, for me it has been the quickest and easiest. Even my Himalayan blunders[4] have seemed trifling to me because I have kept strictly to this path. For the path has saved me from coming to grief, and I have gone forward according to my light."

Devising strategies in his decades-long fight for the rights of men, Gandhi would meditate, sometimes for days, even months before proposing a plan of action. He would often risk many lives, usually astounding and frightening the timid and conventional, but through all this his certainty of conviction allowed him to continue. The strategy was certainly effective: throughout his

---

[3]Translated as freedom from the endless reincarnation cycle of birth and death, perhaps the state of *nirvana*.

[4]This was Gandhi being modest.

career he won victories for the underclass in South Africa and shamed the British Empire into ceding sovereignty to the vast nation of India.

The parable of the Good Samaritan offers a vision which has inspired countless acts of charity and courage ever since it was first taught. In one notable example beginning in 1935, Pastor Heinrich Grüber of Berlin started establishing escape routes to smuggle as many threatened Jews as he could out of Nazi-run Germany. Adolf Eichmann, the architect of the Holocaust, got wind of his activities and called Grüber into his office to try to stop him. The pastor refused to back down in spite of threats and sanctions.

"No one is going to thank you for your efforts," Eichmann warned.

The churchman reminded the senior SS officer about the biblical tale of the altruist who would not ignore a man who was beaten, robbed, and left lying in the streets. "The Lord whom I alone obey, tells me, 'Go thou and do likewise,' " Grüber explained. He eventually spent time in two concentration camps, but survived the war, and was called to testify at Eichmann's war crimes trial in 1961.

The story of the Good Samaritan has inspired countless people to perform acts of charity and courage, even outside the Christian faiths. Written in the Gospel of Luke, the story begins when a man asks Jesus what he has to do in order to merit eternal life. Jesus responds by asking him to recall what the Torah taught.

"Love the Lord with all your heart, soul, strength, and mind," the man answered. "Also, love your neighbor as yourself." But, he asked, who was his neighbor?

Jesus responded indirectly, telling a story of a man traveling from Jerusalem who fell into the hands of robbers. The thugs stripped and beat him, leaving him half dead by the roadside. Two men, one of them a priest, passed by without stopping to help. But a third man passing took pity on the victim, though he was a Samaritan, from a sect with a history of troubled relations with the Jews. Still this kind soul bandaged the victim and lifted him onto his donkey, leading him to an inn for the night. The next morning the Samaritan left money with the innkeeper to continue looking after the victim's wounds.

Jesus asked his follower which of these was a neighbor to the man who was felled by the thieves. He could have indicated either of the first two passers-by, who were Jews and fellow countrymen. Instead he answered, "The one who had mercy on him." The true neighbor was the one who affiliated himself with him, who took time out to care.

"Go and do likewise," Jesus advised, and many since then have attempted to follow his teaching.

⋆　　⋆　　⋆

Many of those who risked their lives helping the persecuted during World War II did so out of strong religious faith or convictions. Unfortunately, too many high religious authorities failed to offer leadership. People looked to the Vatican to condemn Catholic members of the Nazi party for their unholy acquiescence with evil. The Allied nations among others pressured the Pope to take a moral stance. But Pope Pius XII did little to discourage the mass murder of millions. He even stated in 1941 that the Nazi doctrines did not conflict with Catholic theology. To what extent he actively aided the Nazi's efforts or discouraged them indirectly is a matter of debate even today. But there were many individual nuns and priests who deliberately hid children, sheltered refugees on a temporary basis, and offered food or clothing to those in dire straits.

In one unusual example, roughly 300 Jews were saved by the devout Catholics in the Italian city of Assisi, the birthplace of St. Francis. One of these havens developed the ironic reputation of being the only convent in the world to enjoy a kosher kitchen.

Religious faith did not necessarily mean the brave person accepted Jews as equals. Zofia Kossak, one of the founders of the wartime Catholic organization Zegota which helped save hundreds of Polish Jews, was a notorious anti-Semite. Kossak stated on several occasions throughout the war that the feelings of Catholic Poles towards Jews had not softened. Yet she felt strongly that their ambivalence did not free them from the responsibility of condemning the slaughter.

"We do not wish to be Pilates," she said, referring to Pontius Pilate, Roman governor of Judea during the time of Jesus, who supposedly presided over Jesus' trial and handed him over for crucifixion. "We protest from the depths of our hearts, which are encompassed with pity and indignation. God requires this protest from us, God who does not allow murder."

Two Protestant pastors, and most of the village of Chambon-sur-Lignon in southern France, helped as many as 5,000 Jews escape to safety across the mountains in Switzerland. Thousands were saved by efforts such as these, yet millions more were murdered as most citizens looked the other way. There is a famous quote attributed to the German Protestant minister Martin Niemoeller, who ultimately spent seven years in the Sachsenhausen and Dachau concentration camps, much of it in solitary confinement. It eloquently illustrates the pervasive dynamic of apathy, and why it can be so dangerous, not just for the initial victims but for everyone around:

> "When the Nazis attacked the Communists, he was a little uneasy, but, after all, he was not a Communist, and so he did nothing; and then they attacked the Socialists, and he was a little uneasier, but, still, he was not a Socialist, and he did nothing; and then the schools, the press, the Jews, and so on, and he was always uneasier, but still he did nothing. And then they attacked the Church, and he was a Churchman, and he did something—but then it was too late."[5]

★   ★   ★

Mary Dyer was an intense and spiritual woman living in Puritan-run Boston a few centuries ago. If she had lived in recent times, with her temperament she might have become a born-again Christian and spread the good news to everyone she met. Or she might have traveled to India or Tibet, studied in an ashram and come back to teach yoga and meditation. Those roads were not open to her in the 1600s. Instead, like other seekers, she found her way to the new, and in those days considered radical, sect called the Quakers (the Society of Friends). And when she returned to Boston, where she had once lived, but left because of differences in religious interpretation, she felt it was her mission to spread the faith that was so precious to her.

But colonial Boston was a hotbed of religious fundamentalism of a different stripe, and was deeply intolerant of other faiths. The local authorities were

---

[5]This quote comes from Milton Mayer's book, *They Thought They Were Free: The Germans, 1933-45* (Chicago: Univ. of Chicago Press, 1955, 1966), p. 168, and is generally attributed to Niemoeller. There is some controversy about Niemoeller's exact remarks, which were not documented at the time, and many slight variations are floating around on the internet. A good analysis of these remarks is available on University of California (Santa Barbara) Professor Harold Marcuse's website at http://www.history.ucsb.edu/faculty/marcuse/niem.htm.

not at all tempted by the opportunities she preached about. They clapped her in jail the day she arrived, holding her until she could be forcibly transported back to her family in the more tolerant colony of Rhode Island, to the south. But Dyer was not discouraged by her initial lack of success. A few weeks later she was back, evangelizing on the streets of Boston, and was thrown into prison again, this time sentenced to death.

Along with two other Quakers, she was marched to the hanging tree, the three of them holding hands cheerfully, as if going to a party. The executioner tied her skirts around her ankles lest she flash the Puritans a forbidden peek. The two men had already been hanged, and they were getting ready to do the same to Dyer when word came that she was reprieved. She came down from the scaffold promising the crowd she was prepared to suffer as her brethren had done unless Massachusetts Colony repealed its wicked laws against the Quakers.

After a few months spent recuperating with family and friends, Mary felt called again to resume harassing the Puritans. In May of 1660 she was back in Boston, where they immediately threw her in prison. Ignoring her husband's pleadings, the Governor himself sentenced her to death. The following morning she was marched a mile to the gallows, accompanied by a drummer. This was necessary, they thought, to drown out any further attempts she might make to convert the masses.

At the gallows people were urging her to climb down the ladder and repent. She declined.

Cynics might joke that the third time was the charm; realists might call Mary Dyer a misguided fool. Idealists could argue that she did what she felt was right, what her conscience told her to do, spreading the word of God as she understood it, or pushing the narrow-minded to allow freedom for those who believed differently from themselves. Either cause was worthy; in either case she was hoping to rescue others from a horrible (and possibly everlasting) fate, even at great risk to herself.

Whether you view her as an annoying zealot or as a fighter for freedom of religion and speech, she was pushing for something that very few were willing to fight for, in England or the Americas, for a great many years to come. For that we can honor her memory and her strong sense of mission.

⋆   ⋆   ⋆

Fannie Lou Hamer, the irrepressible sharecropper-turned-activist of the Civil Rights Movement, was sustained during those dangerous years by her faith and her community—both church and extended family. One of the first blacks to try—and fail—to register to vote in the early 1960s in rural Sunflower County, Mississippi, she was fired from her job and evicted for her attempts to register and incite others to do the same. "I walked through the shadows of death," she said, referencing Psalm 23. "They shot sixteen times in the house—and it was a foot over the bed, where my head was—but that night I wasn't there....see what God can do?"

Strong spiritual and religious beliefs also firmed up abolitionist Harriet Tubman's resolve, one hundred years earlier. Standing only five feet tall and frequently disabled by seizures, she freed herself via a daring escape from her Maryland plantation in 1849, and made another thirteen trips into slave territory over the next decade, risking her new freedom in order to liberate another seventy slaves and to instruct dozens of others how they could find their own way north.

"I was conductor of the Underground Railroad for eight years," she told an audience at one of her lectures, "and I can say what most conductors can't say—I never ran my train off the track, and I never lost a passenger."

The very image of the Underground Railroad inspired slaves and free citizens to work together for the cause of freedom.

Born into slavery in the early 1800s, the teenaged Tubman was sent one day to the dry goods store for supplies. While she was there she spotted a slave in the process of running away. The man had the bad luck of being spotted hiding, by a white overseer who recognized him. Attempting to chase him down, the white man demanded help from Harriet, which she refused to give. Irate, he picked up a two pound weight from the scale on the store counter and threw it after the fleeing slave. It missed the runaway and hit Harriet instead, cracking her skull and sending her into a deep coma. She was brought, bleeding and unconscious, to her owner's house where she lay for two days. No medical care was provided for her.

She recovered, but from that time onward Tubman fell unconscious at random times during the day. She began experiencing inspirational visions and dreams. She committed herself to Christianity, and especially to Old Testament tales of deliverance. Sometimes she spoke about hearing instructions from God.

Married to a free black man, Harriet gave birth to nine children, but with a slave as their mother, they were born into slavery as well. Three daughters were taken from her and sold away. Three children stolen were three too many. When she heard rumors that her owner was planning to take her youngest son and sell him, she hid the boy with neighbors for a month. When the men finally came to the slave quarters looking for him, Tubman stood her ground. "First man that comes into my house, I will split his head open," she warned. The men fled, and that success may have been what gave her the first hint that she could defy the establishment in the name of freedom.

In 1849 she escaped, travelling at night along the Underground Railroad. The Railroad consisted of a lot of surreptitious movement through the countryside, hiding sometimes, running sometimes, often going without food or water, made feasible only through a series of stops ("stations") at an occasional sympathetic abolitionist household offering food, shelter, directions. It was a path to safety, but a dangerous one, leading her from slave-owning Maryland to free Philadelphia. Once there, she began the lonely and grueling task of working odd jobs, saving money and planning a return to retrieve her family. Over the years she liberated most of her relatives along with a greater number of unrelated slaves, teaching herself essential survival skills and strategies that stood her in good stead.

Most of her raids were made during the bitter cold of winter, to minimize the chance that some unfriendly white leaving a warm home on other errands would spot the runaways. The escapees often left on a Saturday night, since newspapers weren't published on Sunday and thus could not publicize the escape for at least another day, allowing them a head start toward safety. Tubman carried various small disguises with her—a bonnet, a live chicken—and a revolver to protect them from attacking dogs, slave catchers, or even to threaten any of her charges who might consider giving up and turning themselves in. If they did, they'd endanger the entire expedition, because they'd be forced to confess details that could lead the rest of them to capture, torture, imprisonment, or re-enslavement.

Over the years Tubman repeatedly chose a path of danger in order to free others from slavery. There were many moments that would have terrorized almost anyone else. Not Harriet, though. She was cautious but would not let fear disable her. "The good Lord knows where I am," she'd say stoutly. "He'll come find me when it's my time to go, and not one moment before."

⋆   ⋆   ⋆

Not all visions or values that inspire people to courage are religious in nature. Many visions may be idealistic but secular. People have fought for democracy, freedom and fairness; for their clans, countries, brothers and sisters. Values that rally people to acts of courage tend to be idealistic, not hate-filled; they tend to be based on love, affiliation, a sense of brotherhood, and respect for others. They tend to be positive, not negative, spurring people on to good deeds instead of personal gain.

What often rallies people to acts of physical courage is the need to prevent widespread disaster, or some form of vision about saving the helpless.

Values that rally people to acts of sustained moral courage tend to be based on a mission such as righting wrongs, fighting unfairness, extortion, prejudice, or helping the helpless or the weak. Helen Jacobs, a German woman who hid several Jews in her home during the Nazi years, said she did it "to defend democracy and to fight against discrimination—of which the Jews were the greatest victims."

Religious faith plus a sureness of his values kept civil rights activist John Lewis walking directly into the angry crowd that surrounded the bus on the Freedom Ride of 1961 as it pulled into Rock Hill, South Carolina. The violence had been getting worse the farther south they traveled from their starting point in Washington, D.C. Virginians had been moderately polite to them, and when the Riders challenged the segregationist tradition of separate and unequal facilities for blacks, there was little resistance. One man was arrested but the charges were dropped the next day. North Carolinans were fairly mild to them as well. But now they were in South Carolina, just 20 miles farther south, but seemingly an entirely different nation.

At each stop, one of the core group of activists was assigned to be first off the bus, to test the waters, so to speak. Lewis was the one assigned at the first stop in South Carolina, and he could see what was coming, but he was not about to back off. Lewis was a quiet, introspective man, a ministry student from a rural Alabama farming family. There was a mob waiting for them; they could see it as the bus pulled into the depot. Thirty sweaty, shouting, fist-raising young white men surged forward as Lewis and another man stepped off the bus, and the crowd immediately began swinging at them. Reporter David Halberstam depicted the scene as it was described to him:

"Even as Lewis saw it approach, he continued, absolutely without hesitation, to walk right into the surging mob. That was courage, [fellow activist Hank] Thomas remembered thinking, that was what it took to be a real leader in this struggle. John had gone forward without fear as if to accept his fate, the fate of being badly beaten and perhaps killed, the price to be paid for wanting his full rights...[Thomas] wondered if he had that same kind of courage. He wondered if he even had the courage to leave the bus, and then it struck him that sometimes you are more afraid not to do the things that you are afraid of than of actually doing them. In that moment, as he was supposed to get off the bus, Hank Thomas balanced his two fears and found that his fear of cowardice was even greater than his fear of being beaten. He steadied himself and got off the bus."

The key question, some of the Freedom Riders finally decided, was this: were they ready to shed blood if it came to that? Young as they were, would they be willing to die for the cause? If he died, Bernard Lafayette decided, at least it would be for his beliefs. Plenty of black people had died through the centuries, just for being black in America. None of those deaths did anyone any good. But if he died in Alabama on a ride set up to win their freedoms, at least it might do some good. The next day he and the other nineteen with him gave coordinator Diane Nash their hand-written wills to keep, just in case, along with sealed letters of instructions on what to do if they were killed.

★ ★ ★

Values that rally people to acts of psychological courage tend to be based on a need to overcome fears, reclaim dignity, react to bullying, a desire to reestablish the rightful order of the universe. This may include values such as fairness, or the need to help people you care about who can't help themselves.

Sometimes a vision forms to create something new. John Chapman, also known as Johnny Appleseed, had a vision of apple orchards growing throughout what was once frontier, and he proceeded to do something about it. Christopher Columbus' certainty that the world was circumnavigable may have been misguided, but after he spent two decades charting a path to prove it, his determined wanderlust led to one of the biggest population shifts in all of world history.

Some missions may seem completely mythological, or they may be eminently here-and-now. John Basilone was a twice-decorated hero in the Pacific theater of action during World War II. Trained as a machine gunner, he was in charge of two teams defending an airstrip from the Japanese invaders at Guadalcanal. Told by his superior officers that their mission was to hold the airstrip no matter what, that it was a crucial staging area for retaking the network of islands throughout the Pacific, Basilione was determined to hold his ground.

For the Japanese, the territory was equally critical—it was the first line of defense for the far-flung island nation. And their warriors were fully prepared to die for their mission.

In August of 1942, the Japanese Navy outmaneuvered the Americans, sinking four cruisers and routing every other Allied ship in the region. The U.S. Marines, who'd fought so hard to capture Guadalcanal, were isolated and abandoned. After several months of no re-supply, they were growing increasingly short on ammunition and food. The Japanese military forces, in contrast, were already heading out to reinforce their side.

The fighting, when it resumed, was savage and continued over many months. The Japanese made two major efforts to overrun the airstrip but were beaten back. The third and most desperate sortie came in late October, 1942. Just after midnight a Japanese army regiment ran screaming through the torrential rains, pitching their grenades into the Allied gun pits and foxholes. The Americans shot back, holding them off. But frighteningly enough, this gave the enemy a new offensive advantage: They piled the bodies of their own dead soldiers against the barbed wire fencing and used them to climb over onto the airfield.

Basilone was stationed right in the middle of the attack. As his 15 man crew was reduced to a mere three, he began roving back and forth between his two gun emplacements, firing one, running back and firing the other. One of the guns jammed and he had to set it straight in total darkness. When the guns got too hot, he pulled out his pistol and used that instead. Running out of ammunition, he crawled away and ran through enemy fire to bring back additional supplies. At one point he had to reposition the guns because the bodies lay piled too high in front to aim over them. The next day Marine officers counted 38 dead Japanese soldiers lying before Basilone's gun positions.

President Roosevelt himself recognized Basilone's valor. He was awarded the Congressional Medal of Honor, and returned home for a hero's welcome. Sent around the country on a speaking tour to boost morale and sell war bonds, he was soon begging to be returned to battle.

Eventually the brass allowed him to be redeployed. Basilone was sent in the first wave of invaders onto the beach at Iwo Jima. A tiny speck in the ocean 1,200 kilometers due south of Tokyo, the island was another critical target, a stepping stone for the upcoming aerial bombardment of the main islands of Japan. Although they knew it was hopeless, its Japanese defenders were told that every man must resist until the end. Each was to make his position his tomb. The resulting fight was fierce and merciless.

Landing on the beach was a suicide mission for the incoming Americans. Japanese mortars and machine guns blasted away at the amphibious vehicles attempting to unload the poorly-protected warriors. The beach was not sand, which would have been bad enough but at least would have offered traction; it consisted instead of soft black volcanic ash, which mired the tanks and left them stuck, easy targets for enemy fire. Soldiers and marines were dying left and right, many before they even reached firm ground.

One machine gun emplacement was protected by a concrete block building and almost entirely hidden in the sand dunes above them. The Japanese soldiers inside had good visibility and, shooting downhill, were able to control the field with murderous bursts of artillery.

Sgt. Basilone, with more experience under fire than his greener comrades, could see that reaching high ground of the sand dunes was the only hope for his men. He ordered his assault team to burrow into the ashy sand while he ran alone through intense fire, zigzagging to keep his profile elusive. By some miracle he made it to the top. He tossed a few grenades through the small window openings in the concrete wall and, amazingly, silenced the guns from that position.

Basilone yelled back for his men to follow. He led them off the beach and across the dunes toward the Japanese airfield nearby. An enemy mortar fired at them, the shell landing and exploding right in front of him. Basilone died a hero's death, ripped apart on the battlefield, his men around him desperately shouting for the medics.

The airfield was successfully captured by his own unit. The sergeant was honored posthumously with the Navy Cross and a statue in his hometown of Raritan, New Jersey. A Navy destroyer was named after him, as well as a bridge along the New Jersey Turnpike. These days few people pay attention to these dated memorials. But if you ever cross the Raritan River along that bridge, take a moment to reflect on the heroism that it honors, and that brave sergeant from New Jersey.

Chapter 4: Communities and commitments

"The world is a fine place, and worth fighting for."—Ernest Hemingway, *For Whom the Bell Tolls.*

Who's your peeps?
↓
Never let your buddies down
↓
Love bonds—the dark side
↓
Dumbo as role model

When Hemingway wrote of a world worth fighting for, he was not referring to this massive rock revolving in space, but the world of people, connections, and commitments. Love, laughter, and community. Give and take. Back and forth.

Often courage flows out of the desire or need to protect a loved one or a beloved community. When our near and dear are threatened, the crisis calls on a deep commitment to our community. Saving one person is a commitment to a community, even if it's a small one: a couple, a group of friends, a family. To go out on a limb to protect an entire town, a country, or a people is a commitment to a much larger circle. Gandhi's commitment was to India. King's commitment was initially to black Americans, and eventually extended to poor people everywhere. When the environmentalists of Greenpeace place their boats between the whaling boats and the whales, they commit themselves beyond our immediate genetic cousins to saving another species, an entire ecosystem, or perhaps they think of the entire planet and all its organisms.

The bonds of community have weakened throughout much of the modern world for a variety of reasons. Contrast this with the tighter bonds of many tribal cultures, some of which can recite their lineage for six or ten or thirty generations back, and can tell stories of ancestors that all their family remember as true. In such cultures the silken threads of continuity go vertically, many generations back. They also reach horizontally and radially, the network of links encompassing siblings, cousins, aunts and uncles, children, nieces and nephews. People growing up with so complicated an awareness of their connections are well-entrenched in a strong but flexible spider's web of bonds indeed.

For people who are so well connected to each other, courageous actions are often regarded, not as behavior outside the norm, but as what is expected when your family, your clan, or your tribe is threatened. And if a hero's risky behavior on behalf of the clan leads to death, their deeds will be remembered and lauded, their name carried on. In such a society, one person's death is not so dreadful; people are aware (more than we are) of the welfare of the greater group, and are ready as a matter of course to risk their individual necks to protect and preserve it.

Other aspects of such cultures reinforce this in numerous and ever-present ways. Among the Ewe tribe of West Africa, for example, there is a series of communal drumming songs and dances which traditionally are used to prepare people spiritually and emotionally for going into battle. The songs remind them of their common identity, history, and destiny together; the drumming and dancing evoke trance and a shared spiritual experience, thus deepening and reinforcing their bonds together. Some of the dances evoke battlefield tactics, including reconnaissance, surprise attacks, and hand-to-hand combat, thus giving male dancers a chance to practice working as a team. Some honor those who died heroically, marking their sacrifice and inspiring others onward.

These songs and dances are important when going into battle, but they are practiced and performed during times of peace as well. Their power for bonding works even when nobody is threatened, reminding people of their common heritage, their (assumed) common destiny, and honoring those who give their lives for their people.

Thus one community continues during times of peace as well as times of war, reinforcing its common social identity and preparing its members to commit to each other, whenever and however the need arises.

⋆　　　⋆　　　⋆

Through shared hardship and common goals, strangers become colleagues, colleagues become buddies. Buddies become brothers, and brothers become second selves. It doesn't matter if people are male or female, old or young, gay or straight, one race or ethnic group or another; the bonds of community transcend such narrow distinctions. They form and tighten, an invisible but strong spider's silk of connection.

Few of the Nashville students who became the core of the lunch-counter sit-ins and the later Freedom Rides, thought of themselves as brave. John Lewis, for example, who survived his activist years to become a U.S. Congressman from Atlanta, never thought of himself as either strong or courageous. He was arrested more than 45 times for his non-violent activism, beaten and spit on, and yet he and his comrades kept on. Though they may be have been arrayed against the full power of the city of Nashville, the state of Alabama, and the clandestine forces of the Ku Klux Klan, two things kept him going through the various demonstrations: the solidarity of friends and the inner knowledge that they were in the right. He could look around at his colleagues and see how nervous everyone was. Yet they were embarked on an act of faith.

He may not have been physically strong, but that's where he did have tremendous reserves of strength—in his faith. They had each other to lean on; they had faith that none of them would let each other down. They had faith in their teacher, Jim Lawson, and the wisdom of his teachings. They had faith in their cause; they had faith that the country was full enough of goodness that it ultimately would not let them down. They had, most of them, faith in God standing behind them, ready to catch them if they fell. Faith is what they called it, but you could almost as easily call it love, or community, or vision.

Gregory Freeman writes of the American airmen shot down over war-torn Eastern Europe in the 1944 mission to destroy the oil refineries that fueled the German war machine. Hundreds of planes were damaged attacking the well-defended Ploesti oil fields in southern Romania. Many of them were destroyed on impact; a few lucky ones managed to limp back to safe bases in Italy, and some escaped the immediate danger only to fail on the way back to base. Hundreds of pilots, navigators, and gunners bailed out in neighboring Yugoslavia, which was overrun by the German army, but with many pockets of local guerrilla resistors. The ones who were not immediately captured were sometimes lucky enough to find sympathetic civilians to shelter them until they could be passed on to partisan resistance groups.

Serbian resistance fighters moved a number of airmen from village to village, hiding them as best they could from the German army. They could not do this without the help of the local civilians who would feed and shelter them, sharing what meager resources they had. Even at the risk of their own lives, for surely the risk was real; the Germans were known to shoot whole families, sometimes whole villages, for helping their enemies. Yet villagers often offered their own beds, sleeping in the barns with their animals, letting the airmen eat first and feeding themselves and their children only if any food remained afterwards.

As the aviators surreptitiously left a village one morning, hoping to make it safely to the next without being discovered by the Germans, an old woman, dressed in traditional Serbian long dress and head coverings, reached out to grab Texan Mike McCool's hand, sobbing, kissing it, and holding on as long as she could. McCool asked one of the partisans afterwards why she responded so strongly to him, a total stranger. "Many of these people have lost sons to this war," their guide responded in his heavily accented English. "Some have sons in German prison camps. They see you as their own children. Americans especially, because you come here to help us fight. That woman was kissing her son when she kissed you."

Generosity and courage—a way to love by proxy.

⋆   ⋆   ⋆

A commitment to a greater community, when others also commit themselves along with you, lends additional support to a person's efforts. When people work together on a cause, they create a new community bonded by mutual struggle. Pushing together against the rock doesn't just add everyone's efforts together; it multiplies them. Synergy develops, creating a whole which is greater than its parts. This magic arises for two reasons: because efficiencies develop through experience, brainstorming, specialization, and so on; and because ideas and energy start to flow, which evoke additional ideas and energy, amping up the resources available for the effort. A biologist might say it increases the metabolic rate of the group. An economist would say the multiplier increased. An engineer might suggest that it's like boosting an engine's performance with a higher grade of fuel.

James Farmer, the director of CORE, the civil rights activist group that organized many of the non-violent protests of the early 1960s, was torn as he stood watching his youthful Freedom Riders board the Greyhound bus heading into Mississippi. He should go with them, he supposed, but he didn't know if he could. He'd already ridden on the bus for the first leg from Washington,

D.C. through Georgia, but what was coming up would be worse yet. He'd been called away in the middle of the journey for the death of his father, and now he didn't know if he had the resolve to finish the ride with them.

They were so young—19, 20, 21, and they had the kind of raw courage that hadn't yet had to consider a wife, a child, or the demands of holding together a new organization in the face of many pressures to disband. If he were hurt, who would hold them together, organize bail money, keep feeding the all-important national media, and solicit the donations that made it all possible? Who would plan the next campaign? Anyway, he rationalized, his father just died and his family needed him. If he was cut down, what would that do to his mother, bearing up with two deaths in as many weeks?

But there was a pretty 17-year-old girl from New Orleans looking at him, and clearly she was terror-stricken. The first group of riders felt completely wiped out after riding through Alabama: they'd been beaten, clubbed, and pistol-whipped; the bus had been burned to the ground in Anniston, and the volunteers had to be hospitalized for smoke damage in their lungs. One man was left for dead, lying in a pool of blood, though he eventually recovered. Now another batch of intrepid volunteers were boarding the bus, along with six reporters determined to take up the cause of freedom and equality for all Americans.

And yet clearly they were frightened.

"You're coming with us, aren't you, Jim?" the young girl whispered. Farmer was older; big and strong. Somehow, they all seemed to feel, he would protect them.

He started making his excuses, one after the other, but they did no good. She shook her head slowly, eyes wide. "Jim, please," she begged.

Her plea hit him like a fist to the gut. How could he let these brave children go alone and do what he was afraid to do himself? He couldn't, that's all. He couldn't let her down. He couldn't let any of them down.

"Get my luggage," he shouted to another staffer. "Put it on the damn bus. I'm going."

⋆   ⋆   ⋆

If you believe in a cause and all your friends are working for it at your side, then you risk a double hit for failure. Maybe even a triple hit. Because if things do not go well, not only do you risk disappointing yourself and your cause, but you let down your community. And the friends you pulled in to help might also get hurt.

Still, this danger has its bright side in boosting your resolve. When a cause is critical, people tend to put their shoes on and get on with it, even when the cost is high. If the situation is less imminent, or at least, less imminent to those in your immediate circle, that's an entirely different matter. If you'd only be letting down some faceless beings on the other side of the globe, think how much easier it would be to lay down your sword and shield and slink away through the trees.

★   ★   ★

One of the great ironies of World War II was how the Nazi governors used these bonds of commitment to subjugate their subject populations. By threatening extreme retaliation for any disobedience, often on the order of 10 or 100 citizens randomly selected and shot after any attack on a German soldier, and by making it clear that entire families would be wiped out if a single member joined the resistance, they kept whole neighborhoods quietly seething and yet reluctant to revolt. Often only when it was absolutely clear that there was no hope at all were people willing to ignore the threats and attack their oppressors.

In the Warsaw Ghetto, for example, over 400,000 people were forcibly crammed together under inhumane conditions—crowding and starved for food and supplies—in an area suitable for perhaps a quarter that number. Within three years German terror tactics sent more than 85% of those Jews to their deaths. By the time so many had been slaughtered, denial was no longer possible. People could no longer keep hoping their families were safe somewhere. News about the death camps had blasted apart the Nazis' cheerful lies about resettling them in pleasant enclaves where the children attended school, where food and medical care were readily available and people were given decent jobs. Before, the once-booming Jewish populace of Warsaw was torn between resistance and the desperate hope that by going along, they might survive. Before, their messages smuggled out to London and New York might possibly find Allied governments willing to bomb the death camps, or the trains that carried people like conveyor belts of animals to the slaughterhouse.

But by the fall of 1942, with their community so shrunken, with more round-ups every month stealing their friends and family, sending them barreling down the roads to their deaths, it was clear that any such hopes were foolish. They would all be dead within a matter of months. No one was going to save the Jews of Warsaw; in fact no one would save the Jews of Poland, for in every other town or city in the country, a similar fate awaited the Jews who were herded there, not merely to concentrate them, but to make it easier for the SS to murder them as efficiently as possible.

A few of the remaining Jews began meeting in secret to plan their revolt. It no longer mattered if the small group of resisters were leftists or rightists, as uneasy with each other in that time and place as people of widely different political views are today; didn't matter if they were deeply religious or atheists at heart. There were those who didn't think of themselves as Jews any longer—converts, half-blooded or three-quarter-blooded Christians, atheists—yet none of this mattered, since the Nazis and Poles had decided they were Jews, and would share the same fate. Death awaited them no matter which category they fit in, so, while they could, they may as well unite for the common purpose of resisting their murderers.

This resolve to resist could lead to their deaths, and some feared that itself was a betrayal of the meager community which remained. And yet it made sense to risk everything in a revolt. They were going to die anyway. They had no hope of surviving, but they would revolt for the dignity and honor of whatever other Jews might survive the war. The greater community of Jews beyond Poland would honor their bravery—that they would resist in spite of the tremendous odds against them, and would not continue to walk into the gas chambers like sheep.

And if no Jews remained, they would do it for the sake of the rest of the world, who later would be able to point to their time of courage and say, "See, not everyone crumbled under the hateful Nazi regime. Some stood up to them, even at the cost of their own lives. Some went to their deaths willing to stand up for freedom."

And so they began smuggling arms into the ghetto, shooting back at the Germans with pistols and home-made explosives. The handful of poorly armed, near-starved Jews ended up withstanding the German army from January through May of 1943. It was a remarkable but true David and Goliath story.

Thus the surviving Jews of Warsaw chose to destroy their own community in
an extended act of courage, for the sake of a community of people they did
not even know and for the self-respect and dignity they were denied by their
oppressors but which their own daring wrested back for themselves.

Samuel Zygelbaum, a Polish Jewish activist living in London, had been
begging Western governments to organize some form of aid for the Warsaw
Ghetto fighters. The Jewish uprising was the one of the earliest successful
resistance efforts against the Nazis. Yet almost no support came to help
them from abroad. One government after another turned him away, and all
the while his people were dying. When OSS Major Arthur Goldberg turned
him down on behalf of the United States, his last and best hope, he decided
to offer the Warsaw Jews the one thing he could still give them—his own
moral support. He decided to take his own life as a show of solidarity, allying
himself with them and their terrible fate. He would leave letters to the various
governments in the faint hope that shame might move the Allies into action
when reason did not. Even at that late date, he still hoped to save whoever
was left to save.

His method was dramatic, as it had to be, to catch the attention of those
who were committed to ignoring the ongoing massacre. Zygelbaum set fire to
himself in front of the British Parliament on May 13, 1943. The Germans had
been bombing and bulldozing the civilians in the Warsaw Ghetto for weeks
already, and there were very few people or places remaining. His letters to
the world explained:

> "I can no longer live while remnants of the Jewish people in Poland,
> whose representative I am, are being destroyed. My friends in the
> Warsaw ghetto fell with their weapons in hand in the final battle.
> I did not succeed in dying in the same way or together with them.
> But I belong to them and the mass graves there."

He, and his comrades who fought for dignity and revenge, were emboldened
into action because they had no further choices that might let them survive,
nor did they have any real hope of stopping the slaughter. Their resistance,
some say, was more noble and effective than that of all of Poland. The
courageous Jews of Warsaw held out for almost four months. Poland itself
capitulated in only one.

Only two days after Zygelbaum's protest suicide, SS General Jürgen Stroop
declared the end of fighting in Warsaw. Yet those last few resisters still had

hope. Resisting in spite of overwhelming odds, they could at least die in the name of freedom, with honor, in a way of their own choosing, instead of as unresisting victims of evil. In refusing to surrender, by preferring to fight, they preserved their dignity and their humanity. They gave hope to the hopeless and all of mankind. Decades later, even among people of far-different communities, their example gives hope and inspiration.

They stand as bittersweet example of grace under pressure—Ernest Hemingway's favorite definition of courage.

⋆   ⋆   ⋆

People often do courageous things for the community of the future. As Senator George Mitchell continued his labors to navigate a permanent truce between the warring factions of Northern Ireland, a community he was only on loan to, he took off a few days to return home for the birth of his son Andrew. That same day, his staff informed him, 61 other babies were born in Northern Ireland. Mitchell held his new child in his arms and promised his babe that for him and his 61 friends across the sea, he would somehow get the job done. And when he did, he would call it Andrew's Peace.

This forward-looking sentiment was echoed by others who sat with Mitchell negotiating across the table. David Ervine, spokesman for one of the Protestant paramilitary parties, who himself served many years in prison for terrorist activities, kept repeating throughout the talks, "I don't want my children or my grandchildren to go through what we've gone through."

Ervine, possibly the most eloquent politician in Northern Ireland, often pointed out the hypocrisy of some of the hard-line holdouts during the peace talks. Many long-entrenched political leaders on either side of the conflict gathered popular support by posing themselves as strong, defiant, and stubborn. They would stand up, raise a fist and shout, "No, we will never give in!" and the voters would rally behind them. These men (and they were all men) risked losing their base of power if they compromised even an inch. At one exasperating moment in the negotiations, a fellow Protestant turned to Ervine to complain, "If this is peace, let us have war."

"That's easy for you to say," Ervine countered, "safe as you and your family are in the suburbs. But if there's war, it's we and our sons who'll do the fighting and the dying. We want this process because it's the only hope for peace."

Indeed, another negotiator complained that one of the Protestant leaders, a man who stormed out of the talks as soon Sinn Féin[6] joined them, was "prepared to fight to the last drop of everyone else's blood."

Civilization—the very idea implies that some sort of safety, not violence, is the usual state of affairs. Yet the process of knitting together a new society often occurs in the face of extreme physical danger, and it may take the people from the front lines to openly acknowledge how bad it is. At one point, the new government of South Africa, itself knitted together after years of racism, hatred, and outright civil warfare, invited the Belfast negotiators down from Northern Ireland to hold some of their talks in the new African democracy.

The Irishmen accepted, no doubt welcoming a change of scene by that point. The warring factions were put up, ironically, at a former South African missile-testing site. The visitors from the Emerald Isle were astonished to see that real camaraderie had grown between white and black officials of the new South Africa. Whites spoke surprisingly easily with blacks; blacks mixed as readily with whites. And this was a nation where whites had still been throwing blacks into prison for trying to live and work in towns designated for whites just a handful of years before.

The Northern Irishmen saw joking and revelry between a black man once famous for being an African Nationalist activist and an army general from the former white regime's South African Defense Force. These were men who used to plot to kill one another, or at least did their best to cause each other grief. Now they were telling their guests with the assurance of the long perspective of experience that the combatants were the first to seek an agreement—at least partly because they'd be the first to be killed if all efforts for peace failed.

⋆   ⋆   ⋆

The sense of community can, confusingly, be as much a spur to courage as a dampener. We evolved as a species living in hunter-gatherer groups of perhaps 20—40 individuals. More than 40 would be too many mouths for most local areas to support, and too many to sustain enough consistent intimacy to

---

[6]Sinn Féin was the political party long associated with the IRA, the radical terrorist group of Catholics in Northern Ireland who advocated the violent overthrow of British rule.

bind the group together. Fewer than 20 might not be enough to cover all the roles needed—master hunters, tool-makers, apprentices, food gatherers, hide processors, bearers and caretakers of children, plus the children themselves— with some redundancy in case of accident, illness or death. Groups need some genetic diversity to avoid too much in-breeding, and yet related individuals are more likely to be able to cooperate together.

Our evolution may also have allowed for small groups of bachelors or individuals remaining outside the tribal groups for long stretches of time. These were mostly male; it is less likely that single women or mothers with young children would leave the safety of the group to fend for themselves. The group was the most stable arrangement, and the unusually long time our species takes to mature requires a fair amount of stability to sustain or increase the population.

So we evolved mostly within communities, and maintaining those connections represented safety, a sharing of food sources and help in times of sickness. Anything that threatened the community would threaten the welfare of the individuals. This was true for most of our distant past. Yet the most recent several thousands of years have not always selected for such interwoven behavior. For example, in the societies of individual farmers in much of Europe, a more each-for-themselves pattern of life may have sufficed. Competition for land, water, along with the age-old competition for status, sometimes selects for less community-friendly behaviors. Thus we humans have an instinctive, though loose, tendency to rally together when our communities are threatened.

Another tendency that fights against the instinct to step forward and help when a community is threatened is the fear of sticking out. Doing something different than what everyone else is doing is another way of (psychologically) leaving the safety of the group, particularly if people disagree on what is a threat to the community. For example, when some people are certain that a new manufacturing facility will bring additional pollution and thus the threat of climate change, while others see the new manufacturing facility as more jobs for the community and hence more prosperity—or if people around you define their community to be different than you do—as when some in the community have joined the Nazi party and others in the same neighborhood are the Nazi-persecuted Jews—then the actions of some will make them stick out. Way out.

We may have evolved to act quickly when we sense danger to our community, but many dangers are not visible to everyone in the community. And because of our innate need to be part of the group, we have a deep, visceral fear of acting differently than everyone else. Because of this, people may dread stepping forward to take action.

Some feel this more than others. Some may be more willing to act in defiance of it. Some will act but continually have to guard against the fear, though if they can find significant support from others who see the same dangers they do, that will help them to be brave.

★ ★ ★

I keep resurrecting stories from World War II, partly because it has been so well studied, partly because it was a time for great cowardice and heroism both, when people sank to their lowest possible level of functioning, or functioned from the highest of motives. Many of the people who aided Jews during the Holocaust did it for the money; they might have hidden a child or a family for a few days if paid in jewelry or gold, then turned them in to the Germans for a reward. But there were also those who helped people survive from higher motives: religious faith, compassion, empathy for the downtrodden, or personal relationships that transcended the war. Some people rescued Jewish children out of their deep love for young people.

Some risked helping out of gratitude for past kindnesses by the victims or their families. Some were servants who were treated well; others were business partners or tradesmen who remembered a good customer fondly. One teenage girl and her father were saved by patients of his; as a doctor he'd made a number of house calls on the daughter of the family that later saved the two of them. The family took them in because they were grateful that he'd saved their daughter, who almost died of diphtheria.

About 1,800 Jewish men in Berlin were saved by an early and all too rare example of non-violent protest against the Third Reich. These men were married to Christian women who refused to divorce them as they were supposed to under the new, anti-Semitic Nazi legislation. One late winter day the men of mixed marriages were rounded up and held in a detention center prior to shipment to the death camps. By that evening, several thousand of their wives and assorted other relatives gathered in front of the center, protesting. They continued massing in the streets for the following week. Goebbels finally gave in to their demands: he reclassified the men as privileged persons, and they were allowed to stay in Berlin for the rest of the war. Today, the Block of Women sculpture memorializes their courage in a nearby park.

Many Christians in mixed marriages, caught by the war, succumbed to the easier route, obeying the law and thereby abandoning their spouses to a terrible fate. At the other extreme, a few brave men and women refused to abandon their Jewish spouses. Out of love and loyalty they stayed with them, keeping their families intact by accompanying them all the way to torture and death, sharing their fates in the camps.

Surprisingly, Jews who were hidden by Christians during the Nazi era commonly reported that they first approached Christian friends and were, more often than not, turned away. Perhaps some of their friends were not as good as they thought; others had strong and legitimate fears for their safety or the safety of their families. Their own families, after all, would also be at risk, should their illegal sheltering of Jews be discovered.

Many of those who were turned away later absolved their friends. "It was too much to ask of them, to risk their lives for my family," one survivor explained. According to data gathered from the Polish Jews who survived, about half of those who were hidden were helped by people who were total strangers beforehand. A fifth were helped by friends, another fifth by acquaintances, and the remaining tenth by people with some pre-war business or professional connection to the survivor.

⋆   ⋆   ⋆

The motivation behind one extended act of courage which I found in my research was just the opposite—not having any family to be connected to. Arthur Jibilian, an OSS radio operator who agreed to participate in a mission helping rescue downed airmen in enemy-occupied Yugoslavia in the fall of 1944, accepted his posting with the OSS in spite of how dangerous their assignments were. He'd be parachuted behind enemy lines, he was warned, and maybe even get involved in sabotage work. "There's a good chance you won't come back," the recruiter warned.

Clearly the OSS work was riskier than most assignments he might have in the regular army. But Jibilian was an orphan, completely alone in the world. No girlfriend waited for him back home; even the cousin that raised him had recently died. "I'm more expendable," he remembers thinking. "Maybe it's better I take a dangerous assignment than let it go to some guy who has people waiting for him. If anybody is qualified for a dangerous assignment, it's me."

Not only did he help rescue over 500 stranded Allied military men on his first two missions alone, he lived to reunite with other rescuers and evacuees, 60 years later.

★ ★ ★

The dark side of commitments is that they can sometimes interfere with righting the wrongs. An abused woman might not leave her husband, for example, because of her commitments to her children, especially if the husband threatens to harm her or the children if she leaves, or if her earning power is limited and she fears raising them in poverty. In such cases a solution may emerge by reaching out to a larger community for help, for a greater net of linkages to support them.

I had a therapy client once, a young woman sent to me by her boyfriend. She was a secret cutter, someone who would use a knife or some cruder device to puncture or wound herself. Her boyfriend couldn't understand it. She couldn't understand it either, but somehow, she confessed, it made her feel better.

Most seemingly inexplicable psychological conundrums turn out to be complicated tangles of emotion and circumstance. If they were simple, after all, they would work themselves out simply, and there would be no knots to untangle. In her case, as we combed through the mess, the story emerged—a blended family, the mother treating the oldest step-sister horribly; my client feeling a bond with the older girl but unable to stand up to her mother to get her to stop the bad treatment; a step-father who turned on my client in retaliation for his wife's degrading behavior towards his daughter, and a disabled step-brother whose caretaking needs overwhelmed everyone in the family.

My client had accidentally discovered that by inflicting physical pain on herself, a pain she could control, she experienced a certain amount of relief from the myriad forms of psychological pain she was subject to—the anger and hurt regarding her step-father, the guilt about the belittlement that her mother aimed at her step-sister, her resentment of the needy step-brother. Brain chemistry played a part here too: pain brings on the release of endorphins, those lovely home-made opiates that give us both relief from pain and a sense of well-being.

But there were other forms of satisfaction that the cutting set in motion, because of the nature of the bonds she felt within her family. There was a kind of satisfaction for being a martyr; she felt guilty about her sister's pain so she inflicted pain on herself, creating a bond of commonality but also, though ineffectively, attempting to help. She subconsciously tried to use her own pain to draw off that of her step-sister, as if there was only so much pain to go around, so she wanted to grab a greater share of it.

There was also the satisfaction of delivering her own punishment while cutting herself, for the "sins" of resenting her step-brother, and of being too weak, to stand up to her parents. She knew she shouldn't resent her brother—it wasn't his fault that he needed so much attention and so big a share of the family's resources—but she did. And she hated herself for accepting her step-dad's money to pay for college even as she hated him. *Did that make her any better than a whore?* she often wondered. So again, another strand to keep her in place feeling wicked, weak and deserving of pain.

This great tangle had ensnared her partly through her commitment to community: to her stepsister, certainly, and also a commitment to her mother that she stay, helping with the younger stepbrother, although staying came at a big cost to herself.

The great trick, besides untangling all this, was to support her courage to hang in there long enough to devise a solution allowing her to disengage from the unhealthy aspects while honoring her commitment to her step-sister, her mother and herself. The solution included reaching out for a wider community to help, one which included her boyfriend, more social services for the brother, and a scholarship allowing her to move to the dorms at school. It also required her to learn to stand up for herself, to forgive herself, and to forgive others.

$$\star \qquad \star \qquad \star$$

A commitment to communities may be strongest toward the community you live in, though it may extend beyond to include the community of people you work with, work for, or are paid to serve. The light that some people cast may shine for a few inches or a few feet away; for a rare few it may be seen, like a sun, in different places around the world.

One person's commitment might encompass a school or a religious group their family is connected with, fellow members of a political organization, or a volunteer community. Career heroes often develop a strong bond with members of their team (army unit, guys from the same fire or police station) which may transcend the bonds of family, ethnic affiliation, or other communities. Additionally, they identify themselves as fitting the role they trained for, fitting it so snugly that they may not be able to imagine shucking it even when facing the most severe challenge of their careers.

In the fire station at West 100th Street in Manhattan on September 11, 2001, the men were just changing shifts when the call came in to turn on Channel 7. Watching the image of an airplane crashing into the World Trade Center, at first no one could believe what they saw, though it was repeated again and again on the news. Yet they stayed in place, glued to the screen, even those who'd put in a full shift already. No one grabbed their keys to go home.

Both shifts stood around, jaws open. They could see that it would be bad, that many people could never be rescued. Some might already be dead from smoke or from the unbelievable impact of a jet plane smashing into the building. One guy muttered under his breath that a lot of firefighters were going to die that day. And yet they stood there, "like racehorses," says Battalion Commander Richard Picciotto, "waiting to be let out of the starting gate. We belonged down there... this was what we did; this was who we were; that was why we were there."

His men were begging him to get them assigned there. They were, to a man, itching to race down to lower Manhattan when the second plane hit. Regardless of whether they were fresh and rested, or just coming off a 9- or 15-hour shift, they all wanted to be part of it, even knowing some of them may not come back. Yet for some reason the call was not coming in. The commander picked up the phone and told dispatch that they were going. The horrified dispatcher, watching the same news unfold on the TV screen, shakily said, "Okay."

Where does such dedication come from?

At every shift change in most firehouses, Picciotto reports, there are guys who hang out long after they could go home. They stay late, rehashing the stories of the fires they put out, the rescues they made, in no hurry to leave. They go over the details of even the smallest things. They share the awesome, spine-tingling moments as well as the tiny logistics that may have made some little difference, just as other people might stand around the coffee pot rehashing the football game from the night before, or the way they closed a sale.

These men do not readily let go; perhaps they are reluctant to leave when it just might mean they'd miss out on the next adventure to appear the moment they left. Or maybe they hate to leave the camaraderie of the colleagues they are bound to, entrust their lives to, for the cold and empty homes they eventually return to, children at school, wives or partners gone to their own work. Or to noisy households overrun with people who live on different schedules, civilians who are not as well trained to get along, no matter what.

Over 60 of the firefighters who died at the Twin Towers in 2001 were off-duty volunteers who showed up simply because they knew they might be needed, because they thought their presence or their particular expertise might make a difference. They'd already put in their time for the day or the week, undoubtedly on easier shifts, and yet, there they were.

What binds these people together? What creates such loyalty? It is well worth studying; the person who figures out how to bottle it will surely make a fortune.

Most people join the fire department because they want to help people. They may have other motives—a good fit for their innate abilities, a family history of working for the fire department, fascination with fire, whatever. There's the teamwork that binds each group of ornery individuals into a community—the fire department as a whole, or the brotherhood of the guys at each fire station. Such a bond may contain a stew of emotions: Love, annoyance, collective grievances against "the brass," shared worries, fear overcome together on many previous occasions, and a common sense of mission. They make up a feeling of belonging, a sense that they were each part of a team—they worked together, moved forward together. They'd pulled each other out of danger on other occasions. If they had to, they'd die together, and if they did, there were worse fates than that. Dying alone and for no very good reason, for example; most of them agreed that would be much worse.

"Here's one thing I learned that fateful day," Picciotto wrote. "It's better to die with a friend than a stranger. And here's another: It's better to fight and survive with a friend than to die with one."

⋆　　　⋆　　　⋆

Animals, too, will sometimes demonstrate the courage to save their loved ones.

There is plenty of anecdotal evidence of animal mothers putting themselves at risk in order to save their offspring. Drawing away predators so the young can escape, for example, has been documented among giraffes, cheetahs and birds, among others. A work elephant in Myanamar in the 1930s was observed risking her own life twice in one day to save her calf from the rising floodwaters of the Taungdwin River.

This protectiveness sometimes extends beyond animals' own offspring to include other creatures. Scientists have observed such diverse species as gazelles, buffalo, oryx, chimpanzees, birds, and dolphins defending not only their own from attack, but the young of others in their herd. Field biologists who climbed the cliffs one summer along the northern Pacific to band the murre, a medium-sized seabird, often scared most of the adults away. The young could not escape so readily, and usually a few staunch adults would stay behind. The frightened chicks gathered round them for protection, and it didn't matter whether they were related or not. Frequently up to a dozen chicks huddled around the few courageous adult birds attempting to shelter them from those scary two-legged creatures who kept sticking their big, fleshy noses in the birds' business.

Dogs will routinely protect the young children of their masters' families. Such behavior fits well into their evolutionary development, both as members of a pack and as animals bred for such characteristics over thousands of years by humans. Yet our loyal pets are not the only ones capable and willing to risk themselves for the helpless young of other species. In one intriguing series of animal experiments, scientists discovered that many female rats in a laboratory were willing to cross an electrified grid to retrieve baby rats and bring them to sanctuary in the female rat's nest. One rat, perhaps the Mother Teresa of rats, not only brought her own babies back; she kept bringing other babies too. Researchers kept setting more baby rats out, and she kept going—30, 40, 50 rat babies saved. She stopped after 58 only because they ran out of babies to place on the far side of the grid from her.

To what extent this was due to pure maternal instinct, it was hard to say. Still, intrigued at this amazing display of altruism, they devised additional experiments to see not only how deep, but how wide a rat's sense of mother-love was. What else besides baby rats might they embrace?

They began with baby animals that seemed, at least to their eyes, similar. Yes, it turned out that the mother rats were willing to retrieve baby mice calling piteously from across the grid. Next they tried baby rabbits, which are also blind, bald and helpless. Then kittens, which the rats continued to oblige. Researchers tried removing the rescued kittens from the nest but the mother rats struggled to keep their new charges. They were trying to shove the kittens into position to nurse from them, even though their efforts to feed them were doomed to failure.

The scientists tried baby chicks after that, which the rats still kept trying to rescue and tuck into place. The chickens made a terrible fit with the mother rats, though: they became quite agitated, squawking and flapping their tiny, fluffy wings. And who wouldn't, with a big, hairy, smelly beast suddenly looming over them, biting them on the neck and trying to drag them off?

Some scientists scoff at the idea of animals having complicated emotions of any kind. There is a long tradition of reluctance to ascribe feelings to non-humans. Anthropomorphic reaction, most scientists will say, throwing up their hands, and disparage the very idea of any emotions beyond the most basic: fear, jealousy, anger, and pleasure. Yet any pet owner, any circus trainer, or anyone who spends significant time with animals has seen them respond to other animals or to circumstances around them with varying degrees of playful exuberance, reluctance, friendship, compassion, pride, even romantic love. Courage is just one aspect that has been observed by reliable witnesses. Maybe not on an everyday basis, but we do not observe courage among humans every day either.

Yes, people argue, natural selection tends to favor creatures who act primarily for the sake of their own survival and that of their immediate offspring. Yet not every action needs to be for the sake of utility. Not every moment, not every molecule of energy, is necessary to ensure survival. Some actions, whether taken by humans or animals, are useful in their own right, perhaps because it is fun, or feels good, perhaps to establish bonds with a community, perhaps even to bond with a greater commonality that reaches far beyond. Surely there is value to that. Surely there is merit in the heroism of the hated rat, braving electric shocks to save so many bunnies and chicks that she thought were in danger.

And if it is logical for animals to help only themselves, or only their offspring, or only their closest relatives, think: how much of any of our actions are dictated solely by what is logical, by what is best for our health and welfare, versus how many are taken in spite of them not being in our own best interests? If you examine your own activities over the past week, how often did you eat or drink things you knew you shouldn't, but wanted to? How often did you decide not to exercise even though you knew you should? How often did you waste time doing something for the pleasure of it, even though it was in some way not a very good idea?

And if we are such creatures of logic ourselves, why would we assume animals, who arguably have fewer constraints on their freedom than we have, should always do what's healthiest and safest, following the dictates of evolution to the complete exclusion of free will or whim? They too are individuals with a range of possible behaviors. Sometimes animals, like us, may not always opt for the optimal. Sometimes they may just do whatever they feel like doing.

Charles Darwin wrote an account of a monkey in the zoo, forced to live in the same cage with a baboon that absolutely terrified him, yet he rose beyond his fears when a favorite human entered his cage. The baboon attacked the zookeeper, but the little monkey "rushed to the rescue, and by screams and bites, so distracted the baboon that the man was able to escape... running great risk to (the monkey's) life."

Field biologist John Teal, working with endangered musk oxen, once found himself shut up in a pen by accident with part of the herd. Several dogs came bounding toward them, barking away. In a wild and panicky moment, the massive beasts snorted, stamped their feet and ran right at the frightened scientist. He stopped still, his mind leaping in several directions at once. Should he run? Scream and wave his hands? Was he about to be trampled to death, gored among his own research subjects? He was still frozen when they moved around and behind, ringing him inside a defensive circle as they would one of their calves. Apparently they'd adopted him, and were lowering their horns to keep the dogs at a distance. He was safe, and if the dogs knew what was good for them, they would back off so they would stay safe as well.

In the rainy season in Kenya one year, a black rhino and her calf came to feed at a salt lick. The mother moved off to feed farther away, and without her, the baby soon got stuck in the mud. It cried piteously, and she came back, sniffed it a few times and went back into the forest to feed again. Apparently she could not see what he was crying about. Shortly after, a family of elephants came to the salt lick and the mother rhino charged them, protecting her baby. The elephants wandered a short way off and began feeding there instead.

But the rhino babe was still in distress. He cried out again, and one of the adult elephants, a male, moved back to take a look. He ran his tusks over the smaller creature, then knelt down, placed his tusks underneath the poor thing and began to lift it out of the muck. The mother rhino emerged again and came charging at the elephant, who wisely withdrew, at which point she retired back into the woods again, which set the baby off crying once more. Several more times this cycle repeated itself, the elephant coming over to try and extricate the stuck baby, the mother sensing the wrong danger and running him off. Now rhinos are not known as the sharpest knives in the knife drawer, but this was as terrible (at least for the baby rhino) as it was absurd. Finally the altruistic elephant and his herd quit the scene, leaving the baby still caught in the muck.

The following day, with several humans helping, the rhino calf got free and was able to rejoin his mother.

The elephant in this case spent significant energy trying to free a young one in distress—not his own young, not a relative, not even the same species. He risked being speared by an angry beast, with no obvious benefit to himself. Such actions are not common among wild animals or even semi-tame ones, but neither are they common among humans.

That heroism is sometimes displayed by animals as well as people, no matter how common or rare it is, seems amazing. Whether the courageous impulse is based on instinct or whether it stems from some seemingly nobler emotional or spiritual basis is in some ways unimportant. That heroism happens at all is the miracle, not that it happens often or rarely, not that it happens among creatures we might consider somehow less than us.

Nor should we let the fact that bravery is sometimes displayed by animals diminish the idea of courage. It is not that courage is yet another kind of behavior that even beasts might sometimes pursue. It is more that these occasional astonishing acts of bravery are awesome and inspiring; that the brave, no matter who or what they are, should be honored and emulated to the greatest extent that the rest of us poor creatures can manage.

Could Dumbo be a role model? You bet.

Chapter 5: A history of helping

"If we do not lay ourselves out in the service of mankind, whom should we serve?"—Abigail Adams

You are what you do

↓

Serial givers

↓

Why charities keep hitting you up even though you just gave

You are what you do, and not a whole lot more.

Most of us have dreams, aspirations, fears, but these are what you might call edge effects: they do not define who we are. Some people argue that our dreams define us, that a basketball player who dreams of a starring role in the NBA is greatly different than a basketball player of the same abilities and characteristics who has no such dreams, but in general, what such things define is what you are stretching towards, or what hems you in, but not how you function most of the time.

To know who someone generally is, you are better off looking at what they do on an everyday basis. "What do you do?" is the first question people ask you at cocktail parties, and for good reason: it's the fastest way to get a peg on who a stranger is. What we do is what comes to define us, not just in terms of our status in society, but how we look at the world around us, how we process new information, how we respond to our loved ones and colleagues.

You may dream of being an acrobat or a rock star, but doing a somersault occasionally or singing in the shower does not make you one. You may be tempted to steal a piece of candy as you walk through a store, but that impulse does not mean you're a thief. Those unrealized thoughts, feelings, longings are edge effects, and only occasionally make a significant change in your being. Even if you give in to that impulse and steal that piece of candy, you are not necessarily a thief. You may feel guilty and return to the counter and pay for it, mumbling, "Sorry, I ate it already," and showing them the wrapper while counting out your change. Or you may send the store a few bucks anonymously after you get home to cover the cost. Even if you pass up the chance to make restitution, you might resolve never to steal again. The uneasy nights are not worth it.

But if you repeatedly shoplift from stores, there will probably be a day when you wake up realizing you are, indeed, a thief. You may have denied it until then, but something has pierced the veil and you see that's who you are: someone who sees something they want and takes it. Maybe you are not a big-time thief, certainly not a professional thief, and there may be some comfort in that, but a petty thief is a thief nonetheless. You are what you do, repeatedly, over time, and if stealing is one of the things you do, then you are a thief.

You may be other things too: a teacher, a gourmet cook, a salesman, a lover, a tennis player, a wife, a father, a reader, or any of a thousand things that you do regularly and come to think of as aspects of yourself. These kinds of labels also tend to inform the ways we look at the world around us, what kinds of opportunities we recognize, and what we notice as we walk around. The cook, walking through a mall, may light up when he notices a high-end kitchen supply store; the equestrian walking through the same mall may curl her lip in disgust when she cannot find a single store carrying riding boots or saddle soap. The economist, hearing a report on a decline in manufacturing output, might become dour and send warning alerts to her clients, employers, and students; the salesman hearing the same report might decide that this is an opportunity to switch from promoting higher-priced luxury items to lower-priced value goods.

What you do may start out tenuously, but with repetition it etches deeper into your character, scouring deeper ruts. Your everyday situation begins to establish a firm grip on your thought patterns, your use of language, your outlook, your behavior. A beginning chef is conscious of every step along the way—the choice of dishes to prepare, the selection and purchase of ingredients, the handling and storage of foods, and the cookware available for use—every step during preparation, presentation, and the enjoyment of the meals prepared. Success reinforces the sense of identity—*"They liked it! I'm good at it! People will hear about me and someday I'll be famous for this!"* As the new chef develops more experience, these things become almost automatic. He can easily take in stride the occasional variations. His confidence grows because, after all, he is an experienced chef.

A similar process holds for economists, shoplifters, politicians, teachers, assassins, and hairdressers—indeed, for people in any line of work.

The same is true for people doing brave and risky things. Doing one brave thing is wonderful, scary, and exhilarating. It doesn't automatically make a person into a hero; maybe it does or maybe it doesn't. But each time someone does something brave and risky and succeeds, earning the appreciation of others, or at least from themselves, it reinforces the sense that they are a good person, maybe even a hero. Additional brave actions make each additional one a little less tenuous, a little easier, until they develop a degree of ease with it, even if the circumstances continue to be risky. And while many who are called heroes by others resist the label, and feel that somebody else deserves more credit, still they may feel a hesitant sense of pride in themselves and what they accomplished.

In Nechama Tec's study of Jews that were rescued during the Holocaust and their rescuers, the single trait most often cited in the rescuers' pasts was a history of helping others. Some had a lifelong tendency, or at least a long track record, of reaching out with charitable intent to aid the poor and the suffering. She found this tendency to be almost universal among those who helped the endangered Jews survive the Nazi era, though she rarely found it among those who helped Jews for pay of some kind. Other studies have suggested similar results—that those who habitually reach out to help others are often the first to step in during a crisis.

Such patterns tend to persist. People can change almost any behavior, but they tend not to, unless they want to change, feel the need for change, or get tired of their old situations. Hopefully they don't change at all if the tendency is a good one and promotes healthier living, happier families, and a tighter and more cohesive community.

Every non-profit organization quickly learns this lesson. When volunteers are needed to tackle some problem, staff members look to the list of people who've helped out before. Those same few are the ones most likely to volunteer the next time. Calling on this small group generally brings 90 percent or more of the people who eventually agree to help. Calling the entire roster of members may at most bring in another five or ten percent.

Similarly, if a non-profit needs money for an emergency, they typically send a fund-raising letter, not to the general public where a well-written appeal might elicit a tiny response rate (if lucky, in the range of one to three percent), but to their own donors, who are much more likely to be generous for yet another solicitation from the organization that they have already supported. New non-profit organizations often buy the mailing lists of organizations with a similar mission to ensure their requests reach likely new members for their cause.

Whenever teachers need help in class, they tend to ask students who were willing to help previously. Police detectives who have gotten good tips from their contacts seek out those same people when they need more information. Blood banks call their regular donors when the blood supplies diminish. No good deed goes unpunished, people wryly complain.

It is a fact of life: those who have helped out once are more likely to help again when asked. Those people have established an identity which includes offering their time, their money, their contacts, and so on. They may have adopted an interior label which reinforces this tendency—donor, humanitarian, philanthropist, or a more nebulous phrase—*I like to give back to my community, I'm a giver, I'm a good citizen, I like to help out, my family always tithed.*

The rest of the world may not be able to pitch in; they may be able but not willing; they may be willing but not organized enough to find their way to the right location and do what is necessary; they may be organized enough but not stay the course. Or they may not be accessible even to ask for help.

Ask not what your community can do for you. Ask what you can do, and do, and do, for your community.

Chapter 6: Confidence going in

"Courage is fear that has said its prayers."—Dorothy Bernard

School for heroes
↓
Smothered by bugs
↓
Drinking with the enemy
↓
Half full is better

Stage acting is one of those careers that regularly call on reserves of personal courage. Though the physical risks are rare, there is a constant potential for embarrassment and humiliation. Every performance calls on the actor to step outside the normal isolation of anonymity into the spotlight where tens or hundreds or thousands of eyes probe every inch of you. The majority of experienced actors figure out a set of techniques to help them move through stage fright and into the zone of fearlessness from which the best performances emerge.

The best training, for acting or for any demanding task, involves learning the subject and then practicing it many times under varying conditions. Thus police trainees are sent to the academy where they spend time at the shooting range, and even more time doing mock exercises designed to simulate real-world situations that they may encounter. Firefighters practice on abandoned buildings before they are assigned to a fire station; military trainees go through boot camp. Pilots in training will work on simulators and sit with an experienced instructor in the second seat before they are allowed to take expensive aircraft up in the air by themselves.

Training for warriors in times of peace is an interesting subject in itself. Modern nations often keep standing armies, paid to stay in training. This is a new phenomenon in world history, for most societies up through a few hundred years ago could not afford to. They keep their men (and women) occupied and battle-ready with extensive physical exercises, time spent improving weaponry skills, and simulated combat situations. Less affluent societies have not had this luxury; some have adapted lower-cost strategies for maintaining readiness in the event of attack. These include regular physical contests of strength and skill (possibly the origin of the first Olympics in ancient Greece, and possibly the origin of the game of lacrosse among Native Americans), and developing the skills for teamwork, leadership, and follower-ship via other structures within their societies.

Modern armies rarely train specifically to develop courage itself. They rely on developing skills so that the soldiers can function even when fearful and stressed, on building team spirit (unit cohesion), on introducing recruits to tough conditions so they become used to them, and relying on the interpersonal bonds formed by warriors and the resulting reluctance to let their buddies down in a crunch. These efforts are useful and good, but it would be interesting to see if specific training for courage would help win additional ground and secure further tactical advantages in combat missions of the future.

In any case, not everything can be trained for or simulated. And sometimes a crisis comes up for which no one is prepared, in military or civilian life.

Fortunately, people also learn through vicarious experience, by watching more experienced people perform. When long-time Yankee catcher and coach Yogi Berra was suddenly promoted to manager, most of the baseball-watching world was stunned. It wasn't like he'd ever held such responsibility even for a minor league team. But Yogi had long been a protégé of Casey Stengel, who regarded him as his assistant manager, and the catcher had another several months before the promotion would take effect to observe his immediate predecessor in action. After all, as Berra said in one of his famously droll aphorisms: "You can observe a lot by watching."

Indeed, courageous acts do not come only from people we think of as courageous; brave behavior can come from even the most timid or frightened people. Canadian psychologist S.J. Rachman reports on a severely agoraphobic woman who was so anxious that she was housebound for over a year. Yet when her elderly mother became bedridden, the phobic woman forced herself out so she could go grocery shopping, run errands, pick up her mother's medications. Each time she left the house she dreaded it, but she did what she had to in spite of her fears. She gives us a good example of psychological courage; she stretched her own boundaries and did what was necessary in a time of need.

I had a client who came to me for help dealing with her long-standing fear of flying. She had fought it for years with tranquilizers, but she had planned a family vacation and didn't want her children to see her drugging herself. She didn't want to set a bad example, she told me. Instead, on her last flight, she spent the entire three hours digging her fingernails into her husband's hand—courageous by some definitions, though her husband called it annoying. Understandably, she was not eager to repeat that experience. So she came to me for desensitization therapy. We worked on dissipating her phobia for a few months until she felt capable of flying drug-free. She was still somewhat uncomfortable, but no longer disabled by fear. She went ahead and flew, drug-free, doing something she hated to do; a several-hour event of psychological courage. She kept the pills in her purse, though, more as a safety net than something she intended to use.

Rachman points out that the most timid and frightened people can be encouraged to perform brave acts under the right conditions. Undergoing aversion therapy, for example, where someone who is chronically frightened by germs or spiders is exposed to them until they are at least partially desensitized. Though they typically undergo therapy in a supportive environment, the act of immersing themselves is incredibly brave. Many patients drop out before the first desensitization session out of sheer terror of what's to come.

Those that go through with such forms of therapy find it nowhere near as horrible as they feared. Before they climb the mountain, it looks enormous. Once they've succeeded, they can look back and see it wasn't nearly as tall or steep as it looked before.

As President Franklin Deleano Roosevelt famously said in his first inaugural address to the nation, "The only thing we have to fear is fear itself—nameless, unreasoning, unjustified terror which paralyzes needed efforts to convert retreat into advance." He was speaking to in 1933 when the country was lingering in the depths of the Great Depression, and people around the world needed a substantial shot of his optimism to break out of their deeply entrenched fears. One quarter of the country's income earners were out of work, and many others were underemployed; even those with jobs, money or resources were afraid to make a move that might jeopardize their precarious economic position. Almost everyone needed someone credible telling them they could do it. They needed confidence to continue the struggle. They needed someone telling them there was nothing holding them back but this tiny, needless fear.

His speech alone did not do the trick, but it started moving the country and the economy in a new, more hopeful direction which eventually got the U.S. ready to face other fears and challenges, and ultimately to a state of prosperity.

★   ★   ★

Surveys of men serving during World War II indicate the value of working in small groups for keeping up morale in the face of danger. The soldiers' desire to keep from letting down their comrades helped them maintain control over their fears. Studies of combat troops in the Pacific theater found strong correlations between a general sense of self-confidence and brave attitudes during combat. The more self-confident soldiers reported little or no fear going into battle, while the least confident men felt a significant amount of fear.

A study of trainee parachutists demonstrated that training and experience both help to boost courage. Most of the respondents felt at least some fear while performing their first few jumps, but their fears diminished by the fifth jump. By then they knew they could do it, and they were fairly familiar with technique and their own internal warning signals. Successful jumpers persevered in spite of any continuing physiological symptoms of fear (sweating, hand tremors), but their sense of confidence rose as their level of fear dropped, regardless of how dangerous they perceived the jump to be.

A psychological evaluation of the first seven American astronauts showed a similar result. Chosen from among an already select group of military test pilots, all of them had graduated with engineering degrees, were in good physical and psychological shape, and were married with families (at that time—the early 1960's—having a family was considered a prerequisite for being well-adjusted). Each of the astronauts indicated having confidence in themselves during their missions, that enough training and mastery of skills had minimized the fear of going into possible danger.

Though they completed missions in space that no one had done before, these early astronauts experienced exhilaration and remarkably little anxiety or fear. They reported feeling that they'd handled so many emergency maneuvers piloting new military aircraft during previous assignments, and dodged enough threats during active combat, that they had become almost fearless. The study's authors summarized their findings by saying that the astronauts had gained the capacity to control fear and anxiety through "mastery of stress, and through confidence in training and technical readiness."

Training helps–that's why student pilots have to demonstrate, in the air, that they can actually recover from spins and stalls before the FAA gives them their pilots' license. I should know, having barely passed my own. After raising a skeptical eyebrow in my direction, the examiner let me through, but he strongly suggested getting additional training from an instructor before flying solo again.

Studies of British military bomb-disposal operators working in Northern Ireland in the early 1980s similarly report that the early nervousness of new technicians dissipates with training and experience. After a while many of the operators achieved a state of virtual fearlessness while on the job, punctuated by periods of boredom between assignments, exhilaration while focused on the deadly work of defusing explosives, and a sense of calmness overall over their tours of duty. Of twenty operators serving a four-month tour, 20% felt a great deal of fear, but they performed their duties successfully, adapting to the fear and working, courageously, nonetheless. Another 35% achieved a state of fearlessness. The remaining 45% were somewhere in the middle of these extremes, varying in their levels of fear. Sometimes they reported large fluctuations in their anxiety levels, yet they continued to perform their duties.

Unsurprisingly, statistics on fearlessness correlate with experience and training to minimize the risks. Studies of U.S. airmen and regular combat soldiers from World War II variously indicate low levels of complete fearlessness in combat, on the order of 7% of the inductees. Yet 25% of the more highly trained group of paratroop trainees were classified as fearless.

Clearly we cannot assume that courage and fearlessness are the same thing. Some who act heroically are fearless and do what most of the rest of us could not or would not do. We gratefully call them heroes and perhaps even envy them. Others who act heroically are nervous or frightened going into danger, yet they perform under risky or scary circumstances regardless of their fears. They too are heroes, and we are even more touched by their struggle.

Rachman conducted another study to probe this delicate distinction. He and a colleague studied 105 training parachutists and found that this group of soldiers, who were self-selected for a difficult and risky assignment, could be sorted into three groups. About 25% turned out to be what they called fearless performers. They were optimistic, confident, and reported very low levels of fear after finishing the course. The second and largest group, about 66% of the bunch, they called courageous performers, because they felt fear and yet carried on. The smallest group, about 8% of the recruits, had underestimated how scary and dangerous they would find the experience. This minority of men, who were more scared than they realized they would be when they signed up for the task, the psychologists called overconfident. Within these groups, there was a strong negative correlation between fear and confidence, that is, the more confident the trooper was, the less dangerous they estimated it would be, and the less fearful they were when they actually went ahead with the jump.

In another experiment, several groups of people were tested for their performance under stress. Each was asked to make increasingly difficult auditory distinctions, and if they made a mistake, they were given a small shock. One of the groups was made up of people who'd served in the military and had been decorated for bravery. These subjects had a consistently lower heart rate (i.e. stayed calmer) during the randomly painful experiments than a second group of subjects who were in the military but had earned no medals. Both groups showed similar abilities to discriminate between sounds. Both groups of veterans showed less fear of the pain than a group of new trainee soldiers, who in turn showed less fear than the civilian test groups.

One highly encouraging conclusion that we can draw from these studies is that courage under pressure can be gained. Having an ingrained capacity for courage is useful but not necessary. Study and training greatly increase both the attitude (bravery) and the ability to work under pressure (including dangerous circumstances) in spite of any fears the operators had. They are the hammer and nails for the project going in, or maybe the pre-race workouts and the high-carb food and the energy booster drink that the marathoner prepares before beginning a race.

Developing the skills necessary to deal with risky situations increases the sense of self-confidence, and both the skills and the confidence increase courage. Thus having access to realistic, increasingly demanding training is important to promote skills and confidence for people who will be facing danger or other tricky situations. Having good role models or other forms of inspiration or encouragement help as well. Support from a small group of allies is also a plus.

⋆ ⋆ ⋆

Three emotional states are often associated with acts of courage: fear, anger, confidence. Fear can be a barrier, but its presence can also spur people in positive ways by encouraging a wise amount of caution, or through forcing people to prepare more thoroughly in advance. Anger can be a dangerous emotion in the presence of acts of physical courage. Anger can make a person reckless, ignoring all legitimate signals and warning signs, but a finely burning anger is often associated with acts of moral or personal courage, acting as a source of fuel to keep them focused on the target for change. And confidence clearly helps almost any endeavor, as long as it is not completely misplaced.

All three emotions were present and helped fuel the brave, though perhaps foolhardy, response of Richard Felman, the Jewish pilot from New York who was downed in German-held Yugoslavia in 1944 after completing his bombing mission. Hidden by Serbian partisans and peasants, he was being treated to drinks at a tavern in a nearby town one day when he heard a car pull up outside. It had to be a German, because none of the local peasants had the means to support an automobile. There was no time to hide, and Felman was doubly at risk as a Jew and an American military officer in Nazi-held territory. Could he look and act enough like a Serb to survive?

The German officer entered the bar and said a curt hello. The Chetniks with Felman nodded briefly back, not wanting to provoke anything. Felman sat there, trying to decide what to do. He could sit still, trying not to attract the enemy's attention, and hope he left quickly. But so far, at least, the German seemed to suspect nothing. And Felman was feeling a little cheeky, a little angry. There he was, a Jew who couldn't be rounded up and thrown into the gas chambers, he thought, although he could be shot on the spot if his identity were discovered, or sent to a POW camp to slowly starve to death.

Felman pushed a chair out and gestured at the lieutenant to join them. His partisan friends looked at him, clearly convinced he'd gone mad. One of them looked like he was about to jump up and throttle someone—probably Felman; the German would have been a lot riskier.

The officer sat down with them, slowly savoring his brandy. He sniffed it, swirled it in the glass, even bought a round for the table, though the partisans tried to decline—not that they had enough to drink; they never seemed to have enough to drink—but because they wanted him to leave as soon as possible. Felman, in contrast, sat there smiling at his opponent. He was relishing this face-to-face encounter with the enemy. He felt, for the moment at least, that he was the one in power. The deadly deception was working. The man clearly did not know who he was. Or if he guessed, he was outnumbered, at least for now.

When the officer finally left, everyone at the bar sighed in relief. The men at the table were amazed that they'd shared a drink with the enemy, and even more amazed that they lived to tell the tale.

⋆   ⋆   ⋆

A survey by a group of European psychologists found that, given a choice to act or not to act, even courageous people do not choose to act in every possible situation calling for their courage. Not every fireman stops to rescue every kitten in a tree; not every decorated policeman intervenes in the domestic quarrels in his neighborhood. They choose their battles more carefully than that. Certain conditions seemed to increase the likelihood of people stepping in: if they saw the situation as a true and immediate emergency; if they felt some amount of social pressure to help out; if they sensed the goal was worthy and they had some personal responsibility for it; if they thought they had the appropriate skills to intervene; and if the situation made them angry.

These conditions were all present among the college students, the lone housewife, the rabbis, and the ministers who volunteered to travel to the Deep South for the voting rights crusade in the summer of 1964, when the civil rights movement was growing fast and fierce. The nascent activist organizations— SNCC, CORE, and other loosely affiliated groups—knew they couldn't send untrained, naive idealists down into the maelstrom, unprepared for danger. So they set up training sessions in relatively safe Oxford, Ohio, to prepare the volunteers before they sent them into Mississippi or Alabama. Training had worked pretty well for the lunch counter sit-ins and the Freedom Rides, after all.

"We prepared them for exactly what it was like," activist Fannie Lou Hamer remembered, "and it was like you going into combat." She was right— in spite of the training, three civil rights workers were murdered (Chaney, Goodman and Schwerner); churches were fire-bombed; local hosts and out-of-state volunteers alike were routinely harassed, thrown into prison on trumped up charges, beaten—much of it justified by racist whites under the guise of "fighting against Communism." But the activists kept coming, certain that freedom was worth it, that if they didn't do it, all of America would suffer.

Their efforts, their passion, and their blood resulted in more violence, but also drew more attention to a shameful situation. Their collective bravery was rewarded a year later with the passage of the landmark Voting Rights Act of 1965. Within two years of its passage, registration of black Mississippians rose from a paltry 7% to almost 60%, a tremendous change for the better.

Optimism may be another helpful, even necessary trait for courageous action. Optimism often rides along with self-confidence as a silent back-seat partner, the sense that you have the ability to do things and a sense that your efforts usually will be rewarded, either directly or indirectly. Rachman's study of paratrooper trainees found that the most optimistic of the trainees expected to experience little or no fear going in, and these expectations were reinforced when they in fact experienced little or no fear doing their jumps. The larger, middle group of trainees was characterized by mild optimism. The overconfident minority showed a significant decline in self-confidence by the end of the training. They had been too optimistic and confident, going in; when things got rocky, both of those senses took a hit.

Under conditions of fear, some become passive while others leap into action. Taking action can be a way to handle fear by focusing on what you can do to change things. Under challenging conditions, a person who is optimistic by nature may be more likely to respond by taking action than a pessimist, who feels their efforts are bound to be useless.

Yet if you are a natural pessimist with an always half-empty glass, do not read this paragraph and despair. Pessimism has its advantages too. Pessimists can be better at weighing the risks and preparing for them. Pessimists may stay cooler under fire, perhaps feeling that if nothing much matters, they may as well act in a way that preserves their sense of dignity.

★   ★   ★

People may agree to go into risky situations with or without fear. Those who are fearful may, if they continue to face risky challenges, find their fears diminishing over time. They may even come eventually to a state of fearlessness. Increasing skill and experience contribute to their ability to face going into danger; afterwards, their competence and confidence are strengthened by whatever success they had. Those successes, in turn, strengthen their sense of competence and confidence, making a nice positive feedback cycle.

Higher levels of motivation make it more likely that someone will persevere even if they are scared. Fearless people may not need such high levels of motivation as those who are fearful but act anyway, in spite of it. Nonetheless, the combination of competence, confidence, and need is a powerful motivator in getting people to do something that's hard for them to do.

I would argue that all people are capable of being at least an occasional hero. Even the most fearful can be resilient under the appropriate stimulus. Training and good support increase the likelihood that even ordinary people can carry out a dangerous or grueling mission. The particular situation, the need, and a person's level of competence and confidence obviously impact the likelihood that they will step forward and volunteer.

But anyone can do it. Even you. Even me. Even your pet Rover or a monkey caged up in the zoo.

Chapter 7: Responsibility even at a cost

"One man with courage is a majority."—Andrew Jackson

More free will than anyone can handle

↓

Turning on a dime

↓

Dancing to the death chambers

↓

Solace and sirens in science

↓

The economics of altruism

↓

Whistle while you work

Every day we make choices, little or big, and those choices in part define who we are, where we're going, if we'll continue to be what we were or choose to become something new. Sign up for flying lessons, and you become a pilot; take that same money and time and spend it at the racetrack, and you don't.

Most of the time we fail to recognize the large number of choices we have, and that other roads branch off from the path we are walking on. Old habits, a strong focus on where we're heading, distractions of all kinds play their part in blinding us to the wider set of possibilities. But often what keeps us from seeing how many choices we have is a kind of timidity toward change.

Being timid has good sides as well as bad, but timidity results in a tremendous amount of inertia. In the course of a long life, the amount of time people take deciding on their direction is small indeed. Some might argue that you need a period of reflection only a few times in life to decide these things, and that may actually be true for many, but at the other extreme it is possible to reflect daily on your path. Certainly there is a spectrum of possibilities in between.

Sometimes this narrowing of focus is for the best, sometimes not. Think and judge for yourself the merits of each case: the mother of young children who longs to run off to Broadway and become great actress, but instead stays home with the kids. The doctor, invited to treat a tyrannical dictator for cancer, who won't consider using the opportunity to inject the tyrant with a lethal drug because when he became a doctor he swore to do no harm, even if this one death would save the lives of millions.

Now consider the passengers of United Airlines Flight 93 on September 11, 2001, none of whom were trained in the art of anti-terrorism, all of whom were on their separate paths in life. Yet they veered onto a completely different path within the course of a few terrifying minutes when they conspired to force their plane to crash and kill everyone on it, rather than accede to the terrorists who were trying to aim the plane as a weapon at the U.S. Capitol or possibly the White House.

Of course it is rare to be presented with such immediate and dire circumstances. Usually there is the luxury of time to think about the choices we face, to embrace or to ignore them. Some, torn between alternatives, might cite necessity as the reason for plowing ahead without shifting course. "I can't become a great actress because I have to stay at home with the kids," or "I can't take a life; I have sworn the Hippocratic Oath." A few might decide that they very well can.

There is room for free will, they might argue. No unbreakable iron shackles bind me. Other mothers have run away from home, or found ways to juggle two very different possibilities. Other doctors might choose to break their oath in order to serve the greater good. Those that do, follow a morally ambiguous path also trod by people such as Mata Hari, the courtesan who (arguably) used her intimate relationships to ferret out top-secret information from enemy officers during World War I, or Yael of biblical times who offered hospitality in her tent to Sisera, a commander from an invading army, and then attacked and killed him when he fell asleep at her feet.

Such constraints are real. And yet they leave room for interpretation, should the person feel compelled enough, torn enough, adventurous enough, energized enough. Take the example of a man or woman who escapes from a burning house, emerging outside to find that one of their children is still within. Up and down the block people emerge sleepily, rubbing their eyes, wearing their bathrobes and slippers; the fire department is called but hasn't arrived yet. One of the parents prepares to enter, but a neighbor pulls them back. "You can't," they cry, "you'll die! You're not trained for it. The fire department will be here in two seconds. Wait for them to do it!"

Some parents would take "You can't!" as a command, and stop in their tracks. Others would see it as a senseless plea for caution and ignore it. The direction they go depends on their nerve, their sense of duty, guilt or connection to the child inside, their experience with danger, and so on. They may secretly want to be stopped, but feel they have to at least try going to that child's rescue. In that case the neighbor's interference would be a relief. They may secretly want to be stopped but go ahead, wanting to show everyone how devoted they are, in which case the neighbor would still play a welcome role as a witness. They may be weighing the risk of leaving the rest of their family without them forever against the probability of success. Or they may need to save the child no matter the cost, in which case the neighbor is an obstacle to shake off and ignore.

Bravery and courage may be one factor shaping the degree of personal freedom, expanding its boundaries in ways and places that many would not think to do.

Take, for example, the path to the gas chambers at the Auschwitz concentration camp. Prisoners were directed to the right or the left: one path led to a temporary reprieve, working as a slave-laborer, but life nonetheless; the other path led immediately to an ugly, undignified end—strip searches, people herded naked *en masse* into the gas chambers, crushed in against each other, half an hour of suffocation, people crawling over each other desperately seeking for a tiny air vent which did no one any good.

In neither case did the victims have any meaningful choice. For the vast majority of the unfortunates brought there, nothing they did would change the outcome of their lives. They might try to bribe or cajole the official making the selections, but it rarely did any good; more often they took the bribe and sent the person to die nonetheless. They might offer their services if they had some unusual talent, though most of these offers were ignored; there was a glut of victims to choose from, after all. And even if their offers were accepted, the life expectancy of a new inmate in the concentration camps could be measured in days or weeks, given the poor sanitary and medical conditions, and the starvation rations they were allotted.

And yet some chose to walk the path of doom in their own individual way. Some, selected to live in the slave labor camps, threw themselves back into the line snaking toward the gas chambers in order to remain with their loved ones. Others, begged by their relatives to choose to live and carry on their name, did not. Some held their heads high and kept their dignity, even as their lives were being snatched away. Some of the Hasidim, an ecstatic sect of Orthodox Jews, actually danced on the way to the gas chambers. Each moment of life was a gift from the Lord, they believed; every moment could be celebrated, up until the very end of life. And there were others in the concentration camps who in their own ways spat at their tormentors, snatching a small personal triumph, retaining some sense of their human worth even in the face of degradation and death.

Were they heroes or fools to do so? The question could be argued from now until forever.

Perhaps the very act of exercising choice, elbowing aside the constrictions to create even a small degree of freedom, was another way to be a hero. Even knowing you might have to pay the ultimate price.

★   ★   ★

Brave actions may carry with them certain obvious costs or risks. Situational heroes don't agonize about these things in advance because there *is* no advance for them, just the moment of the action itself. But the ongoing heroes and the career heroes have excruciating amounts of time to do just that. Perhaps this is part of the reason they are so few; perhaps many of us start down the road to deeper behavior, and the amount of time we have to contemplate, to second guess and pull back, to decide we've done enough, means that the ranks of heroes thin out quickly.

So the question of what makes some people hang in when others drop out in big numbers bears some investigation.

The Great Influenza Epidemic of 1918–1920 was, to date, the biggest epidemic in the history of the world. An uncountable number of people died due to the flu and its complications, estimated between 50 and 100 million people, possibly as much as 5% of the world's population at the time, more than twice as many as died in the First World War.

Misleadingly named "Spanish Flu," the pandemic began in rural Haskell County, Kansas in February of 1918. The likely cause was a virus that had long lived in farm animals, mutating to be viable in human hosts, and spreading fast when a handful of recruits from the Haskell area reported for military duty at the nearby Camp Funston Divisional Training Camp.

Within months, 24 of the 26 largest Army training camps were fighting influenza outbreaks, and by April the virus had spread overseas to the armies on both sides of the war. The disease continued moving eastward around the globe, swamping hospitals as far as Bombay and Shanghai by the end of May.

Germs were fast-attacking and nasty, and for the first few months people sickened, but most of them recovered. Over the summer the virus worsened— mutated perhaps, or swapped genes with another, more lethal virus. By August of 1918, public health specialists were reporting a dramatic spike upward in death rates. Most flu viruses spread evenly throughout all age groups, and the worst hit are the most vulnerable people; thus flu deaths tend to be concentrated among infants and the elderly. But contrary to the pattern with most influenzas, this particular flu seemed to hit disturbingly high proportions of young men and women in their 20s and early 30s, normally the heartiest group facing any disease. Ultimately almost 10% of the world's population in that age range died over the next several months from this terrible outbreak. And those who didn't die took weeks or months to recover.

In heavily-hit Philadelphia, there were so many victims that the hospitals had to close their doors. In spite of precautions—scrubbing, wearing surgical masks, wiping feet before entering a new room—many doctors and nurses were also falling sick and dying. The city's death toll ran so high that the undertakers ran out of coffins; cemeteries could not keep up and had to bury people in mass graves. The city's board of health entreated retired doctors and nurses to come back to work. Five local medical schools dismissed classes, releasing students to man the emergency hospitals that were being hurriedly set up in schools and empty buildings everywhere. Yet none of the known treatments were working—not masks, not disinfectants, not the sera or vaccines that served against other diseases.

Patients were feverish, turning blue with cyanosis, coughing, delirious, dying while attempting to clear their throats of the pervasive blood-tinged phlegm. Often the illness came on like a tidal wave, completely overwhelming its victims. Some died less than twelve hours after feeling their first symptom.

As the epidemic raged on, scientists and epidemiologists were desperately searching for a cure. They and their allies, the doctors and nurses, risked infection and death every time they reached in to swab a dead or dying mouth or nasal passage, every time they attended an autopsy to collect samples, every time they leaned over a microscope, breathing in pathogens, studying tissue or saliva or blood. And yet the work had to be done.

A few trained personnel broke or fled, but most stayed on task, even as the civilian population shriveled and isolated itself in fear, so many of them ignoring the daily calls for volunteers. So many people refused to leave their own homes that businesses simply shut their doors and the streets were empty of people.

Yet as doctors died, other medical professionals redoubled their efforts. Twenty student nurses arrived from distant Vassar College, and even after two of them succumbed, the rest vowed to work all the harder. Other city professionals also rallied as the emergency deepened. The police department, once completely dominated by corruption, volunteered extensively for menial tasks like removing the decomposing bodies from private homes and loading them into coffins.

How could so many scientists, laboratory technicians, doctors, nurses, orderlies, and unlicensed medical students stay the course, risking their lives every day for months at a time? This is the same question we could ask about firefighters, Coast Guard rescue personnel, people who marched for civil rights, or those who hid slaves from the slave catchers or Jews from the Nazis.

For many, the answer was as simple as this: this is who they were. This is who they saw themselves as being, this is what they trained for and worked hard to become: doctors, nurses, people serving science, people serving humanity. This was their vision of themselves, which was powerful enough to overcome their natural fears. They did it because "that's what Clara Barton [or Florence Nightingale, or some other role model] would do." Reading their accounts, you hear variations on these same themes—they considered it an honor, perhaps even a deep emotional or spiritual need, to be able to pursue their professions, to put their skills and expertise to serve mankind in its time of great need.

For this, they had pulled themselves through years of training, to do this very kind of tough and demanding work. They worked even through the worst of times, perhaps especially in the worst of times, even when their families, friends, communities needed them the most. This was what they were hired and paid for, and yet can anyone ever be fully compensated for risking their lives and the welfare of their families, all in the name of a career? For those brave people, this was less like a career and more like a mission. Dedication in the face of terrible odds almost inevitably has to come from outside the everyday system of economic rewards.

These people had trained for it, investing themselves in their careers, often studying for years. Ambition may have played into it for some, for anyone who discovered the bacillus or virus responsible for the spread of the most ravaging disease in all of history would surely be lauded by their colleagues.

Yet pride alone did not burn fiercely for everyone. Some of the scientists found themselves spending hours sterilizing glassware and other such menial tasks. Such simple duties were absolutely crucial to doing good science and obtaining results they could believe in. Poor hygiene might result in contaminated procedures, so even the most basic steps had to be rigorously supervised.

Many of these scientists and medical personnel had spent years nurturing some vision of themselves as the calm one in white whom others had to turn to for help: the caring nurse, the benevolent doctor, the scientist in the lab coat impartially dedicating himself to the pursuit of knowledge. Such a self-image can be a powerful factor in strengthening resolve during a tough situation. Without such a vision, many would fold in the face of the long hours and the frustration. But with such vision lighting the way, many things become obvious, and thus more possible, even in the face of obstacles or opposition.

The most successful ones had some kind of network or team of other like-minded people working with them. If they were lucky, the staff around them united to work well together. Scientists working in Philadelphia, New York, within the U.S. Army and Navy, at the National Academy of Sciences, and at major universities began contacting each other to share information and hypotheses, so even those working alone in a particular city could draw on distant colleagues for emotional or logistical support. Working with others, even loosely, offers a kind of community where achievements are cheered, efforts noticed, and failures are set in a context where they are easier to bear. People shore each other up in well-functioning communities, and thus lend strength where it is needed.

$\star$ $\star$ $\star$

Indeed, support from others in an organization can be vital to keeping people going in the helping professions. A study of certified nursing assistants (CNAs) who work in long-term nursing facilities for the elderly found that the CNAs who enjoyed more support and respect from their organization were less prone to emotional exhaustion and burnout. Thus they were better able to cope with additional stress, more able to endure the grueling conditions they were often called to work in.

Yet in the case of the scientists researching the Spanish Flu, each had colleagues who did not step up to shoulder the burdens. Some crumbled under the strain; others let their own or family sickness lure them away, and did not come back even after they recovered. Someone had to attend unrelated research, after all, and the routine medical cases of those suffering from broken bones, heart attacks, and tuberculosis. Yet there were surely some who fled in the face of great distress.

For others, responsibility or duty came into play, even if those principles were not ordinarily major factors in their lives. There was a sense that some principle needed to be honored. This same sense may explain whistleblowers, people who work in organizations that should be fulfilling some particular mission—expanding scientific frontiers, protecting children, defending the nation—which have been diverted by human greed or expedience. If there are one or two instances of wrongdoing, people with a strong sense of fairness, duty, or mission may overlook it, perhaps trusting that others will take care of the situation, or hoping that the bad behavior will be self-limiting. But when corruption become pervasive, the most dedicated people either leave, attempt to take on a leadership role, or start to consider blowing the whistle.

Donna Howard did the latter. An administrator at a highly respected Ivy League university's psychiatry department, she was horrified to notice a number of irregular practices in some of the university's research. Her department hosted a major center conducting clinical trials of drugs for treating adolescent depression, but it did not appear to be following the usual high standards of disinterested science.

New drugs must be tested rigorously before receiving FDA approval for sale to the public. A typical double-blind test involves random assignment of test subjects to two groups, one of which gets the drug being tested, the other getting a placebo. The researchers analyze the different groups to determine whether the drug is more effective at treating the condition than receiving no drugs at all. But instead of the carefully contrived procedures designed to minimize bias, what Howard was seeing was deliberately skewed results. Study participants who experienced bad outcomes from the drugs (in this case, depressed teens attempting suicide instead of recovering from depression) were removed from the study and marked "noncompliant"—as if they willfully stopped taking their medication, rather than dropping out because they tried to kill themselves.

Suicidal behavior was a clear indicator that the drugs were not working, or even worsening the condition they were meant to treat. Even a few of those misleading characterizations would distort the results enough to allow the drugs to pass FDA screening so they could be sold to unsuspecting consumers. Bad science would result in doctors and psychiatrists prescribing medication that may or may not help some, but clearly posed a deadly risk to others.

When Howard began questioning why certain people were pulled out of the studies, she was warned to keep her mouth shut. She tried speaking with the director of research administration, which resulted in a half-hearted internal investigation and even an interview with the FBI. Yet nothing changed. She ended up copying papers and documenting her allegations, taking them finally to the *Boston Globe* and the New York Attorney General, which eventually resulted in changes in the pharmaceutical industry and its regulators. Today, partly as a result of Howard's insistence on outing a painful truth, all clinical trials and their results have to be made accessible, whether their findings are positive or negative, so that doctors prescribing drugs have access to information on the side effects and efficacy of new medications before prescribing them. Of course, whether busy doctors have the time or inclination to dig beneath the summary statements for the extensive explanations underneath is another question.

During the course of these investigations, however, Howard was pressed to resign her university position, as well as a subsequent position in a non-profit organization devoted to mental health, before finding work in another field altogether where the influence of the drug companies was negligible. Howard never felt threatened physically, but her credibility and reputation were tarnished for years.

Yet it was important enough to her that she kept pushing, even knowing it risked her career. She and her daughter both suffered bipolar disorder and she knew firsthand how much of a difference an effective medication could make in someone's life. The community of the mentally ill was a community she had ties and and felt loyal to. She was convinced that it deserved more loyalty than her own employer. A commitment to truth, a devotion to doing the right thing—these were responsibilities she held tightly to, even if it cost her security.

Linda Howard's bank account may have suffered for her principles, but at least she slept better at night.

⋆   ⋆   ⋆

My inner economist wants to discuss the issue of cost here, so for those who hate abstraction, feel free to skip a few pages ahead.

Traditional economic theory would say that heroic behavior makes little rational sense. Risking your life to save an unrelated person from a burning building, for example, is irrational because the hero would be trading their time, risking loss of much or all the time remaining in their economic lives, for no material gain. Yet often there is utility in doing things your own way, following your heart instead of doing things as society says to do them. For the sake of discussion, let us call this phenomenon "deep behavior," or behavior that follows some deeper instinct than the everyday exchange of a person's time for money. In fact we could propose an economic utility function showing the utility of deep behavior.

Let us say that in a standard utility function, an individual trades hours of their time for some amount of dollars per hour, which we think of as their wage rate. The mathematical function describing the trade-off looks like Figure 1.1.

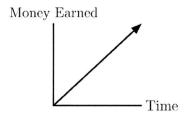

Figure 1.1: Standard utility function representing an individual earning money for their time.

Here, the y-axis measures money earned and the x-axis measures hours spent earning that money. Following the arrow, you can see that at zero hours spent, no money is earned. But going to the right and upward along the arrow, the more hours the person spends working (using values that go farther along the x-axis), the more money the person earns (using the associated values going higher on the y-axis).

Now instead of money, you can also use the y-axis to measure a broader measure of well-being, which we will call utility. Utility is a catch-all phrase that lumps all kinds of good things together, possibly including money, status earned in the community, a sense of self-worth, good relationships with others, a whole host of things which might gratify someone.

Similarly, instead of using number of hours on the x-axis, you can substitute instances of deep behavior. So, using the same function as above but re-labeling the y-axis to measure the person's overall utility, you can say that, starting with zero instances of deep behavior, never doing things according to their own inner beliefs and feelings, a person would derive no utility at all. But as soon as they start doing things according to their own values and convictions, the more utility they are likely to derive, and so, the more engaged and content they are in their lives.

You could argue that some are too fearful to follow their inner convictions, and for them there would be negative utility (i.e. actual discomfort) spending time doing things in any way other than the most socially acceptable ways. And for others you could argue that their happiness will not keep increasing but will plateau out after a while as they get used to doing things their way. However, for simplicity we will start out with the mathematical function $y = f(x)$ as above, with a simple positive correlation between a person going their own way more of the time (deep behavior being a proxy for courage) and utility (a proxy for contentment in life).

Now when a person goes their own way, there will undoubtedly be costs associated with that approach. Some of these costs will be economic, whether direct, as in sending money to feed the hungry, or indirect, such as the loss of income as the person devotes less time working and more time volunteering for social justice causes. Other costs will be non-monetary: social, emotional, or spiritual costs, such as having less time for family and friends, any guilt they might feel as a result, loss of prestige in the community for doing things that others cannot comprehend or accept, and so on.

Any of these costs may start with the very first step outside the socially acceptable circle of behavior. The costlier and riskier the behavior, the farther afield they go from behavior that is expected, so the cost or risk function is likely to look something like Figure 1.2.

Comparing the two – rewards vs. costs – we might predict that, for the first few instances of deep behavior, a person is likely to experience increasing utility.

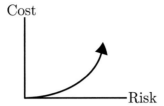

Figure 1.2: Cost or risk function for a person whose behavior becomes costlier and riskier.

But at some point the costs or risks get more than proportionally higher, and additional instances of deep behavior bring less and less satisfaction. We might call this phenomenon "burnout."

Again one could argue that the costs initially are higher than shown above, or that the slope is steeper at first and then not as steep. Once people think you're an oddball, additional weird behavior will not change your reputation much. But we will ignore such fine-tuning of the mathematical functions in order to keep the discussion simple.

Adding in a risk factor reduces the utility of an action because of the possibility of failure, costs or harm. And the greater those risks are perceived to be, the greater the reductions. Because of the high and increasing costs of non-standard behavior, the risk-adjusted utility function may end up mostly in negative territory. In other words, a person doing something courageous will pay for it in one way or another. Thus most people choose not to do brave and unexpected things very often.

In fact, most people are risk-averse, preferring to pay a premium for certainty even if it is unpleasant, rather than surfing the unpredictable tides of life. This widespread risk-aversion is the basis for the entire insurance industry, for the optional service contracts many people pay for when they buy new computers, appliances, or cars, and for the widespread patronage of chain restaurants and hotels among travelers who have no way of knowing which local eateries might have better or more interesting food, or which hotels will wash the sheets regularly.

But there is a minority of people who are risk-takers, or at least willing to take risks for particular, selected purposes. Risk-takers may actually derive greater enjoyment (utility) than most from the adrenaline rush, the contrary stance, or other aspects of their non-standard actions. Thus the perceived costs of potential deep behavior may be significantly lower for some people, even negligible. Or it may be lower at first, even if it increases as they get further away from the norm.

For such people, the first few steps outside of normal, risk-averse behavior might bring positive utility, though less and less as they move farther out. Deep behavior brings its own rewards, at least until the costs rise too high. Yet to some extent people may be willing to stay the course, even as the perceived costs rise, if they continue to feel the importance of the work they are doing, if they can see an end in sight, or if they find allies to share the costs and thus partially allay them.

How is it we can understand brave behavior in the face of obvious costs? There may be some who simply cannot bear a conformist life. Their utility functions may be modest until some aspect of risk creeps in. For people who enjoy taking physical risks, or for people with strong moral beliefs and values which differ from the norm, the costs of living within the status quo may be too high. For them the utility of working to subvert the established norm, and creating social change, may be enormous. For them, bringing about a new world order is Eden once again.

Chapter 8: Character

"The battle, sir, is not to the strong alone; it is to the vigilant, the active, the brave."—Patrick Henry, 1775

↓

Politicians with character—an endangered species

↓

Leadership costs even more

Navy SEAL Commander Richard Marcinko stepped out of the airplane, readying himself to pull the cord on his parachute. His target: a tiny swath of jungle on a small Caribbean island, four miles below. The mission: to attack and disarm a 30-man terrorist cell holding a single engineer hostage, along with a hijacked nuclear weapon.

The jump went smoothly. His men were suited up and ready; the plane made good time, their position on target. A number of his men lined up ahead of him, going through the door. Finally the jump-master signaled Marcinko's turn. He stepped out into the empty sky, blowing him a mocking kiss as he went. Now he was clear of the plane, plummeting through the icy night air, 100 pounds of specialized equipment strapped to his back. He pulled the rip-cord, felt the usual lurch on the harness as the parachute he had personally selected and packed deployed. Everything was as perfect as you could hope it to be.

Except for the sudden veering, steeply to his right. He was spinning uncontrollably, and rushing too fast toward the ground.

This was no longer the expected course of events. Marcinko looked up at the silk canopy above him. One of the cells had collapsed in the sharp cross-wind, and all his tugging of the guidelines failed to shake it out and fill it with air.

Two more air cells collapsed. The chute started folding in half. Clearly it would not bring him safely to the ground.

Hey, no problem. Like most paratroopers, he carried a spare. Methodically he cut away at the faulty chute, letting himself free-fall for several more seconds. A quick glance at his altimeter—15,000 feet to go—assured him there was plenty of time left. Another yank on another cord, a second lurch skyward. He could sense the reassuring feel of the reserve chute slipping free of the backpack and moving outward, behind him.

It was opening up nicely above. Or was it? No, something felt wrong. Twisting his neck, he took another glance upward. Oh, God. This one was folding in half and collapsing too, just like the other one.

There was no third chute to fall back on.

He had a satellite communications receiver in a pocket of his combat vest. He could call up his boss, a brigadier general, and say goodbye, or maybe deliver a solid string of curses as he hurtled toward the ground.

At times like this, you could laugh or you could scream.

But no. Absolutely no. He was not even 40 years old, and had a lot more living planned for himself. He'd built his Navy SEAL Team 6 painstakingly, selecting and training the men over a long stretch of grueling months. He had stepped on a lot of toes to build up what many regarded as the best counter-terror force in the world. Here they were on their first mission, and after all that, he was not about to miss out on the fun.

He dragged at the lines with every bit of strength he could muster. More. Even more. Keep it up. Finally two of the far-right air cells began filling with air. The crazy spins slowed, ceased, and his plummet became a lazy swirling, slow enough now for him to correct his course and catch up with the rest of his men.

Attitude is one big aspect of character, and equally of courage.

⋆   ⋆   ⋆

No one would argue that we are all exactly the same. From the moment of birth we already have individual characters, some of us fussy or reluctant, others sociable, adaptable, eager to try new things. Our characters develop with experience, sometimes seemingly set in concrete, sometimes making unexpected U-turns.

But the character we bring to the situations we face can make a big difference in the ways we respond.

A weaker man than Marcinko might have given up in mid-air. A more pious man might have said his prayers; a sentimental man might have called in a message of love for his wife and children; someone more by-the-book might have radioed his next-in-command. All of these reactions would have had differing outcomes, none of them absolutely correct. There are no right answers in the tests life throws at each of us; there are only answers which are more deeply right for us. The gritty Marcinko chose to keep struggling to survive, and ultimately he prevailed.

Physical courage seems to draw on strength and confidence, grit, a certainty of response, and an endurance to stay the course. Other forms of courage may draw on many of the same traits, though the form that strength takes may be emotional or moral, instead of sheer muscle power and an intrepid spirit.

Political courage, on the other hand, requires grit, independent thinking, voting for legislation that seems right, and refusing to back down out of fear of losing an election. The annals of winners of the John F. Kennedy Presidential Library's annual Profiles in Courage awards are full of such men and women. Charles Longstreet Weltner, for example, the Georgia Congressman who was the only representative from the Deep South to vote for the Civil Rights Act of 1964, supported it even though he knew it would alienate him from the vast majority of his conservative constituents.

Weltner was from an old Southern family, with a long tradition of white supremacy. He was named for James Longstreet, a leading Civil War general from South Carolina; he counted among his own ancestors the man who authored the Confederate constitution. Weltner not only went against this extensive tradition, he went against it in a big way. Even as a supporter of fairness to all races, he could have been more cautious. He could have abstained from voting at all on the Civil Rights Act, and quietly supported the legislation behind the scenes. The roll call was alphabetical, so by the time his name was called, the bill already had enough votes to pass. But instead of ducking the issue, he decided to make a speech and announce his support to the world.

Why? It seemed like the right thing to do at the time. Maybe, just maybe, he could rally the South to a higher standard of behavior. And so from the floor of the House of Representatives he spoke out to the hate-filled wielders of high pressure hoses leveled against civil rights marchers in Selma, Alabama; to the Klansmen bombing black churches in Birmingham; to the angry blacks denied their civil rights; and to the tentative voices for change in both communities.

"Change," he told them,

"swift and certain, is upon us, and we in the South face some difficult decisions. We can offer resistance and defiance, with their harvest of strife and tumult. We can suffer continued demonstrations, with their wake of violence and disorder. Or we can acknowledge this measure as the law of the land. We can accept the verdict of the Nation... Mr. Speaker, I will add my voice to those who seek reasoned and conciliatory adjustment to a new reality. And finally, I would urge that we at home now move on to the unfinished task of building a new South. We must not remain forever bound to another lost cause."

Voters in his district reviled him for this stance. Months later, he explained:

"how well did I realize that whatever career might be ahead for me would fall into grave jeopardy. But my career was not the question; my safety was not the cause. There was a greater issue, a larger question, a higher cause. Indeed, at stake was the highest cause in the affairs of men—the cause of simple justice for every American. And so, on that afternoon in July, when the bells rang in the House Chamber—on that day when they called my name, I voted 'aye.' "

Another politician who swam against the tide of his own constituency, yet who survived for eight terms in the House of Representatives, was Congressman Mick Synar of Oklahoma. He voted to protect huge swatches of the Alaskan wilderness against the wishes of the powerful oil and gas companies in his district, and voted for a variety of gun control measures, even though his entire family were hunters. He voted against exempting agriculture from gas rationing and for raising fees paid by ranchers who ran cattle on public lands, thereby alienating the ranchers who made up a large bloc of his constituents (though he himself ranched, as did many in his family), and refused to support pork-barrel projects, though they would have won him political support.

Synar even refused to participate in extracting hand-out projects for his own district. He hated the hypocrisy he saw so often, with voters angry at high taxes and denouncing the evils of big government, yet lining up for their own share of federal goodies. "Don't tell me again you want a balanced budget," he told a local politician, draping his arm collegially around the man's shoulder. "Not if you keep asking me for all these things."

Synar voted his conscience, always sure he could go back home afterward and explain it to the fair-minded folks in his district. They didn't always agree, but for 16 years they voted him back in office. Campaign manager Amy Weiss described a common response. "People would say, 'Goddam Mike, you're totally wrong, but you're standing up for what you believe in and I'll give you my vote.'"

His luck ran out in 1994 during the Clinton doldrums, as Republicans around the country swept into office. Yet he left with grace, telling the media, "I have had the opportunity of a lifetime."

In his last year in office he described his motivation to a reporter. "I have a responsibility to move my district, my state, my country forward," he said. "You've got to be looking down the road. We're trying to push the envelope to the very, very end."

Mike Synar died less than a year later at age 45, as cancer invaded his whirling, scheming, irrepressible brain.

As Vaclav Havel used to say, "I simply take the side of truth against any lie, of sense against nonsense, justice against injustice." Havel was a Czech playwright, another example of someone who practiced deep behavior, whose non-violent civil rights activism helped break Czechoslovakia away from its decades-long domination by the USSR. Havel's activism forced the Communist government to ban his plays from being performed in public; his continuing political action campaign led them to throw him in prison for years. As his country worked its way out of the yoke, Havel became its first president in 1989, and has since been awarded the International Gandhi Peace Prize, Amnesty International's Ambassador of Conscience Award, and the Presidential Medal of Freedom.

★   ★   ★

While we are speaking of character, I will add a note about the character of those who take on leadership roles for difficult and heroic missions. Teamwork is a big help in accomplishing anything complicated, but it requires that someone take charge. The leader's role requires its own forms of courage. Rick Marcinko writes about how his life and perspective changed when he went from being a Navy frogman, concerned only with completing his assignments,

dangerous or not, to being the one handing out and leading those missions
after he graduated from Officer Candidate School:

> "Somewhat to my surprise I discovered that leading is not easy. It
> takes the same sort of confidence you need to jump out of a plane
> to order a man to do something that may prove fatal to him—
> and have him carry out the order instantaneously and without
> question.
>
> "On a more mundane level, leadership is learning how to make
> a decision, and then sticking by it even though you are heckled,
> nagged, pleaded with, and cajoled to change your mind. The first
> time I canceled my crew's short leave because there was work still
> to be done on the boilers was one of the toughest decisions I'd
> had to make to that point in my life. Why? Because I had been a
> sailor, and I knew how much a night out meant to them."

Chapter 9: No other choice

"Many are brave when the enemy flies."—Italian proverb

Between rocks and hard places
↓
The bind of battered women
↓
Kids in wartime
↓
The heroic Sgt. Coward

The USS Blessman, a high-speed troop transport ship during the battle for Iwo Jima, was bombed by Japanese aircraft right down the middle. The blast set the ship on fire. Dozens of sailors, a highly trained demolition team, the ship's ammunition, and 30 tons of the demolition team's high explosives were all at risk. The power was out, and none of the water pumps would start. If the crew didn't put out the fire, the ship might blow up at any time. The men formed a bucket brigade, throwing buckets and helmets over the side, filling them with seawater and hauling them up to toss them on the blaze. It wasn't much, but it was all they could do. And the effort kept them focused instead of panicking.

Fortunately, the nearby USS Gilmer steered over and offered up their firehoses, running them off the Gilmer's pumps. One of the Blessman's firefighting crew had already refused to go down and help. Though firefighting was not his job, demolitions expert Lt. Andrews went through the hatch down into the hold, accompanied by another demolition team officer. They sprayed water across the bulkhead between the fire and the explosives, getting there just barely in time to stop Armageddon. The paint was already blistering with heat. Fire was spreading into the ammunition locker, next to where the explosives were kept. Bullets and shells were starting to go off, fragments ricocheting off the steel walls, projectiles and fragments bouncing around, each one potentially lethal.

Andrews didn't feel like he had a choice. "If that much explosives went up, it wouldn't matter where you were aboard ship," Andrews said later.

"Everything would be gone. That kind of action I don't think took heroism. It was either do it or get blown up. Somebody had to do it." So he did what he had to, and the fire was contained.

★   ★   ★

There are times when people begin to feel that something simply must be done, that things are so bad that they may as well go out fighting, because there is so little to lose. Some of those people turn to therapy, to political protest or badgering their congressman. Some of them take direct action.

And of those who act, it is instructive to understand what helps them choose to act.

Battered wives (and husbands) may find themselves stuck for years in a dangerous marriage based on a complicated mixture of love, fear, and denial. Often they find themselves believing they somehow deserve the punishments their spouse inflicts on them. Or they cling to the wistful hope that they can change the situation by changing either themselves or their partner.

Her husband may have told her he loves her, and she tries hard to believe him. And surely if he loves her, the battered wife keeps reminding herself, he wouldn't want to hurt her, would he? So she must have forced him to beat her, or at least done something to deserve it. Thus she comes to see herself as a bad person, a bad wife. Punishment is her due; why would she ever try to escape what she fully deserves?

Research suggests that battered women have a higher than average tolerance for cognitive inconsistencies. They may be more adept at ignoring mixed messages; they may enjoy high self-esteem at work, where they get praise for their achievements, even in the face of a loved one beating them in the privacy of home. She may try doing nothing, hoping it will get better by itself; there may be the inertia of habit or a reluctance to break up the home for the children; her husband may have threatened to go after the children if she leaves—many factors help keep an abusive marriage together. A wife and mother threatened by domestic violence is in a scary and dangerous place with no clearly good options.

The uncomfortable fact is that, though it is dangerous to stay in a violent marriage, the risks shoot up dramatically as the woman takes steps to leave it. A variety of reports validate this common-sense fear: one study reported over 70% of abused women seeking emergency medical services were injured after leaving the battering husband; 65% of intimate-homicide victims had separated from the perpetrator before the murder; separated women were 25 times more likely to be victimized by their spouse than married women. Other studies conclude that the mere threat to leave will often provoke an attack, sometimes a lethal one.

Surveys indicate that the majority of domestic violence cases come from low-income, low-education households. Yet there are alarming numbers of cases in even high-income professional households, where the woman has the additional burden of wondering how she of all people could have gotten herself into such a mess, where police and social workers are skeptical about her troubles.

I began looking into cases of domestic violence, thinking they'd be good examples of people gathering up their courage to act because there was no other choice. And that happens in some cases, where women leave because they know the next injury may kill them, or kill one of their children. Yet it turns out that what usually begins the process of leaving the marriage, even in the face of credible threats, is that over time they begin to **change the vision** they have of themselves and their marriage.

She may find a friend, therapist, co-worker, possibly even another battered woman who is sympathetic and patient enough to allow her to tell her story, and in telling it, hear it herself for the first time. Over time this process allows her to begin reconstructing and revising the story she sees herself living in. This is sometimes the first step on the road, leaving behind the old self-image of "victim," "bad wife," "ungrateful bitch," or whatever hold her husband has used on her. Gradually she can see that she does not deserve such treatment, that she can create another and better life for herself and her family. Only then will she begin to break free.

As Dr. Susan Weitzman of the University of Chicago describes it, "Only when the woman can see what's wrong will she sense what could be right." Only when she has a clearer vision of something she can *run toward*, not just a clearer vision of what she should *run away from*, can she brave the gauntlet and risk the lives of herself and her children in leaving her deranged and violent husband. As we discussed in a previous chapter, vision is one of the things enabling people to find the courage to act.

Women who leave battering husbands or boyfriends are at 75% higher risk of being murdered than women who stay with them. And of course one of the biggest reasons they stay is economic—most often in order to keep their children from poverty. Which is its own form of courage, is it not? Though it comes at great cost. Many who leave (assuming they survive) say it was the best decision they ever made.

Professor Sarah Buel of the University of Texas is a former battered woman; she left her abuser several times before finding a way to afford to stay away. The first step for her was to go on welfare with her three children, thus trading safety for poverty. It is a conundrum. More domestic abuse victims are killed when fleeing their attackers than at any other time. So they can leave and maybe die, or stay and keep getting hurt, possibly killed, while the kids grow up watching the violence, and run a high risk for becoming victims or victimizers eventually themselves.

If they leave, there is often little money and nowhere to go that feels safe. Buel points out there are twice as many shelters for stray animals as for battered women in this country. Many shelters allow the family to stay for only a limited time (30 days is common, which is often not enough to find housing or a job to pay for it); many shelters do not even accept children. If a woman finds a shelter which could in theory accept her family, there may not be an opening. 70% of women applying to get in are turned away, resulting in 80% of the children getting turned away as well. Friends and family may be afraid to take them in—a legitimate fear because an angry, abusive husband may threaten them to get at his wife or children. And, like the Holocaust-fleeing Jews whose own friends would not shelter them, most of the battered wives understand and do not blame them.

The first step toward leaving, Buell points out, is to develop an action plan detailing how to stay alive; the next is to extract the most crucial belongings before physically leaving. A good exit plan includes taking or making copies of every important legal document (marriage certificates, insurance policies, tax returns, school immunizations, drivers license, passport, medical files, etc.), finding safe places to stay in advance, figuring out how to make yourself secure going to and from work and while at work itself, making sure the children have safe places to run to if they need, and overall, finding enough money to tide the family over with the basic costs of setting up in a new place. Indeed, all this takes courage as well as resources. This key combination is acknowledged by the non-profit Amy's Courage Fund, named after Amy Lynne Latus who lost her life to a domestic batterer in 2002; the Fund offers up to $2,000 of aid for women leaving violent domestic situations.

One former wife batterer named Donald (no last name reported to respect confidentiality) was thrown into jail three times for attacking his wife. Released after a single night in prison the first two times after his wife backed down from pressing charges, the third time he was sentenced to prison and released only after completing an alcohol education program. Additionally he was required to enter into a battering prevention program. He could have paid lip service to their requirements. Studies estimate only 40% of batterers manage to refrain from violence for a year. But Donald was motivated. He was horrified when he noticed his daughter witnessing him getting hauled off in handcuffs; he was humiliated at missing his other daughter's first birthday celebration because he was in prison. It was tough, submitting to group therapy and learning to reveal himself to a group of strangers. The instructor "told us stories that made my skin crawl," he confessed. "They made me take a good look at myself. It put a real bad guilt on me." Thorough psychological change takes courage, persistence, patience. It is not always a straight road to the new Paradise. But, Donald says hopefully, "I don't think I'll ever relapse. I know I'd lose everything—this house, these kids, her—everything. . . I'm not going to blow it this time."

★   ★   ★

Often with an "it's gotta be done" situation involving moral or social wrongs, there is a great deal of anger and frustration with the status quo, where someone finally can't stand it any longer, or something happens to bring it to a head.

In the slaveholding days, most Southerners valued saw African-Americans as property, valued only for the work they did for their masters. After slavery was abolished in America, it took many more decades to win full freedoms for the descendants of slaves. In any disagreement between white and black, blacks had little recourse, for the sheriffs, mayors, and judges were all white and would almost inevitably side with other whites. The entire system was designed to allow hateful behavior to go unchecked in a virtual reign of terror against blacks. The most successful strategies for blacks were to flee the area or to keep their heads down and try their best to avoid trouble.

Ned Cobb, a black Alabama farmer, spent a lifetime trying to shrug off the blatant discrimination and occasional random violence against him. One incident in the early 1900s helped him set a course of deliberate opposition, or perhaps it could be characterized as asserting his manhood in the face of belittlement and outrage. His wife asked him to take two of their children into town on that day for new shoes. At the general store, the clerk, a white woman, began helping him. Another clerk working at the store tried to badger Cobb into buying a pair of broken-down shoes instead of nicer new ones. When Cobb refused, the man grabbed a shoe and struck Cobb, who deflected the blow with his arm.

Frustrated, the salesman picked up a shovel and ran at Cobb with it. Cobb yelled out, "Don't you hit me with that shovel!" The man swore and yelled at him to leave. For a few long seconds, Cobb held his ground. Another clerk joined them, threatening Cobb while the first one grabbed a shotgun and began loading it with shells. The woman clerk gave Cobb the nicer shoes and he left.

One of the male clerks followed outside, signaling a policeman to come over. The policeman accused Cobb of carrying a concealed weapon, then grabbed him and marched him to the mayor's office. Fortunately the mayor knew Cobb for a decent, hardworking farmer. Waving the others away, he advised him to leave town immediately to avoid trouble.

That advice was reinforced by common sense and a lifetime of small and large indignities from the white community. Yet something in Cobb decided not to give them that satisfaction. Perhaps it was the presence of his two children who he feared would be stunted by a lifetime of lessons in giving in. Perhaps it was the knowledge that he'd done nothing to deserve such harsh treatment. Perhaps he'd had a particularly strengthening breakfast, or his biorhythms or the stars lined up appropriately that morning. Whatever it was that gave him that extra burst of determination, Ned Cobb decided to set aside caution and stand tall. Instead of skulking away through backstreets, he sauntered through the middle of town, walking slowly and defiantly in full knowledge that he was in the right and hadn't hurt anyone in any way.

He survived into his eighties, farming his own land and working to organize black sharecroppers to help them live life on their own terms as well.

★   ★   ★

Two stories of brave children in war-torn Europe demonstrate how a strong connection to **values at variance with the dominant culture** can give someone the courage to risk themselves. Jayne Pettit's book *A Time to Fight Back* discusses a young Belgian boy, Peter Brouet, who grew up with inspiring tales of his grandfather, who was shot during World War I for editing an underground paper that preached resistance to the German invaders. When Peter was small, he and his father played, taking turns pretending to be editor or delivery boy of the paper, sending secret messages and hiding them in unlikely places in their clothing or throughout the house. When Peter was eight, his parents gave him a toy printing press for Christmas. Playing around with it, Peter wrote a sample article about the notorious German dictator Hitler who might one day invade Belgium.

During the early war years, as food was diverted from the local markets to trains heading for Germany, as Jewish neighbors were rounded up and sent who-knew-where, the Brouet family got busy. Peter's father revived the underground newspaper that his father had edited. Madame Brouet smuggled copies to women in the marketplace. The now 12-year-old Peter and a group of his friends waited until after curfew, then went door to door pushing papers through mail slots, melting into dark alleys whenever they heard or saw a German patrol. The boys willingly took these risks in spite of several well-known incidents of children being executed for resistance to their Nazi occupiers. The Nazis considered their actions treasonous, but to the Brouets and other members of the Resistance they were the height of moral behavior.

Similarly, Pierre Labiche was a deaf-mute orphan living with his aunt in the Normandy region of France. Like many people who lose one of their senses, his others sharpened to compensate. One evening, as his aunt came into his room to say goodnight, Pierre saw the flash of anti-aircraft fire through the window and, moments later, a wisp of white drifting down from the sky. Signing rapidly to his aunt, he threw his clothes back on and went out into the nearby forest to investigate. Yes, he was breaking the curfew imposed by Germans, but they lived on a small farm on the outskirts of the village, and he figured he could get away with it.

A short while later, Pierre spotted a British airman folding his parachute, revolver and flash aimed at him. Pierre ignored the gun, lifting a finger to his lip to warn the man to silence. Boy and man worked together to hide the chute, which, if discovered, would start a manhunt and possible reprisals against Frenchmen suspected of harboring the enemy. When they were done, Pierre led him silently through the woods, stopping once to hide when two German officers came, searching the area. Back at home, Aunt Paulette found some old clothes for the airman to change into, and she hid him under a trapdoor in the woodshed.

Pierre passed messages back and forth between his aunt, his school teacher and the local pharmacist, both connected to the Underground, and the pilot was moved to the next stop along a fairly well established rescue line helping downed Allied airmen escape. The grateful aviator tried to give Pierre his watch in thanks, but Aunt Paulette insisted he keep it; if anyone found an English watch in their home, they might be shot.

A week later a coded message arrived. The airman was safe, back at his base in England.

Another war story has reached us about a man whose values were at great variance with the society in which he dwelled. The ironically named Charles Coward, a British sergeant major captured in 1940, made nine escape attempts before ending up in the POW camp at Auschwitz. He spoke passable German and so was given responsibility as Red Cross liaison for the POWs, thus enjoying some freedom of movement through the camp.

Most of the POWs, though sympathetic, were too busy surviving on their own meager rations to reach out and help their even less fortunate fellow internees. But Coward was different. He began smuggling food to the starving Jewish inmates and even managed to supply the Jewish crematoria staff with dynamite, which led to one of the few even-partially successful uprisings in the concentration camps.

Coward developed another complicated scheme of collecting chocolate from his fellow POWs and bribing the guards for dead bodies. He gave their stolen identities to the Jews every night when they returned from the slave factories to their barracks in Auschwitz. Now registered as officially dead, the lucky few were given civilian clothing and smuggled out of camp. Something like 400 Jews were saved through his efforts.

Coward survived the war to testify at the Nuremburg trials. An English film was made based on his exploits in 1962, although like many films that are "based on a true story," it took plenty of liberties with the truth. Perhaps we should all be grateful anyway; any celebration of courage reminds us of how rare and precious it is, and hopefully inspires more of the same.

Chapter 10: Darker motives with good side effects

"Courage is a quality so necessary for maintaining virtue, that it is always respected, even when it is associated with vice."—Samuel Johnson

The ambition of Chris Columbus
↓
Ends and means
↓
Honoring courageous creeps

Although Christopher Columbus' name evokes a mixed set of emotions today, he undoubtedly had courage. Without it, he never could have set forth with three ships and a mixed crew of sailors and felons who were released from prison on condition that they ship out immediately with him. Along with his courage, he a good set of navigation skills, great confidence in his own abilities, and a sense of the rightness of his course. What else did his courage rest upon? Ambition to make a name for himself, and perhaps a false sense of security. Though no one knew for sure at the time, he made a number of critical mistakes leading him to greatly underestimate the distance from Europe to Japan and China, where he thought he was going.

Ambition also played its role among the negotiators hammering out the Good Friday peace accords in Northern Ireland. Most of the participants were politicians, who are ambitious almost by definition, standing for public office in order to achieve some greater status, salary, job security, or political agenda.

David Trimble was one such ambitious man. Representing the Protestant paramilitary Ulster Unionist Party, back in the days when Catholic and Protestant extremists were car-bombing and shooting each other across Northern Ireland, he'd already been punished once for advocating a peaceful power-sharing agreement. During his first stab at moderation, he tried convincing his Protestant, right-wing, Vanguard party to join with the moderate-leaning, predominantly Catholic, populist Social Democratic and Labor Party. Many of the rank-and-file were uninterested, and the entire party fragmented. Trimble lost his forum and could not get elected to public position for another ten years.

Slowly he worked his way back into Parliament. For several years he lingered on the fringes of power without getting anywhere. This all changed in a single moment of serendipity. Trimble seized the hand of the wildly popular Protestant politician Ian Paisley during a confrontational march through Ulster and they walked together, hand-in-hand, crowds cheering, for a short time. This symbol of friendship was captured by local photographers and the resulting publicity buoyed him to leadership in his Ulster Union Party.

A few years later, during the Belfast Agreement peace talks, Paisley was the senior member of the various Protestant factions, and everyone, including Paisley, assumed he would dominate their side of the table. Predictably, the confrontational Paisley was one of the most obstreperous of Chairman George Mitchell's detractors. At one point he walked out of the talks, refusing to participate any longer when Sinn Fein, representing a significant 15% of Northern Ireland's Catholic voters, finally agreed to stop the violence and join the rest of them negotiating for peace.

Paisley said he refused to deal with terrorists "as a matter of principle," a principle which would likely have resulted in continuing the civil warfare around them. Another, smaller Protestant party representative followed Paisley out of the talks, and Trimble had to decide whether to follow them or stay. His own party was split, with many feeling as strongly as Paisley, though most of their leadership was eager for peace.

Weighing in the back of his mind was the punishment he'd had two decades before, when trying to affiliate his constituents with the long-hated Catholics. What should he do this time? His career might very well hang in the balance. His life, as well. Hard-liners viewed compromise as surrender. And "no surrender" had been a rallying cry for the Northern Irish Protestants for hundreds of years. Many of the negotiators felt an oppressive shadow of fear, looking over their shoulders for possible assassins after every new development was announced.

A lot of brooding went on, but Trimble finally decided he'd rather lead the remaining peace-lovers at the conference than follow Paisley's obstinate protest. Following him would be the coward's way, the way that kept children dying. Following would trigger a collapse of the entire peace process, and blood would continue to flow for years to come. He didn't feel ready to speak directly with the representatives of the hated Sinn Fein, but he would stay in the talks. If he had to, he'd address Sinn Fein through intermediaries, of which there were plenty at the table with him. "I know my own leadership was at risk," Trimble confessed, but "playing safe was not an option."

There were moments he almost regretted his decision. There were times his constituents and his colleagues in the party regretted it too. But he didn't want to lose sight of the goal, which was to bring the Irish people into a state of peace, even with risks on every side, even when extremists threatened to topple the precarious agreement process with car bombings and murder. "You can't just walk away from this," he explained later. "You have to reassure yourself and other people you did the right thing."

Trimble's ambitions were rewarded before long. He shared the 1998 Nobel Peace Prize with John Hume, one of the negotiators from the Catholic side of the talks; he served twice as First Minister of Northern Ireland, and was given a life peerage and a seat in England's House of Lords where he represents his country as Baron Trimble of Lisnagarvey.

★   ★   ★

Researcher Nechama Tec identified a small subset among the Christian rescuers of Jews in Nazi-run Poland whose actions may have been primarily fueled by *guilt*. Unlike the bulk of the rescuers in her study, whose motivation stemmed from a lifetime of helping those in need, this was a group of politically active, anti-Semitic Catholic intellectuals who before the war had been outspokenly anti-Jewish. Yet watching the mass murder of the Jewish people gradually began to horrify them, especially those who had been active in other humanitarian aid charities.

In spite of their prejudices, as the Jews began to appear less like hateful competitors and more like starving, helpless victims, the group began offering secret help despite their personal dislikes. Guilt that their public statements may have inflamed the climate that allowed mass murder to be carried out was a frequently cited motive for their rescue activities.

Zegota, mentioned previously, was organized by several of these activists, and ultimately saved as many as 2,500 Jewish children, helping perhaps tens of thousands of other Jews with temporary food or shelter, and even some weaponry.

Career heroes may derive **enjoyment** out of their jobs. Firefighters, for example, often cite the adrenaline rush of fighting the fires, the pleasure of "riding the hose," the thrill of looking into the face of danger, and cheating death. They value the frat-house camaraderie, and the respect their children have for them, knowing how brave their fathers are. Police officers are sometimes suspected of getting secret thrills out of their close associations with criminals.

Certainly non-career heroes have the same possibility for mixed motives. Oskar Schindler, whose generosity towards threatened Jews during the Holocaust was memorialized in the book and movie *Schindler's List*, seemed to derive satisfaction out of being a hero figure to the hundreds of people he championed. He'd had a reputation as a ladies' man, frivolous and insubstantial, for years, and suddenly he was needed, admired, loved for his audacity and his steadfast adherence to principle. It was a remarkable change, which seemed to surprise and gratify him in almost equal measure.

In any case, it is hard to begrudge them their other pleasures, as long as the result is so admirable. Humans inevitably have a mixture of feelings, habits, behavior, both good and not so good. Why not channel these not-completely-admirable motives and put them to good use?

Even if you prefer your heroes to be lovers of flowers and butterflies, do not be surprised if some of them tend toward worms and beetles. There is plenty of room for worm-lovers in the panoply of courage.

Chapter 11: Preparing for courage

"Let us therefore animate and encourage each other, and show the whole world."—General George Washington, 1776

Buck up, buttercup

↓

Samurais, gunslingers and pilots

↓

Remind me why I'm doing this?

Preparation can take many forms. Planning in advance, training, efforts to inspire people to move forward, developing bonds with allies and reminding them of common values—all these can be crucial forms of preparation. Some require thinking, while others are more emotional, social, or spiritual in nature.

Figuring out a strategy, coming up with the appropriate tactics, breaking the plan up into manageable pieces and assigning people their various parts: these kinds of preparations represent the logical, thinking approach to preparations. This form of preparation is largely done beforehand, but how much of it to undertake will depend on the complexity of the project, the number of people involved, the importance of the task, and the difficulty getting it done.

Besides the obvious usefulness of figuring things out in advance, for some, such preparations can be a soothing prelude in the anxious build-up to more heart-stopping action. Advance work is helpful to all but the most spontaneous acts of courage, where the process of thinking may kill the impulse to step in. Planning in advance works best for complex projects, although it still carries some risk of getting caught up doing too much. A particularly anxious person might keep telling themselves they need more preparation before they begin. It may or may not be true, but it can provide a completely credible excuse—until it is used once too often. A famous example comes from the Civil War, where Major General George McClellan, in charge of the Union Army, spent so much time meticulously raising, organizing and training the army, putting off attacking the enemy all the while, that President Lincoln wryly said, "If General McClellan does not want to use the army, I would like to borrow it for a time." McClellan was finally removed from command, still insisting his troops needed further training before going into battle.

A more intrepid leader, General Colin Powell, once suggested the following process instead:

> "Dig up all the information you can, then go with your instincts.
> We all have a certain intuition, and the older we get, the more
> we trust it. We do not have the luxury of collecting information
> indefinitely. At some point we have to decide. The key is not to
> make quick decisions, but timely decisions."

The trap is that decisions and plans are usually developed in the face of many uncertainties. Risks could be greatly reduced with better information, but that information may not be available until it's too late. Crisis waits for no man; further misery rains down while people hesitate, paralyzed by the desire for more and better preparations. "Analysis paralysis," this trap is often called. In every crisis some balance needs to be struck between the pressing need for action and the desire to reduce the painful price of actions taken. Powell thoughtfully provided his own formula: keep digging until you have enough insight to achieve at least a 40% probability of success and then move forward. If you had to wait until you had more than a 70% probability of success, it would have been too late.

And yet, in the most desperate situations, waiting until you achieve a 40% chance of success may take too long.

★   ★   ★

Maintaining resolve through long-term crises often requires steps taken to keep up your strength, courage and commitment for extensive periods of time. Just as an engine may need boosters to keep the vehicle moving when the route goes uphill or over rough terrain, our internal engines may find that the ordinary fuel that keeps us going through more mundane circumstances may not be enough to carry us through extraordinary times.

A recent survey conducted by psychologist Dr. Cynthia Pury found that 82% of the respondents, when describing a situation where they had acted courageously, remembered doing something beforehand to increase their courage going in. But the kinds of measures they took were different for the various kinds of challenges.

People who displayed physical courage most often relied on practical, problem-focused coping methods to bolster their courage before the fact. Just over a quarter of them used strategies such as gearing up for action, reminding themselves of their training, or mentally rehearsing their plan of attack.

In contrast, about half the people who performed psychologically courageous actions used emotion-focused strategies as they approached the situation. These included keeping a positive focus going in, reminding themselves of all the reasons not to be afraid, and soliciting and receiving encouragement from others.

Of the people who demonstrated moral courage, 93% used what she calls outcome-focused coping strategies to increase their resolve and gear themselves up beforehand; these included considering the people being helped, reminding themselves of the rightness of the cause, and thinking about their obligation or duty to help.

Training for the Freedom Rides used a mixture of all the above. Organized by the Congress of Racial Equality, the week-long training session began in Washington, D.C. in April of 1961. The training started with an orientation which included an overview of the mission, its goals and possible outcomes, good and bad. An attorney spoke next, outlining federal and state laws regarding interstate transportation, the recent Supreme Court rulings outlawing discrimination that were being ignored in the Deep South, and the Riders' legal rights in the event of arrest. People discussed what was likely to happen, then began a series of role-playing exercises simulating the experiences they had with the lunch counter sit-ins and then the upcoming bus ride through the South. Each session was followed by discussion and some revision of their tactics. Interlacing all these activities were reminders of their common beliefs and ideals, reviews of previous successes, references to the rightness of their cause, and a lot of encouragement to go the distance. A week of such preparations was followed by a celebration dinner, which someone nervously called "The Last Supper."

That training, on top of the experience that some of the activists had from previous demonstrations, paid off. The first segment of the Freedom Riders' bus journey was ridden by a group of volunteers, many of whom had never done anything like this before. They were good, kind, and well-meaning people, but some of them were utterly unprepared for the chaos, the beatings, the arrests. Many of them—especially the older ones, the ministers, rabbis, and ordinary middle-class citizens who came because they wanted to support the young activists—were emotionally wrung out and had to leave halfway through; even a week of training wasn't enough. But for others, that week may have been what it took to get them through.

In any case, their numbers were important: without enough people at risk, the media might fade away; without those numbers they'd be much more vulnerable to mob violence and the lawless police actions in the most racist jurisdictions.

The Nashville lunch-counter veterans on the trip made some quick phone calls to their friends, some of the battle-tested ones who'd survived a few rough demonstrations already. Enough of them joined that they could continue on the harrowing journey and make it a success.

Attorney General Robert Kennedy was stunned at their equanimity in the face of danger, remarking to one of his Justice Department aides, "My God, they're really fearless, aren't they? They're really willing to die there, aren't they?" Some historians argue that the turning point, where the Kennedy administration finally decided to offer active assistance, came when these young students won RFK's reluctant admiration on the journey from Washington to Jackson, Mississippi, making him an advocate for their cause in front of his brother, the President.

★   ★   ★

Of course people might use any of the above strategies, or a combination thereof. Their use may more often be unconscious rather than deliberate, though as they come to understand how useful certain practices are, including mental and emotional preparations, they may begin to adopt a pattern of thoughts, prayers, meditations, and so on prior to entering the fray as did the ancient Japanese samurai or certain Native American warriors on the eve of battle.

Each situation may call for its own particular mental and physical preparations. Situations that require special equipment (weaponry, tools, radios, maps, etc.) will inevitably require preparations that include inspecting and correcting any flaws in the equipment and supplies beforehand. Pilots of small aircraft typically follow a checklist of procedures—personally inspecting the plane's tires, the fuel, the electrical and navigation equipment—and the process of methodically going through the checklist can have a calming effect on the nerves. Gunslingers of the Wild West would check their revolvers; doctors going out on house calls would peer into their medical bags to make sure everything was in place. Firefighters check their hoses and fire trucks daily, and may review procedures in their minds while riding towards a fire.

People immersed in morally courageous endeavors may sometimes have to take additional precautions. They may find it necessary to routinely isolate themselves from family or friends who are opposed to their work. Often they create a small bubble of supporters around them, because they need that cushion of belief to protect them from the constant barrage of resistance—the hatred, the threats, the screaming insults—to the change they represent. Allies surrounding them feel the need to be supportive, which may involve upbeat discussions of the cause and the people who've been helped, a chronic reviewing and renewing of the commitment to the ends they serve, and venting sessions, whose function is to let off steam but also affirm the rightness of what they do for the world.

Good leadership can do a lot to boost a sagging resolve. But what if the leaders themselves need a bucking up?

They may have to pull themselves up by their bootstraps, if they don't have other sources (prayer or meditation, a place to retreat for refreshing the spirit, friends and family to lean on, favorite maxims, and so on). And they may have to hide their own uncertainties. "People want to share your confidence, however thin, not your turmoil, however real," Colin Powell once said. "Never let 'em see you sweat."

Sometimes a bit of acting comes in handy. If you don't feel confident, at least you can fake it, which might lend a much-needed shot of confidence for others. James Farmer, a leader of the Freedom Riders, describes being thrown into jail in Mississippi, otherwise known as Hell to many of the blacks in the movement. His fellow Freedom Riders kept descending on hate-filled Mississippi, and the sheer numbers of determined activists began to overtax local prisons. Jackson's city facility soon filled, and so the wardens sent the activists walking through the streets on foot, in shackles, to the county jail. The men were afraid; after all they would not be able to defend themselves if the locals attacked, and their guards were more likely to join in the violence than to protect them. "I led the procession," Farmer later recalled, "trying my best to exude confidence for the benefit of those who followed. The sweat dripping from my face was from the Mississippi heat, I hoped all would believe, not from anxiety."

Courage, he reminded himself, was not being unafraid, but doing what needed to be done in spite of any fear.

$\star$ $\star$ $\star$

A friend of mine, the folk-singer and storyteller Joe Aronson, was an activist during the Civil Rights era, taking part in the lunch-counter demonstrations and other fabled events. I asked him once what struck him as the bravest act of courage in that time. "The Freedom Riders," he answered, unequivocally. "They were riding the buses knowing they were going to be get beaten, maybe even killed. They'd enter these little towns all through the South. You know how there's often a sign at the outer edge saying, 'Welcome to our town,' and it's signed by the Rotary Club or the Elks? Well down there, they used to say, 'Welcome to our town,' signed by the Knights of the Ku Klux Klan."

So I grew interested in learning how these people prepared themselves, which lead to reading about Jim Lawson's workshops prior to the lunch counter demonstrations which were offered, somewhat modified, for the Freedom Riders. Lawson was a student preparing for the ministry. Lawson was an activist who had been recruited by Martin Luther King, Jr. to continue his studies at a southern Bible school so that he could lend his talents to the cause of integration and social change. He began offering his workshops in the fall of 1959 on the campus of Fiske University, a black college in Nashville. Drawing students from many other schools, it became a place for like-minded people—dedicated to integration, impatient with the glacial speed of social change even after the Supreme Court had ruled against segregation in several decisions—to talk, vent, and plan. It became a support group for activists, as well as a forum to distill their ideas and harden themselves for the battles ahead.

Lawson was a graduate student himself, but he'd been hardened by three years in prison for being a conscientious objector during the war in Korea; he'd also gained depth, working as a missionary and disciple of Gandhi in India. He was sure that an individual acting on their own deep convictions could accomplish much in the world. Indeed, personal empowerment was one of the first lessons Lawson taught, for though the students were still nobodies, once they began acting on their consciences, they were sure to be transformed into leaders and heroes. Ordinary people who acted on their beliefs and took on terrible risks did not stay ordinary.

The second lesson he taught, though perhaps it was an outcome of holding his workshop rather than a teaching itself, was that deep and abiding bonds were forming between them. In studying together, in establishing common values, through practicing nonviolent techniques and holding endless discussions, his students were fast becoming their own little community.

The trust that these bonds engendered was helpful in creating another important outcome of the workshops: the men and women who attended them began shedding the pervasive sense of shame and vulnerability of being black in a white-dominated society. They had all grown up with a kind of blaming-the-victim attitude, that being black was always worse than being white and they didn't deserve fair and equal treatment.

Lawson knew that this attitude would hold them back, and he began teaching them pride in themselves. He felt sure that only when they had begun to learn to rise above the anger and hatred, both towards themselves and their oppressors, could they begin to embrace the non-violent philosophies of Jesus and Gandhi, based on mutual respect and love, even toward those who opposed them. A powerful step down that road was forgiveness of their enemies.

"They had to come to terms with their own dignity," concluded reporter David Halberstam, who covered the civil rights movement in the late 1950s and early 1960s:

> "their own belief in themselves, and their own motivation before they dealt with those who would oppress them. As they accepted themselves, as they accepted that this condition was not their fault, only then would they have the strength to be more tolerant of those who oppressed them. They were to be teachers as well as demonstrators. If they accorded others dignity, there was a great chance in the long run that fair-minded people would accord them theirs."

They had to reverse the old social order of diminished dignity and sense of self-worth for blacks everywhere. They had to learn to value themselves, and to let racial insults like "nigger" bounce off them. That was a word, Lawson taught, that said bad things only about the person who said it, never the person it was said about.

Their planned acts of moral courage for the sake of the whole country first had to grow out of a groundwork of psychologically courageous personal change.

Words and teachings were followed eventually by role playing and physical acting of simulated experiences. They began to play out various roles—the white racists who attacked and harassed them, the black victims of the attacks, the police who might or might not provide protection. They practiced dropping into a fetal position to protect the vital areas if they were beaten. They learned to use their bodies to shield one another. They practiced hurling insults at each other until the words stopped pricking their pride.

His students eventually came to regard this as Lawson's greatest victory— that he turned the very insults which had been a source of shame and weakness into a new source of strength, a tool to harden them and get them ready for the battles ahead.

⋆   ⋆   ⋆

Doing unto others, it's been said, is a way of doing it unto yourself. When your followers need to be reminded of the merits of the cause, you reiterate them, and in doing so, you hear and learn it too. When your helpers and associates need to hear how much they're appreciated for the work they do, you tell them. This nourishes them emotionally and spiritually, and they will often reciprocate with their own appreciation, and nourish you in turn. The more you give, the more you receive. As many parents have learned, they often receive the parenting they wish they'd had through the very act of raising their own children.

"I listen to my own soothing words," one of my therapy clients used to tell me, "when I tuck my children into bed. Those are the words I wanted my mother to tell me every night, which she never knew how to do. But I get soothed in the act of soothing my little girls, and that makes everything seem right in the world."

Chapter 12: Maintaining focus

"Why not go out on a limb? That's where the fruit is."—Will
Rogers

When tunnel vision is a good thing

↓

Learning to ignore a stimulus

↓

Mohawk braves take on the sky

Lt. Picciotto and his aide raced through Manhattan on the morning of
September 11, 2001 in the fire chief's vehicle, sirens blaring. "There was a part
of me, deep down, that felt like I was driving off to battle," he later wrote.
"Like I was heading out to do what I had to do, what needed to be done, but
that I wasn't coming back." And yet that feeling did not stop him. Instead
he began preparing for the job of a lifetime by reviewing the details of what
they'd probably find once they got there, where they'd go, what they should
do. In other words, he began the process of focusing on the task ahead.

The image of going into battle comes up frequently in firefighters' conver-
sations. Some ride to the scene of a fire praying, some review procedures in
their minds, some give themselves pep talks. (*You can do it, you've worked
this fire and that fire and came through them safely; you'll come through this
time too.*) Most stay silent in the fire trucks on the way to the next job, and
while gathering in front of the blaze awaiting orders, to unite for a moment
before entering the fray.

Once in the danger zone, what the experienced firefighter does is largely
what they have been trained to do in advance. They know what the goal
is—to deliver enough water to quench the fire, to pick up any unconscious
bodies and bring them outside to safety, to get out alive. With their goals
in mind, they keep looking ahead for the next step and the one or two after
that.

Myron Walsh, part of a Demolition Unit at Utah Beach, one of the
Normandy landing sites on D-Day, describes landing in the first wave of the
invasion. There was no one yet on the beach and nothing seemed to be moving.

A shell hit close, and he dove into the hole it created, taking cover. He waited for the next shell to land, and then let himself move into it, waited again and so on, repeating the process, using the enemies' own ordinance to create safe zones for cover. Since they rarely aimed at exactly the same place, it seemed the safest way to move onto the beach—jumping from hole to hole, all the while being chased inland by the tides.

Their job was to blast away any obstacles so that the next wave of landing boats had a clear path onto the beach, allowing the main body of troops to land. His group gathered up the unexploded ordinance, directed pilots around the remaining obstacles, ducked whenever they could to avoid being shot. "Doing all this, so much was happening that you didn't really have time to think about what you were doing and where you were," he explained. "We were all cold, wet, and miserable, though we did wonder just how badly our wounded man was hurt."

$$\star \qquad \star \qquad \star$$

At his seminars in Nashville, James Lawson instructed his students that nonviolence was not merely a tactic to use as one of many, but a principle to live by. They would need complete inner certainty, enough to be able to withstand an enemy flinging rocks at them, grinding a burning cigarette into their necks, whatever evil they might do to try and break the activist from his or her chosen stance. All the while, they'd have to keep love in their hearts for that enemy, regardless of the enemy's fear and hate toward them.

Lawson trained many of the early civil rights activists in the use of sit-ins and other techniques. A good thing, too, because his disciples had to endure pain and extreme harassment as they stepped outside the realm of complacency and into the visible forefront of change. During the Nashville sit-ins, the Freedom Rides, and the 1963 March on Washington, they were faced with endless streams of crazed hatred aimed at holding them back.

The first three lunch-counter sit-ins were relatively peaceful. Police were called and managed to restrain the hecklers until the students, having made their point, adjourned to a nearby church. The fourth demonstration was different. Police arrived late on the scene, long after the rights activists had been pulled off their seats, beaten, and one thrown down a staircase. But not one activist struck out in return. They stayed true to the code of non-violent resistance, worked out in advance, running through some of their minds like a mantra during the event: "Don't strike back or curse if abused. . . Show yourself courteous and friendly at all times. . . Remember love and nonviolence."

Training helped. Having their friends with them helped. Having something to keep reminding them of their purpose helped as well.

Fellow activist Reverend C. T. Vivian, imprisoned with Lawson's students during the Freedom Rides, felt they had become a community of conscience inside an alien prison. Vivian was surprised to realize that the prison doctor, some of their jailers, and other members of the white community were all prisoners of the same bad system, whether they understood it or not. Understanding that was one of the ways he began to accept the teachings of non-violence, to avoid the destructive side-path of hating the enemy, and to find ways to love even the men who struck them.

For him, developing this big picture perspective was another way to maintain the focus. Until the forces denying their civil rights were shamed and bullied into retreat.

★   ★   ★

Men of the Mohawk tribe have been involved in the hazardous trade of ironworking on high-rise construction projects since the 1800s, working on everything from the Empire State Building to the Golden Gate Bridge. It is extremely dangerous and demanding work, and often outsiders ask them how they do it.

Manual dexterity, some suggest; others say they must stay in good physical condition for climbing and balance; genetic advantages, a few insist. But the likeliest explanation is that they are better than most at handling the fear.

Dr. Solomon Cook, a former chief of the St. Regis Mohawks, was asked in an interview if the ironworkers were afraid of heights.

Of course they were, he answered. They were human, like everybody else. When you're standing on a beam swinging a sledgehammer, 200 feet up in thin air, he said, "you'd damn well better be afraid of heights. . . What Mohawk steelworkers have is an unusual ability to concentrate on what they were doing. Probably they developed that during their early training in hunting and tracking from their fathers and uncles."

"We're not [simply] construction workers," explained Jerry McDonald of the Wolf clan. "It takes a special man to walk a beam and climb a column without losing your life." *Weekday warriors*, they sometimes call themselves, and the nickname stuck, appropriate both for the courage displayed and for the pattern of going off the reservation during the week to work on the construction sites and bring back what it took to feed their families.

Focus seems to be even more key. "I try not to look outside the building," ironworker Kyle Beauvais said. "I try to look just at the beam I'm walking on, that's a trick I found... it's hard sometimes, a piece of steel is coming at you and you gotta look up and the clouds are moving; you gotta catch yourself. As I go up higher it doesn't bother me... if I fall three floors I could die the same as if I fell 40 floors; that's what I keep in mind."

So many Mohawks had participated in building the World Trade Center that they felt it was their duty to participate in the relief efforts after the towers were destroyed. All that mangled steel, and some of them, or their fathers and uncles, had helped build it thirty years before. Fifty Mohawk men volunteered for duty that was perhaps even more hazardous than erecting the towers had once been: searching for survivors, clearing the rubble, cutting apart the twists of steel girders. Over the next several months they were put to work climbing piles of unstable rubble, using their acetylene torches to cut the massive beams, steel rods, and rebar into manageable pieces so they could be hauled away, allowing access to the next layer of rubble.

"You didn't know how deep it was where you were working," Jerry McDonald recalled, "or what was under you. You had to cut and slash, and watch out for bodies. It was perilous. The steel can be half-melted, bolts might be sheared. You had no idea of the integrity of the steel when you were walking on it."

The whole time they were mindful of the special spiritual aspects, working on-site at the Trade Center turned mass gravesite. For Mohawks who practice traditional beliefs, it is important to honor the dead. They carried ceremonial tobacco and offered silent prayers as they worked.

Such work always has its spiritual aspects for those who are receptive to it. "When you're up in the air, sometimes you have to call on an eagle," McDonald says, "when it gets windy, or if it's raining or you have to work on ice. The eagle is closest to the Creator, and when the Mohawk builds a skyscraper, he is close to the Creator."

Chapter 13: Inside the zone of fear

"Cowards die many times before their deaths. The valiant never taste of death but once."—Shakespeare, Julius Caesar

Fight, flight or freeze

↓

Being one with death

↓

Singing through the danger zone

↓

The beds go marching one by one

Lieutenant E.F. Andrews of the U.S. Navy, who served with distinction in the Pacific theater during World War II, once explained:

> "Fear is something everyone feels. Anyone who has ever been in war has been afraid... anyone who says he has never been afraid is a fool. A hero is not somebody who does something he isn't afraid to do. A hero is someone who does something he is afraid to do. And I don't know anyone who isn't afraid of being shot at. So in wartime, of course you feel fear. Somebody is out there trying to kill you, and they aren't trying to kill anyone else at that time... it gets very personal then."

In a moment, circumstances can change from benign to frightening. And in that moment a person has to decide to fight, to flee, or to curl up and accept whatever consequences come to them. Typically this moment of decision seems lengthy, even endless, although it is usually quite brief. Often more thought takes place during such timeless moments that you can believe could have fit into such a small interval of time.

Yet whatever decision you make may have less to do with logical thinking than with personality, propensity, and perspective. Until the moment comes, Fire Department of NY's Lt. Picciotto says, you cannot predict which way you'll go. You make an assessment of your chances, looking at the tiger staring you in the face, not sure if you can make it safely home or whether you're better off swinging a weapon at him. In a moment one of those reflexes kicks in—fight or flight—or you stay, unable to decide, freezing and doing nothing. But that propensity can be influenced in advance, through training, through the use of mental rehearsals, through developing a strong sense of mission, through investment into the community you are fighting for, and so on.

It helps to have a good relationship with the concept of death. We've made so many advances against the ravages of famine and drought, disease and violence, that people are shielded from witnessing death. They rarely think about it, which is more a form of denial than of acceptance. In earlier days, death was more common and more visible. Children grew up seeing their dinners slaughtered in front of them; parents buried children who died before they learned to walk; children buried mothers who died bearing their siblings. Cotton Mather, the influential Puritan minister in colonial Massachusetts, had 17 children, only two of whom lived to adulthood. He conducted most of their funeral services himself.

Today there are only a few professions in which lives are regularly at risk. Beyond those, most people have little personal experience with death, and so have trouble coming to terms with it. One hospice nurse estimated that only 25% of the deaths she witnessed were what you might think of as "good deaths," where the patient has come to terms with dying, made peace with their families, and has some equanimity about the process. In those fields where people have more acquaintance with death or dying, they still may not accept their own mortality.

Yet some in the military, the fire departments, and the medical professions come to accept that death is part of life, that it will be part of what they do. Though it may still come as a frightening shock when actually faced with mortal danger, they may have accepted it well enough that they can put the fear aside and function in the face of grave personal risk. Picciotto writes, "I don't know too many firefighters who spend much time worrying. Planning, yes. Considering every eventuality, yes. But worrying? Nah. What the hell's the point?"

When he headed out for a job, the thought sometimes crept in that it might be his last. But he set the worry aside, let it go, and thought instead about what had to be done. Focus is a good thing for banishing such anxious, fruitless thoughts.

At least until you come to one of those heart-stopping moments, the moment when you know there's nothing you can do but pray, or wait and see if you'll survive. People who inspect the black box recorders after an airplane crashes report that the most frequent last words they hear are, eloquently, "Oh, shit!" This may be a common reaction in other extreme situations as well. Picciotto reports that the North Tower of the World Trade Center fell while he and a large number of other rescue workers were still in the stairwells. He blurted out, "Oh, shit, here it comes," on his bullhorn, voicing for everyone what they were probably feeling.

And yet, he reports, there were comforts in that moment. For the time being, they were trapped and there was nothing they could do. In that moment he had a vision of his wife and kids, smiling, not a pose he'd ever seen, just their images, cheerful and safe, comforting.

In that moment, with nothing more he could focus on to do, he found himself feeling both sad and grateful. Sad that his kids would lose their father before they were grown, sad his wife would have to cope without him, yet grateful for the love they'd shared, the time they had together, grateful that his pension and insurance would provide for his family once he was gone.

He wasn't afraid of dying, though he was afraid of suffering, of the possibility of a long and painful lingering with no food, no water, no hope of rescue. He found himself praying, frenetically, his mind jumping from subject to subject, but praying above all that his end be quick.

⋆   ⋆   ⋆

There is another kind of courage. In dire circumstances, where people may be elbowing each other aside to survive, there may be some who choose with dignity to stay put, letting others move ahead. They may be motivated by a sense that their time to die may be soon anyway, that other lives may have greater responsibilities than they do, that the lives they would be returning to are not what they want, that there's a good chance they won't escape anyway so they may as well meet death in a way of their own choosing. The musicians sitting on the deck of the sinking Titanic, for example, who played hymns and other comforting music for those who could not find seats on the lifeboats. Rescue workers on doomed missions. The Jews during the Holocaust who, knowing about the death camps, chose the short, hard lives of revenge as partisans. The passengers on September 11's Flight 93 who chose to die, not as victims, but as heroes, wresting control of the airplane from the terrorists and forcing it to crash on a farm rather than doing more damage at the nation's capitol.

All what you might call extreme grace under pressure.

⋆   ⋆   ⋆

You train until your muscles can respond automatically, you think and prepare scenarios in advance, but all the planning in the world won't prepare you for every contingency. But you get good enough—especially after the 10,000 hours that Malcolm Gladwell estimates it takes to become a master in your field—that your response is like that of a dancer, able to navigate a crowded dance floor even when others keep shifting their positions all around, even when your partner makes a misstep.

"You do your thinking *before* you get up at bat," explains Yogi Berra, named baseball's Most Valuable Player in three separate years. "We used to do a lot of talking and a lot of thinking about batting. We just didn't stand there thinking when we were up to bat. You can't stand up at the plate trying to think when the ball is coming at you—you do your thinking *before* the ball gets there."

In Berra's playing days, he used this wisdom not only to benefit his own team, but to disadvantage his opponents by disturbing their focus. Berra was known for his gift of gab. In his days as a catcher, he crouched close behind each opposing team member when they were up at bat. Cleveland Indians' Larry Doby was warned about Berra. "If we were playing in Cleveland he'd say stuff like, 'Where's a good place to go for dinner after the game?' If you try to answer while you're trying to hit, you're thinking and hitting at the same time—which Yogi said you cannot do."

Slugger Ted Williams once had a pithy reply to Berra's chatter: "Maybe just shut up, you ugly bastard."

⋆   ⋆   ⋆

People can use music and song to help tamp down their fears so that they can keep moving ahead. Jewish partisans fighting the Germans in World War II would often sing *Hatikvah* (The Hope) or and other Zionist movement songs.

Poles and other nationalist resistance groups would sing folk songs from their cultures to affirm that, in the face of the prevailing Nazi negation of their worth, they were indeed forces to be reckoned with.

The Freedom Riders of 1961 also used music to give them strength. Things had been relatively peaceful in Virginia and North Carolina, but as the bus ventured furthered into the South, the nasty incidents mounted. In South Carolina, two white thugs beat up a black Freedom Rider while a city policeman stood by. Only when he crumpled to the ground did the cop encourage the aggressors to move along. The Freedom Riders rode unmolested through Georgia, but the next stretch of road through Alabama was a nightmare, including riots, beatings, and a fire-bombing of the bus.

The Greyhound bus was pulling off the road, right on the border between Alabama and Mississippi. As bad as Alabama was, they expected worse in Mississippi. The driver got off and was replaced. The six Alabama National Guardsmen who'd been grimly sharing the ride, rifles with fixed bayonets at their sides, stepped off while guardsmen in Mississippi uniforms boarded. An Alabama government official climbed the steps and whispered at the six reporters who were riding along. Five of them stood up and sheepishly left. The remaining reporter told Farmer that the bureaucrat warned them the bus would be ambushed and destroyed when they cross the border.

The Freedom Riders looked at each other, a sick smile crossing their faces. After a few tense minutes one of them broke into song, if only to relieve the tension. It was an old church hymn, slightly modified for the occasion:

> "I'm a'takin a ride on the Greyhound bus line.
>
> I'm a'ridin the *front seat*, to Jackson, this time."

Everyone in their group joined in for the chorus:

> "Hallelujah, I'm a'travelin, Halleluja, ain't it fine?
>
> Hallelujah, I'm a'travelin down freedom's main line."

All of them were singing by the end. The music reinforced a feeling of solidarity among them. Song had stiffened their resolve and broke the hold of the fear that had become ever present on the ride.

When they were arrested in Jackson, Mississippi and locked in the patrol wagons on the way to jail, they sang a rousing chorus of "We Shall Overcome."

"We sang loudly," Farmer later recalled, "to silence our own fears. And to rouse our courage. There is no armor more impenetrable than song."

The singing picked up again after they were fingerprinted and locked into a series of small rooms. Farmer heard the same song coming from one of the other rooms further down the corridor, but it was stilled when prison guards started beating up the Freedom Riders. In the room Farmer was in, the guards panicked, waving their billy clubs and shouting, "Cut out that noise. Cut it out now!"

Defiantly, the activists finished the stanza before falling silent. "We felt good... That we had obeyed the command to stop singing did not bother us at all. The cops suddenly seemed irrelevant. We had the boost we needed. We could face anything now. We were not alone."

Later they were sent to the notorious Parchman State Prison. Singing continued, in spite of threats to make them stop. At one point the Deputy Warden told them the guards would remove their mattresses if they didn't shut up. The singing stopped, and silence reigned while the activists thought it over.

Finally Bernard Lafayette, a 20-year-old black theological student whom the others had nicknamed "Little Gandhi," rallied them with the reminder of what they were trying to accomplish. "We're all worrying about these hard, stupid mattresses because that's all we've got in this place. But those mattresses aren't anything but *things*. Things of the body. And we came down here for things of the *spirit*. Things like freedom and equality. And brotherhood."

Fellow activist Hank Thomas started calling for the guards. "You get my mattress; I'll keep my soul."

Again the refrain started up.

The guards came rushing in to remove their bedding from the cells. But in the contest of wills, freedom was what finally prevailed.

Chapter 14: Teamwork

"It was the nation and the race dwelling all 'round the globe that had the lion's heart. I had the luck to be called upon to give the lion's roar. I also hope that I sometimes suggested to the lion the right place to use his claws."—Winston Churchill

Don't handle these horses

↓

Be there for your buddy

↓

The glues of joking and drink

↓

Drumming for democracy

↓

It takes a village to escape a village

If you want to understand how teams function, you could do a lot worse than to study elite sports teams, either Olympic contenders or professional franchises. And one of the better ways to understand teams is through studying their coaches—the men and women who pull them together and keep them going through thick and thin.

Red Auerbach, the venerated coach of the Boston Celtics, praised one of his own coaches, a man named Bill Reinhart who coached college-level ball. His strength was in handling his players, Auerbach insisted, but he didn't actually handle them. "Players are people, not horses," Auerbach explained. "You don't handle them. You work with them, you coach them, you teach them, and, maybe most important, you listen to them. The best players are smart people and a good coach will learn from them."

In other words, great coaching and teamwork arise from training, encouragement, communication, and mutual respect. You train them in the skills they need, you rehearse all kinds of possible scenarios, you make sure they understand their mission, and at some point you have to let them go after it, performing as best they can, improvising whenever they have to, as undoubtedly they sometimes will.

Hymie Perlo, a paratrooper who jumped into enemy-occupied southern France during the Battle of Anzio in June of 1944, was one of 550 men who jumped that day. A tragic miscalculation caused over 300 of them to land in the Mediterranean, where many of the heavily laden troopers drowned. Perlo, luckily, landed on the ground but was immediately shot in the leg by an enemy sniper. He started hobbling toward safety when he spotted another of his squad members still in the water, also shot, and unable to help himself get onto the beach. Perlo was bad off, but he forced himself back, dragging himself into the water, and carried his buddy to safety.

"I was lucky," Perlo said, from the safety of a lunch counter in Washington D.C., many years later. "I did what I had to do, what I was supposed to do, what I'm sure the guy would have done for me. Nothing heroic there. The most heroic thing I did was live. I didn't jump into the Mediterranean Sea and I got out of there alive."

Modesty, as discussed earlier, is a pretty common trait among heroes. Too often they measure themselves against those few they knew who did even more, or for longer, or who died trying to do more.

⋆　　　⋆　　　⋆

The strength of the Navy SEALs, according to their commanding officers' philosophy, came from working together. And so the men trained together, vacationed together, and developed a sense of family. By the time guys paired up, especially for underwater work, they were deeply invested in looking after their buddy, and their buddy looked after them. No matter where they went or what they did during an operation, they were aware of where their assigned buddy was and never lost sight of them. That was the first rule among the teams.

Especially in dangerous situations, which might mean being underwater, or during any work in enemy territory, they dedicated themselves to taking care of their buddy, no matter who he was. Each man's buddy was the best friend he could ever have, even if only for the duration of the job. Even if there were personal differences between them, they were put aside for the duration. Everyone understood that. Each made sure nothing happened to their buddy, regardless of the cost, and could count on their buddy watching their back as well. That deep personal trust was a bond, an attitude penetrating the entire group, but was especially strong between each pair of buddies.

One SEAL, Edward Ashby, remembered a strong feeling of team spirit.

"If you were just there for the glory, you weren't going to stay very long...Everyone was important in the team, and it took everyone working together to get the job done...Friendship isn't a good enough word for what we felt for each other in our team. What we did and how we did it was a real bond between us. There was a relationship between the members...that seems to have been stronger than the bond between a married couple."

To get into the SEALs, after all, took a strong will, a capable mind, and a high degree of physical fitness. But to stay on the SEAL teams took a good heart and a sense of values, another veteran stressed. Without those, nobody wanted to work with you again, not when things could get critical at any moment. They had to be able to trust you.

Bonds can form in spite of many obstacles, including extreme differences in background and communications difficulties. General Colin Powell described the bond he felt as a young officer assigned to advise a squadron of the South Vietnamese Army in the remote A Shau valley. "I had taken the same risks, slept on the same ground, and eaten from the same pots as these men and had spilled my blood with them, shared death, terror, and small triumphs. All this linked me closely to men with whom I could barely converse."

Still there might be plenty of good-natured (or not-so-good-natured) teasing between members of a team. Seebee Charles Lewis described being sent into the late-winter ocean at Iwo Jima without a cold-water suit. "When my ensign told me it was my turn to get wet, I just put on my mask and fins and rolled into the water. Of course, I managed a little payback. On the pickup, my ensign was the man on the sling. Now he was a pretty good-sized lad...when it was my turn to be picked up, I set my fins against the water and braced myself. It was my ensign who was pulled from the boat instead of me!"

Horsing around plays its part as well in bringing teams together. In fact, laughter can develop a bond which otherwise might not exist. Freeman shares a story of Tom Oliver, an an American airman shot down over war-torn Yugoslavia in 1944, who was lucky enough to be picked up by partisans. But the partisan groups were not always pro-Allied, and with little common language between them, it wasn't completely clear if they would shelter an escaping American or turn him in. The Chetnik soldiers who picked him up were good about pouring brandy down his throat but not so good about telling him where they were taking him, or why.

One day, the drink flowing, a partisan pointed to the two knives Oliver carried, one at his belt and a spare strapped to his leg. He was puzzling how to explain the idea of a spare, relying on his few common words and a lot of gestures, when another partisan started laughing. "Ahh, Hitler," the man said, pointing to the first knife, then mimed the slitting of a throat, and a dramatic fall to the ground. Then he pointed to the second knife, saying, "Mussolini!" and repeating another dramatic death scene. Everyone joined in the laughter, which allowed Oliver to relax for the first time in days.

$\star \qquad \star \qquad \star$

The invisible bonds of affiliation can run amazingly strong and deep. Why else would Lt. E.F. Andrews go into the hold of the ship, as we read about earlier, to put out a blazing fire that was threatening to spread to the explosives stored there, when the navy's firefighters refused?

His job wasn't to fight fires. His job was to wait until a path needed to be cleared for the boats to land, then to scout the hazards along the way and destroy them, one by one. Until then, his assignment was to stay put, preserving his highly specialized group for when they were needed. There might be days or weeks when his men were idle except for exercising and checking their equipment, but the Navy felt that was a small price to pay to have their skills available.

His commanding officers would have ordered him to stay put and let others handle that fire. But the ship's firefighters froze in the face of danger, as sometimes happens even with well-intentioned, well-trained people, especially the first time they find themselves in crisis. Andrews recognized the situation for what it was—the choice between a frying pan and the flame itself. He might die either way, but one of the ways gave him a chance to save most of the men on the ship, whether or not he himself survived.

The trained firemen could see only the immediate danger, and panicked in the face of it. Trained to do a job while danger looked over his shoulder, even if it wasn't that particular job, Andrews saw a gamble with odds he could accept, and accept it he did.

And besides, a number of the wounded were members of his team. If the ship blew, he might be able to escape by swimming to another ship nearby, but his buddies would die a cold and lonely death, bleeding out into the vast, dark ocean. He couldn't leave a single teammate behind like that. They wouldn't leave him, if the roles were reversed.

So for him there was no choice at all. Once he understood the need, he had to give it a shot. And, to the undying gratitude of hundreds of men on the USS Blessman, he succeeded.

$\star$ $\star$ $\star$

The power of the group was confirmed for one of the Nashville Freedom Riders, Bernard Lafayette, when he rode the bus home from college for the holidays. "Riding while black" on an interstate bus through the Deep South with a large group of your comrades was tough but manageable, but doing it alone was just tough and scary. As his bus rode through the endless series of rural southern towns in the middle of the night, he could not let himself fall asleep. Every time the bus stopped at some small, deserted depot and an unknown white person approached the bus, he was on guard. He knew that blacks were pulled off sometimes and were never heard from again.

The absence of the same group was deeply felt by Diane Nash when her friends prevailed on her to stay behind, back at the office, while they went on the dangerous Freedom Ride through Alabama and Mississippi. She longed to join them; sheÕd trained to join them, but they insisted someone had to keep answering the phones and rallying the media to cover their mission, or it would be all for nothing. Someone had to solicit money to post bail for them and pay for lawyers when they were arrested. Someone had to speak to the Justice Department when Attorney General Robert F. Kennedy kept calling to try talking them out of what was becoming a political embarrassment for the new Kennedy administration.

David Halberstam reported that Nash

"was constantly exhausted by what she was doing, more, she later realized, emotionally than physically. If she made even the smallest mistake, if she was not careful, someone might get killed because of her. The strain of that was terrible. But mostly what she remembered from those days was the loneliness... In Tennessee they had always had each other. Now she lacked the comfort of that special community. At the beginning she cried herself to sleep every night. All the people she loved and cared about were completely at risk."

What Nash instinctively felt was the cutting of that tie to the ones you were responsible for, how vulnerable you felt when it was suddenly severed, and how bad you knew you'd feel if something happened to them while you were somewhere else, safe.

★   ★   ★

Teamwork comes easily to well-coordinated groups who have practiced working together extensively. But there are times when amateurs join forces to fight a common battle. As a team they can do more than one or two could do together—and yet there is more risk among such loosely-bound groups. Trust may not have had a chance to develop enough to ensure the feeling of confidence that they can count on each other. Paid professional teams have the additional motivations of monetary incentives and punishments, but with untrained or volunteer groups there is often little discipline to go on.

One of the most useful sets of instructions I have read about how a group of people can begin to form a sense of teamwork—a sort of collective instead of individual functioning, comes from a book of instructions on performing West African music entitled *Songs of West Africa*. Attempting to explain the African sensibility of music to a Western audience, author/musician Dan Gorlin had to grapple with bridging a huge cultural gap he didn't realize existed until he tried teaching around it. Westerners are socialized to function as individuals, separately from each other. We leave our families as we mature, often leaving our home towns as well, and only return once in a while. We are not expected to bear much responsibility for either family or hometown. In contrast, Africans are traditionally reared to be active participants in a coherent whole. The family, the village, the tribe—to a tribal African, each of these has its own personality, and members are woven into them.

This subtle but vital difference impeded his Western students' abilities to join in the musical experience, because the egoism involved in individual-driven behavior—the tendency to show off, to seek attention, to use whatever level of accomplishment you achieve as a mark of status—tended to ruin the beauty of the performance, diminishing or destroying the natural bond-forming tendencies of music.

So Gorlin was forced to teach the notion that the purpose of the music was not to provide background sounds for the dating scene, nor mere aesthetic appreciation as an art form, but a spiritual and emotional event designed to draw people together as a coherent community. Instead of gratifying individuals and providing them with yet another way to compete, drumming and dance events were more like combinations of sacred religious celebrations and high school pep rallies. His lessons for beginning students of West African music can be applied to the development of any team:

First, he says, people can and should use their voices to shore up the voices of the people around them. Especially if a neighbor's voice is weak but their own is strong, they can reinforce their sound and both will feel more confident. "Don't think about how your voice sounds alone," he advises, "only how the two or three sound together, and make the most of that sound."

Each individual's job in such a setting "is to contribute what you can to the success of the group. What your fellow singers need from you is not so much sound or technique, but *spirit*. As you sing, look around you and notice where the enthusiasm is, and where there could be more. Sometimes just sharing a brief smile with someone can have amazing results. Don't try to do more than you're comfortable doing. . . you're supposed to contribute *what* you can, not *more* than you can. . .

"Finally," he writes,

> "a word about confidence. When you sing, let your confidence come from the pride you feel for the group, not for yourself. You sense of self worth may come and go, belief in your own abilities may waver, but community pride is something you can always count on. Try to identify more with the group than with yourself."

So, in order to become part of a great team, each person may have to step back a bit, dial back their awareness of their own needs in order to work on behalf of the whole. Yet this does not negate the importance of each member of the team. Basketball coach Sidney Goldstein, author of *The Basketball*

Coach's Bible, draws out this point also. In discussing how to teach skills to a team, he urges that coaches use his number one rule: "Teach each individual as though everything depends on it. (It does.)"

★   ★   ★

In the middle of combat, a fire, or any difficult collective effort, there is comfort in knowing you can count on your buddies to do their jobs while you are doing yours. And if someone gets hurt, each of you knows enough to pick up where someone else left off. When you understand the overall mission and have practiced most of the contingencies that might come up, you develop enough confidence to go forward into even the most terrifying of missions. You proceed, learning *in situ* the rough combination of skills, ability to improvise, and some variation of trust in your luck, fate, or the hand of God.

In the Nazi concentration camps, trust was a rare commodity; sadism was king and blood-lust was given full license to roam. The few Jews who held positions of trust in those hells often did so at a terrible cost: the goldsmith who was kept alive so he could turn the gold teeth ripped from his murdered grandfather's mouth into jewelry for the wives and mistresses of the thugs who guarded and beat him; the teenage girl, raped and forced to become the mistress of the man who ordered her mother's and sisters' deaths; the cobbler who made fine leather footwear for the commandant after witnessing his predecessor's murder because the commandant's son did not like the way his new shoes fit.

Sobibor was one of three camps established by Heinrich Himmler in Poland to mass-murder the Jews of that country—and by the autumn of 1943 they had almost succeeded. Before the war, over three million of Poland's citizens were Jewish; by the middle of the war more than 90% of them were dead. The railroad spur that brought the cattle cars crammed full of victims to the camp every day, now sat in disuse except for a once-a-week transport of new victims from occupied Holland. Rumors swept through the camp that it was scheduled to be dismantled, possibly as soon as mid-October. And once it was dismantled, they were sure that every last prisoner would be liquidated. The Nazis were not likely to transfer them carefully to other camps.

For months, members of the Jewish underground had been working out potential mass escape plans. Several earlier, uncoordinated escapes had ended in disaster, both for the escapees and the people left behind. Any show of resistance brought reprisal killings of other, randomly selected Jews. Furthermore, the escapes forced the SS to strengthen security measures at Sobibor. They increased the number of guards. They cleared the perimeter around the camp of any cover and planted land mines in random patterns around the periphery. To Leon Feldhendler, a leader among the prisoners (played by Alan Arkin in the 1987 TV movie of the uprising), it was clear that all escapes had to be discouraged until they could break out, *en masse*.

But how to break out all at once would be a challenge in itself. Three different schemes were devised, all of which had insurmountable problems. One key difficulty was that none of the prisoners had ever killed anyone. Before they were rounded up, they were doctors and lawyers, craftsmen, tradesmen, rabbis—peaceable people caught up in the war. Escape would require killing a number of guards, no matter which plan they used. Feldhendler's people knew enough to set up an escape, but he wasn't sure any of them could actually kill, even to save their own lives. What they needed were a few men with military training, people who had actually killed before. Maybe also someone with experience leading people, who might know how to plan not just for an escape but to lead them toward some place where they could survive and join the resistance, once they were outside the camp.

His prayers were answered on September 23, when a train carrying 1,700 new prisoners arrived from Minsk. Most were immediately murdered in the gas chambers, but one of the few allowed to live was Lt. Alexander Perchersky, a large man in a dirty green Russian officer's uniform, a Jewish prisoner of war who'd already spent two years in Nazi-run prison camps. Though he'd been a bookkeeper before the war, Perchersky had been through a number of battles. If armed, he would not be afraid to strike back at his captors.

At his previous work camp he had learned the hard lessons: how to finagle or steal extra food, avoiding the slow starvation that most of his comrades faced, and how to survive random beatings and torture. He was already deep in plans for his own escape with several Russian POWs when the Germans ordered him and the other Jewish slave-workers onto the train for Sobibor.

Newcomers sometimes broke under the shock of learning that their newly assigned task was gassing and burning the bodies of the innocents coming in on the death trains. Those who survived the shock often turned to a strategy of self-preservation at all costs, becoming hardened and cynical. If Perchersky had adapted this way, he would not be someone they could trust. And what could be more important than trust, when they had to develop a plan in total secrecy to liberate the several hundred poor souls remaining in the camp, or resign themselves to being shot or gassed as the Germans attempted to clean up all evidence of mass murder before the Russian army, now only a few hundred miles away, overran them?

The lieutenant, on his side, had to satisfy his doubts. Could he trust Feldhendler not to betray him? To even hint that he wanted to escape might get him executed. Could the man provide information that might make the difference between futile defiance and a mission with even a small chance of success?

On September 28, Feldhendler arranged a meeting. It went well enough that the two met twice more, finally agreeing they could work together.

Their first decision was to agree on a goal. Were they seeking vengeance against the bastards who had decimated their families, their villages and towns, and their way of life? Such a plan would involve grabbing weaponry and remaining in camp to kill as many Nazis and collaborators as they could, until they themselves were gunned down or beaten to death. Were they looking to destroy the machinery of death, wrecking as many of the buildings and equipment as they could before they were stopped? Or were they looking to break as many prisoners free as possible, and then put distance between themselves and the camp?

Escape became their priority, not vengeance or destruction, and that decision shaped their final plan. All other components were debatable: who could they trust? How many should be told in advance of the breakout, and how many left to figure it out once the fences were broken down? Which SS men and collaborators absolutely had to be killed in order to get away?

Trust was one of their biggest issues. In the divide-and-conquer system used by the Nazis, betrayal was often a way to stay alive a little longer: give up someone's secret and earn an extra slice of bread, turn someone in and earn a chunk of sausage or a stay of execution for yourself. Beyond the every-man-for-himself rule, there were alliances that both bound and divided the community of survivors—ethnic loyalties, kinship, language and cultural differences.

The leaders of the revolt thus chose their allies carefully, those who would help overpower the guards, seize weapons and break down the fences. Everyone else would have to fend for themselves, and once the fences were breached, they could decide to leave or stay. Indeed, about half the inmates ultimately stayed in the camp after the uprising began. Some stayed to fight and avenge themselves. Others stayed out of fear that the land mines, the Polish peasants, or the dangers of the unprotected forest were worse than the dangers inside the camp. Some tried to escape but failed, overpowered by the guards as they tried to break through.

Feldhendler chose the men who would set up ruses to take out a few key SS men and *kapos*.[7] Perchersky selected the Russian POWs who would hide in place so that, once those key men were lured indoors, they could be killed or silenced.

Breakout day was fast approaching. Tensions mounted, but the men tried to keep each other calm. On October 13, two days before the date an informant told them the camp was supposed to be shut down, a trainload of SS officers arrived unexpectedly, which forced them to call off the escape. They had enough manpower to overwhelm the key officers in camp, but not for this additional barrage of trained and armed sadists.

Fortunately the outsiders left that evening for another camp eight miles away. There was some hesitation about resuming the plan. Secrets were hard to keep. Did anyone give them away? Would the SS officers they counted on to be on vacation return in the morning? October 14 was the Jewish holiday of Succot; would the Orthodox Jews be willing to fight on a holy day?

"The Nazis kill Jews on holy days," Perchersky decided. "We can kill Nazis on them too."

For all their planning, a few unexpected developments forced them to improvise. The next day a sympathetic kapo was sent to a different part of camp under armed guard; an SS sergeant they were planning to put out of commission noticed one of the conspirators wearing sturdier clothes than he was supposed to have. Another SS sergeant resisted the bribe which was supposed to lure him away to a back room where they planned to silence him; instead he returned to his office in the Administrative Building.

These changes made the leaders uneasy, but there was no more time for delays. The next day the camp would be shutting down and they might all be machine gunned to death. They had to risk going ahead. Perchersky sent a

---

[7]Kapos were prisoners who were trusted by the Nazi officers. Often they were criminals, transferred from German civilian prisons, who were allowed to supervise work details or become wardens in the barracks. Many kapos were notorious sadists, and were prosecuted after the war for their participation in the mass murders.

messenger boy to Feldhendler telling him to handle the changed circumstances as he saw fit. "Happy hunting," he told his confederate.

The power and phone lines to the camp were severed. The Assistant Kommandant was led into the tailor shop, ostensibly to be fitted for a new suit. While the tailor was hovering around him, a man came up from behind and split his head open with an axe. The camp's hatmaker, swept up in the excitement, picked up a scissors and started stabbing the Kommandant, shouting the names of his murdered wife and children. He had to be restrained so that the noise wouldn't alert the guards still moving freely outside.

By five o'clock, most of the solo targets had been killed or disabled. Perchersky signaled the barber, who put a bugle to his lips and blew. The Jewish prisoners lined up, four people to a row, attempting to look like a normal line-up to the guards still manning the machine guns in the towers. Feldhendler led the line, marching them to an area of the camp behind some of the barracks. They'd already stashed a ladder there tall enough to scale the fence, in an area they were fairly sure would let them skirt around the land mines.

Several mines exploded anyway, eliminating any possibility of surprise. Guards opened fire with machine guns, but many of the prisoners escaped safely to the woods beyond.

Back in the middle section of camp, Perchersky couldn't believe his luck. He was certain he'd have been shot and killed by this time. "This is it," he told the sympathetic kapo who was to play the next part. The kapo blew the whistle, though roll call wasn't scheduled for another few minutes. When another kapo complained, he was knifed to prevent him from alerting the others.

This changed things enough, however, to out their secret. Perchersky jumped atop a table and shouted to the prisoners milling around, "Our day has come. Most of the Germans are dead. Let us die with honor."

One of the guards ran to alert the SS. Two young boys spooked and ran, and an SS officer began shooting. Jews ran in all directions, some heading for the fences, some for the main gate. A guard on a bicycle began yelling, but the Jews knocked him down and proceeded to slash at him, using knives made with scraps of metal in the craft shops. Russian POWs assaulted the armory but were held off by the SS. Some got away, though others fell, wounded or dead. A third escape route opened up when some prisoners with wire cutters snipped the barbed wire behind the SS quarters and crawled through.

Over 160 Jews were still alive and trapped inside the camp, but approximately 300 escaped. Dozens more lay dead in the yard or the fields, gunned down by the SS and their guards. Eleven SS officers were killed, plus a number of the hated guards.

Over the next several weeks, many of the escapees were captured and killed by the Nazis, or by anti-Semitic Polish partisans and citizens living in the area. Some of the prisoners banded together and began carrying out guerrilla warfare against the Germans. Others went into hiding. But just because they were outside the camps did not mean they were safe.

About 50 of the escapees survived the war. Feldhendler was murdered in January 1945 by members of the ultrapatriotic Polish Home Army in the doorway of his own apartment. Lt. Perchersky led a group of men eastward into Russian territory, though the Germans still occupied the region. He joined a group of Russian partisans and began dynamiting German troop trains. Eventually his luck turned: he stepped on a land mine that tore away much of his leg. Taken to a hospital, the surgeons saved the leg and sent him home to his wife and daughter. Deep enough in Russia to be safe from the Nazis, he was caught and imprisoned by the Soviet secret police, who charged him with treason, for the crime of having let himself be captured by enemy troops. Sentenced to a labor camp, an international outcry eventually resulted in his release.

⋆ ⋆ ⋆

Any experience offers lessons, and the Sobibor escape is no exception. What worked for the freedom fighters, and what didn't?

Their efforts were helped enormously by the good and careful choice of allies. Their lives depended on each other, and any careless slip could have gotten them executed long before the break-out. They were lucky, too, that none of his fellow conspirators were discovered committing some minor infraction and shot, which might have left them missing some key component of the plan, or tortured, which might have resulted in someone giving them up. Feldhendler was also lucky in that the men of action he knew they needed were delivered by train, with just barely enough time to plan and carry out a revolt.

The youth and strength of the men involved were a factor, and yet they were unremarkable in that environment. The men who planned the uprising ranged in age from 16 to 33. A few younger lads were involved in the revolt—carrying messages, handing guns out a window—but not in the planning itself. Age was not a telling characteristic for courageous action under the Nazis because there were few outside that age range left alive in the camps. There were no children: Nazis sent children to the gas chambers with their mothers. There were no older people, who were usually selected to die as soon as they arrived at Sobibor. The SS plucked the young and strong from the sea of victims, and from those kept only the ones with skills the Germans could put to immediate, profitable use.

What hindered them most were shortcomings that became apparent, not during the breakout, but in the hours and weeks that followed. The Sobibor uprising was a huge success, given the adverse circumstances. The bravery demonstrated by the conspirators was enormous. That half the survivors in the camp escaped to the forests, having killed most of the top administrators, represents tremendous success. Once they broke through, however, the severe lack of information about where they were and whether there were any safe zones nearby, plus the lack of allies in highly anti-Semitic Poland, led most of them straight to their deaths, many within the first 24 hours of their escape. Three hundred bbroke out, but less than 20% survived the 18 months until the war's end.

They broke out, most of them carrying no more than the clothing they wore, and maybe a crust of bread. The prisoners had no money, no food, no weapons or tools, sometimes didn't even speak any Polish to communicate with nearby farmers and townspeople. Unlike the downed Allied airmen shot down over France or Belgium, who were sometimes lucky enough to be discovered by an underground partisan prepared to run them along escape routes back to friendly territory, the escapees were surrounded by a hostile world where soldiers were actively hunting them down, where the locals were afraid to hide them for fear of reprisals, and many were happy to accept a reward for turning them in.

On the other hand, while the Sobibor Jews were still prisoners, most of them felt they had little to lose. They knew they would be shot or gassed soon by their tormentors. There was a remote chance that the Russian army would arrive and beat the Germans into submission, but few of them held much hope for that. Progress at the front was slow, and the Germans too efficient. They were likely to die anyway; why not do so while making a difference?

Perhaps their deaths could slow the machinery of murder; perhaps other Jews might live a little longer if the Sobibor Jews revolted. If they could take a few of the evildoers down with them, at least there would be some purpose to their deaths. If their actions drew the world's attention to this God-forsaken corner of the world, maybe the Allies would do something to put a halt to it. Years of oppression had created huge pools of anger and frustration within them. Yes, there were still a few, even in the camps, who were in denial, and others who were so beaten down that they could look no farther than their own broken feet. But there were plenty who were willing to risk themselves if there was a chance it would make a difference. These motives were the base of their courage.

What else helped, in addition to the bonds of teamwork, the sense of responsibility to others, and the sense that there was little to lose? This was a clear us-versus-them situation as long as the Nazis held themselves on top and trampled the Jews underneath. Yes, there were collaborators who were exceptions to this rule, who hoped they could cling to their overlords and survive. Most of them didn't. Among the rebels, some may have drawn on their religious faith for the inspiration or the strength to rebel. Certainly there are accounts of religious faith giving some in the camps the strength to survive. Others may have looked to the future, wanting to leave some kind of memorial, so that future generations would look back at them and be proud that they stood up and said, "No!" even as most others had been too badly beaten down and so, could not.

As with so many other exemplars of courage, we cannot help but be proud of them.

Chapter 15: Sustaining courage

"Courage is fear holding on a minute longer."—General George S. Patton

"We shall not flag or fail. We shall go on to the end, we shall fight in France, we shall fight on the seas and oceans, we shall fight with growing confidence and growing strength in the air, we shall defend our island, whatever the cost may be, we shall fight on the beaches, we shall fight on the landing grounds, we shall fight in the fields and in the streets, we shall fight in the hills; we shall never surrender."—Sir Winston Churchill

Serial bravery

↓

The energy sag

↓

It ain't over 'til it's over

You often see courage in people not once in a lifetime, but as a repeated choice. Courage, for some, shows up again and again in the course of a lifetime, each occurrence building those deep emotional muscles stronger until they can clear away the biggest obstacles and open up the pathway for all.

First Lady Eleanor Roosevelt stuck her neck out often enough for others that, eighty years later, she is still remembered as a woman of great moral courage. "You gain strength, courage and confidence," she once said, "by every experience in which you really stop to look fear in the face. You are able to say to yourself, 'I have lived through this horror. I can take the next thing that comes along.'" She urged people to push against their own boundaries, saying, "You must do the thing you think you cannot do."

In every firehouse, every police station, there are a few individuals known for their willingness to face the very worst circumstances: the fires that have the others trying to stay back at the truck feeding hose to the ones at the front, the domestic disturbances or urban riots that set an officer in unpredictable danger, risking his life. There is no mistaking that these people are courageous, and a well-run society depends on them. Yet they are paid for their time and gain a certain status for their efforts. If they burn out, it is understood (though not happily), and the hierarchy tries to support them with counseling or a lateral move to a position on the sidelines. Some may argue these career heroes are not paid enough, or do not receive the status they deserve, but at least their efforts are acknowledged and applauded to some extent.

This is in contrast to certain moral heroes like Harriet Tubman and others who acted in the face of social and legal obstacles to courage. They risked not only their lives and livelihoods, but also potential rejection by their communities even if they succeeded and survived. And they didn't act courageously just once, but over and over again. They are serial heroes; if only they received the same attention, the same box office appeal in Hollywood, the same number of feet on the bookshelves as serial killers do.

Another example of serial bravery was the Japanese consul in Lithuania, Chiune Sugihara, who in 1940 signed more than 2,000 visas for Jews who were desperate to escape the Nazi invasion, in spite of his government's direct orders not to do so. Japan was an ally of the German government that was murdering millions of Jews; showing them sympathy, let alone aiding their escape would embarrass the diplomats of his nation. Thus every morning that Sugihara made the decision to help, every time he picked up a pen to sign another visa, he acted heroically, doing what he knew was right, each time risking his career and possibly his life. At the end of the war his actions were not lauded, even under the new Allied-approved administration. He was fired from the Japanese civil service and had to find employment elsewhere.

But Sugihara, like Tubman, was no one-shot wonder. He had made a series of choices throughout his adult life that indicated a tendency to think for himself and act according to his conscience. As a teen his father pushed him to enter medical school; he deliberately failed the entrance exam so that he could go instead to Waseda University and study English literature. He entered the Foreign Service and was eventually posted to Manchuria where he became Deputy Foreign Minister. When the Japanese invaded Manchuria and began ruling it through a puppet government in the 1930s, he quit his post to protest their increasingly harsh treatment of the native population. He was a man who tended toward serial acts of moral courage; a lifetime of increasingly tough choices hardened him for the task.

⋆   ⋆   ⋆

Former terrorist turned president Nelson Mandela is another hero who has taken a lifetime of courageous stances. He dedicated his life to fighting the unfair restrictions on black South Africans throughout most of the 20th century, who could not own property or vote, and whose mobility and choice of where and how to live were vastly restricted by the white European settlers who colonized their country. Yet even while working night and day toward their liberation, Mandela lifted his eyes up toward ever broader horizons, affiliating himself with not only the cause of the blacks of South Africa, but an ever wider group of people, acting on their behalf and advocating for their welfare.

Born the grandson of a king in the Thembu tribe, son of a chief and educated to be privy counselor, Mandela could have acted most of his life for his own benefit. Many people would have made that choice and enriched themselves in the process. Or he might have taken on the greater cause of the Thembu, or the entire Xhosa-speaking peoples, and been known among them as a great leader. He chose bigger, wider, and deeper instead.

One of his early heroes was a tribal poet who electrified the students at Mandela's proper, British-run boarding school when he appeared in a ceremonial leopard-skin cloak carrying a spear in each hand. The man's native-language poems celebrated Xhosa culture and values. This was a breathtaking break for the teens whose curriculum included British history, science, and other Western subjects, and completely ignored African studies of any kind, though their students all lived in Africa. The poet opened the young Mandela's eyes to the possibility that his fellow Africans might deserve some dignity and respect.

Later, as a young man Mandela traveled around the country, and eventually to Ethiopia and Egypt, enormously broadening his horizons. Joining the African National Congress (ANC), which was formed in 1912 to bring chiefs, church people, and ordinary Africans together to defend their rights and freedoms, Mandela began to think about fighting a system run by a British colonial government that seemed entirely designed to shut the natives out of power, both political and economic. In his early adulthood he turned his back on other down-trodden groups—the substantial Indian minority and those of mixed races—but by his mid-thirties he was welcoming their support for the ANC and advocating on their behalf as well.

Make no mistake—this was a form of courage as well, taking up the cause of these other peoples, when so much more work was needed to promote his own. Many of his black African colleagues resented the mixed race and Indian populations, whose restrictions were nowhere near as harsh as those on the darkest-skinned Africans. There were times when Mandela had to withstand attacks from within his circle on this very issue. Yet he kept widening his affiliations to embrace even more of those who needed help. His activism was labeled "terrorist activities" by the government and he was thrown into prison, where he fought the authorities for a greater degree of respect and better treatment of all prisoners—whites, blacks, and those of mixed race. All the while he was writing, dreaming, and politicking to extract equal rights for all South Africans, as well as agitating for reconciliation and forgiveness across tribal, racial and socio-economic fault lines.

He had a big heart and a lot of endurance, but it was his embracing of forgiveness which is the most memorable aspect of Nelson Mandela's life and character. He could have chosen an easier life; as one of the few well-educated blacks in South Africa. He could have earned great wealth and status as a lawyer or advisor to tribal kings. Instead he chose to fight for the dignity and rights of his people. Thrown into prison on charges of treason by the impossibly racist system of apartheid, he could have pleaded for his life, but he chose to put the government itself on trial, a strategy which everyone predicted would earn him the death penalty. But he continued to stick his neck out for the welfare of others.

Repeatedly rejecting amnesty when it was offered to him, he spent 27 years in prison. When the politics of his country finally softened enough to allow his release, as well as the decriminalization of the ANC, he could have resumed a safe and lucrative life as a lawyer or public speaker. His cause was won, and people everywhere honored him for it. Instead he rolled up his sleeves and reentered the public world. Again he refused the easy, safe route. He could have advocated the obvious and easy positions—power for his people, payback from the former white establishment which treated him so brutally for so long. He did, after all, spend almost three decades of his adult life in prison. He missed years in his wife's arms; he was not allowed to bury his mother when she died; he missed watching his children grow up. He was not even allowed a furlough to attend the funeral when his firstborn son was killed in a car accident.

Instead he embraced the white community along with the black, using his growing stature to encourage forgiveness, reconciliation of grievances between black and white, a sharing of respect and power. Without Nelson Mandela, many agree, South Africa would have devolved into civil warfare. Without his courage and compassion, blood would have flowed down the streets of Soweto, revenge would have wreaked havoc in Johannesburg and Witwatersrand; throughout South Africa chaos would be king.

His five years as president instead allowed his nation to prosper as one of the best-integrated, best-run countries on the continent of Africa, the continent which long ago gave birth to us all, which apparently still has things to teach us.

Including the courage to forgive.

★   ★   ★

At its most basic level, fear is the body's visceral alarm system. When the heart starts pounding, the armpits sweating, the hands or stomach muscles clenching, these are all calls from the subconscious mind interpreting the present situation as an existential threat: *hey, listen, it doesn't feel safe here!* Fear says gird yourself for danger. Sit this one out if you can, or go forward cautiously if you have to, instead of running away. This reaction kicks in no matter whether the situation represents a physical risk or an emotional one.

When the fear response is set off, a series of physiological processes are triggered. The *locus ceruleus*,[8] an area within the brain stem, begins to fire. The more unusual and potentially dangerous the situation, the more intensely and prolonged those neurons will discharge. This activates the autonomic nervous system, releasing adrenaline and norepinephrine from the adrenal glands, increasing heart rate, blood flow to skeletal muscles, and releasing glucose (a chemical form of energy) from various storage reserves in the body. All this stimulates what has come to be known as the fight-or-flight response.

If the person who feels endangered responds by fleeing the situation or confronting it, or if the danger is averted or at least shifts, the biochemistry

---

[8]Latin for "blue spot", so called because of its slightly blue color.

eventually returns to normal, their body flushing the residues from the system in the normal fashion. But if the person cannot respond by either fleeing or fighting, trapped in chronic danger, the body responds in several dysfunctional ways. The stress of long-held fear which is not dealt with and allowed to dissipate leaves its track, often in the form of diseases such as ulcers, asthma, skin rashes, heart conditions or certain forms of cancer. It may also manifest in emotional reactions such as insomnia, nightmares, dissociation, or depression.

Fear can thus be the unwanted gift that keeps on giving. It may become a black hole that sucks you in, whose enormous gravity holds you prisoner, outside of ordinary space and time, until you implode or someone outside the hole sets up a rescue mission.

Implosions were often what brought therapy clients into my office. "I can't sleep" was a common one, when the new patient came in after a bad car accident or some other disaster. "I can't seem to get myself out of bed most mornings," I might hear on the first visit, for the client who couldn't make themselves go to work, whose life was falling apart. They might feel suicidal, or tell me, "Nothing makes sense any longer." All these could be outward symptoms of a person who got stuck somehow in a situation which they were not ready to deal with (too frightened or too confused) until the slow dustfalls of time eventually buried them under a mountain of muck.

What entrenched them was often a need to remain in a bad situation—a dependent child of an abusive parent who felt helpless to stop the abuse, a man or woman held in a difficult marriage by their religion, economic dependency, the needs of their children, or fear of the unknown—which outweighed their distaste for the wretchedness of the known situation. Yet sometimes what held them in an unpleasant state of suspended animation began to release its grip as circumstances changed, as the children left home, as they began to doubt the wisdom of their religion, when the person could finally afford to consider either a fight (or at least a confrontation) or taking flight.

One client came to me who suffered from terrifying recurrent nightmares. A student from a local university, he was becoming afraid to sleep at night for fear of seeing these scenes: a violent creature ripping flesh; himself, powerless and cowering in the background; flickering firelight. His face was pale and his hands trembled; he had an air of deep weariness about him, and he was having trouble focusing on his studies when he came in for help.

We did several sessions of Gestalt therapy work together, and the story that emerged was extreme. As a young teen growing up in an alcoholic family, he had witnessed plenty of disasters, but one of the worst was seeing his father beating his younger brother to death in a drunken rage. The man had stormed off, and my client's younger self had kept himself hidden, afraid that if his father realized he was there, he'd get beaten too. By the time he finally felt safe enough to emerge, his brother had bled out on the floor before him. Years passed, my client going through middle school and high school in a daze of post-traumatic stress syndrome. Now in a psychology graduate program, he was drawn to working with troubled teens in abusive alcoholic families, but for some reason he couldn't focus well, he couldn't sleep at night.

The subconscious mind can be a puppet master, pulling the strings to keep the person functioning, stopping them from functioning when it is not safe, and starting up when it's time to begin again. For years he'd suppressed this frightening, guilt-inducing scene. Even the memory of his younger brother somehow seemed to fade out, and for good reason: The 12-year-old boy had to live with his father, yet who could live with the person who murdered his beloved sibling? No one, and so that was who he became—no one, a shell of a person, until he was off on his own and strong enough to begin dealing with that horrific combination of emotions and events.

He lost years of his life this way, but it allowed him to survive, and now the memories were beginning to emerge, indirectly, through the dream, but coming back often enough to insist he begin paying attention. Instinctively he'd begun reaching out for help—getting training through his psychology studies to bolster his ability to understand and cope, developing a circle of friends for the first time in his life, and finding an ally/therapist to begin the process. He was starting to get a grip on that old, bad situation which had been too overwhelming to attend to when he was younger. Now, at 23, he was stronger, braver, more capable of coming to terms with knotty questions like whether his father was evil or merely sick, and whether he'd ever be able to sit across a table and eat with him again, now that he had the choice.

Psychological fear and psychological courage are in many ways parallel to physical fear and physical courage. There are stomach-dropping moments and moments of pause, where the person wonders if they can do this, and other moments of plunging ahead. There are moments of strength and moments of depletion. Courage for confrontations can be strengthened and supported through training and preparation in advance, through experience, through a good choice of allies, by clarifying the sense of what greater rightness you are working towards, and by having a community of supporters to cheer you on and acknowledge your success.

★   ★   ★

As we have said before, one thing that works well for sustaining courage is to build on previous successes. Longevity is often the key to winning a metaphorical marathon. As filmmaker Woody Allen famously said, "Eighty percent of success is showing up."

But it's not just showing up or hanging in there, it's also using what you learned in the past to sustain the present action. Harriet Tubman learned more of the back roads with each successive slave raid, making each trip safer than the last. Nelson Mandela grew to know his opponents' weaknesses and capitalized on them; firemen develop a special sense about fires from working on many in the past. Experience tends to make brave actions more efficient, safer, and more effective over time. And success in the past can smooth down the pathway to success in the future for many reasons: it creates a sense of confidence that the next obstacle can be overcome too, it attracts allies because more people are willing to help when it looks like their work will have a reasonable chance of success, it strikes fear in the heart of the enemy, which weakens the opposition they face.

The students who became the core of the Civil Rights movement in the early 1960s built on each success or partial success to keep the momentum going. Once they succeeded in their first lunch-counter sit-in, the students organized more, which led to a day when several thousand people marched to confront the mayor of Nashville on the courthouse steps. Diane Nash, leader of the student group, found enough confidence, based on their small but real series of successes, to demand that he use his influence to end racial segregation. The mayor looked out over the crowd, annoyed at feeling ambushed by her, and yet he found himself agreeing to do just that. Within a few days it was a done deed—the downtown department stores of Nashville began serving white and black alike.

Success at the lunch counters in Nashville gave the activists the courage to push for integration of other public facilities, which encouraged them to go on the Freedom Rides, which led to the voter registration campaigns, the passage of the Civil Rights Act of 1964 and the Voting Rights Act of 1965, the push for equal opportunities in employment, and the multitude of laws and regulations that make the world today a much more fair and equal place than it was in the fall of 1959, when those students first began meeting in a back room on a quiet, shaded college campus to discuss the nature of non-violent protest.

Chapter 16: How common is courage?

"We are the world
We are the children
We are the ones
To make a better day."
—song by Michael Jackson and Lionel Ritchie

The impossibility of statistics
↓
Start with 7, dream of 100

As people read through all these facts and anecdotes, they may find themselves asking "How common is bravery?" and "Can anyone be a hero?" and, often, "Do I have what it takes to be a hero?" This chapter explores the first question; the chapter that follows discusses the second, and both chapters, in their different ways, attempt to answer the third.

Fire stations are populated by self-selected groups of people more likely than most to risk their lives in order to save others. Yet even among them, not everyone is known for their courage. There are always a few in every firehouse, police station, and military barracks who are known for being brave, for standing out, even in a crowd already known for courage.

Among the general population, the incidence of heroism is understandably much smaller. It is difficult to measure how common courage is because of the many varieties of courage. There may be some who will risk themselves to pull a child out of the street when a car careens down the road toward them, but who would be reluctant to report a fellow employee stealing from their company. The woman who separates from an abusive husband, even as he threatens to kill her and their children, might be unwilling to take on a different set of risks.

Some may have courage for a single instance, while others might have enough to risk safety, status, or reputation again and again. These variables make it hard to determine how many of us would be brave if we had to.

The Holocaust, one of the most heavily studied periods in history, was a crucible that burned away the superficial qualities for many, while revealing or exaggerating other people's true personalities. Persecution was especially intense against the Jews, but Gypsies, homosexuals, leftists, members of the clergy with particularly strong consciences, and anyone opposed to the Nazi Party were also targeted. Resisters were sentenced to death and might be shot on the spot. If allowed to live a little longer, they often awaited their sentence under conditions so terrible that they might be relieved when death finally came.

In many towns and cities no one was willing to shelter the persecuted. The result was that 5.7 million Jews were killed, as well as close to 1 million gypsies, and countless other civilians who were murdered by government fiat and the inaction of civilians who let it happen. Yet here and there in every country a few courageous souls refused to allow this to happen without protest. Some objected through civil action, others through quiet words or deeds of kindness. Some offered food or a place to hide for a night, a week, or even the whole war, and thus several thousands out of the millions being hounded towards their deaths were saved.

It is impossible to estimate how many or what percentage of the population were courageous in this way. Many went unrecognized except by the ones whom they helped, and often neither of them survived the rest of the war. Some historians suggest that for every Jew who survived, there were ten who reached out at some point to help them, for they may have had to change hiding places several times, may have needed shelter or directions, food or weapons at multiple points over those years.

Anecdotally, several books have attempted to catalogue the righteous (and the sporadically righteous) who volunteered to help. Often mentioned are the handful of diplomats such as Chiune Sugihara, who ignored orders from their various governments and saved as many as 20,000 people before war shut the borders tight between countries.

Other anecdotes mention this town or that where five or twenty thousand Jews lived before the war, and a few of them were hidden while the majority were shot and dumped into mass graves. Occasionally a heroic person or family managed to help dozens or more, like the Christian handyman at the synagogue in Bialystok who broke a window in the rear of the building after the SS herded hundreds of Jews inside and set the building on fire. This simple humanitarian action allowed a few dozen to escape through the rear window, though many of the survivors were rounded up later.

In one eastern Polish town, it became known that if a slave-laborer could escape the concentration camp nearby and find their way to the family of dogcatchers who lived outside of town, they could stay for a night and get directions to join the partisans. Dozens escaped that way until that family was caught and slaughtered, their property burned to the ground.

When the 20,000 Jews of the Ludomir ghetto in eastern Poland were being killed, fifteen Jews were saved by two brothers, farmers who kept them safe in various outbuildings on their land. The brothers were remembered for their thoughtfulness, going out of their way even beyond providing the basics of survival, to make sure the refugees had ceremonial candles to light on the Sabbath, which they made for them, dipping thread in tiny pools of precious oil, which they nestled in hollowed-out potatoes.

The collaboration of diplomats and humanitarians resulted in permission for several trainloads of children to escape Germany and go to Britain and North America, though most of their relatives perished in the camps. A number of nuns, priests, and ministers in war-torn countries hid Jewish children, though many of these children were converted to Christianity, raising questions about how disinterested the clergy's altruism was. Most of one village in Southern France organized to hide hundreds of children and move them across the mountains to Spain. Other children were saved in the ones and twos by people who adopted them as family at the risk of their own death.

The organization Yad Vashem, headquartered in Jerusalem, has spent enormous time and energy documenting and publicly honoring those who risked their lives to save Jews during the Holocaust. Over 22,000 people have been recognized through 2008, most notably over 6,000 people from Poland, 4,900 from the Netherlands, 2,800 French, 2,200 Ukrainians, and 1,500 Belgians.

The following table uses their research in a very rough attempt to address the question of how common heroism is. Note that the overall population estimates are highly approximate in some cases. Additionally, these honors only include those who risked themselves to save Jews. In each of these countries there were undoubtedly other courageous souls who were heroic in battle, among the resistance underground or in other situations during the same period of time. However, with statistics we sometimes have to take what data is available and let it shed whatever feeble light it can.

Table 1.1: A stab at estimating the variable incidence of heroes. (* Rough estimate.)

Top 10 countries for Yad Vashem Honorees	Number of Honorees	Jews as a Percentage of Prewar Population	Est. total Wartime Population in Millions	Honorees per Million People
Poland	6066	10	35.1	173
Netherlands	4863	2	7 *	695
France	2833	0.6	45	63
Ukraine	2213	6	40	55
Belgium	1476	0.8	9 *	164
Lithuania	723	7	2 *	361
Hungary	703	5	9.3	76
Belarus	587	10	9 *	65
Slovakia	478	3	3 *	159
Germany	455	0.3	50 *	9

To whatever extent we can make use of these rough statistics, we can see there may be large variations in the incidence of courage. These variations may be due to many causes, including different levels of poverty, education, values, historic circumstances in these countries. Poland had the largest number of honorees, but only a mid-level number of honorees per million of population. Tiny Netherlands had the highest rate of bravery. Germany, with the largest population of these countries, had the lowest incidence of heroism. One could spend much time and energy debating why, for each of these. And yet what we also see is that great heroism is not at all common. Yet this should not dampen a desire to encourage bravery through whatever efforts we can devise.

As mentioned above, these numbers under-represent the incidence of courage. Even the country with the largest representation, Holland's 695 honorees per million people, represents only seven hundredths of one percent of their population.

The study of soldiers mentioned in Chapter 6 found that 7% of the population displayed physical bravery. These men may be as good a proxy as we are likely to get for the average male population. Most young men either volunteered or were drafted during World War II; only the unhealthiest, or those needed for farming or key industrial work, stayed behind. Of course the smarter, better educated, better connected people would have removed themselves from the group entering the lowest ranks of the military in order to become officer candidates; still we can tentatively consider 7% as a possible base-line estimate for the incidence of heroism among a population untrained for risky action.

At least it's a more optimistic estimate than seven hundredths of one percent.

Psychological courage may be more common; moral courage possibly less. But if we additionally estimate that psychological courage is found, at least once or twice in a lifetime, among 80% of the population, and moral courage demonstrated by 3% of the population, if we find that situational courage is available to 75% of the population if faced with the right circumstances (threats to our own children, for example); if we agree that the occasional brush with heroism may increase the potential for a person to be brave in future situations, and that exposure to good role models, training, encouragement, and teamwork increases the potential, it begins to seem that almost anyone might, under some set of circumstances, be a hero.

All you have to do is want it, prepare yourself, and be ready to dive in at the right time.

Chapter 17: The basis of heroism

"O Great Spirit,
Whose voice I hear in the winds
And whose breath gives life to all the world,
Hear me...
I seek strength not to be greater than my brother or sister,
But to fight my greatest enemy—myself."—prayer of Lakota Chief
Yellow Lark, 1887

The feeling mushroom
↓
Mirrors in your mind
↓
Barriers to compassion
↓
Too busy to stop
↓
Which wolf do you feed?

In Nechama Tec's study of Polish Holocaust rescuers, the trait most often cited in the rescuer's biographies was a history of reaching out to help the needy. This tendency was almost universal among the heroes offering help who weren't doing it for gain. Other studies have suggested similar results—that those who habitually volunteer their help are usually the first to step in during a moral crisis.

And yet if you want to become more morally courageous, you can easily overcome the absence of any history of volunteerism. All you need to do is start offering to help others in need. You can do this in any capacity—offering to help neighbors in a crisis, reading to sick kids or the elderly, stepping up when a teacher or a community leader asks for a hand. By cultivating the habit of reaching out, by going beyond your own comfort to help others in need, you will find you are creating a stronger sense of community.

Why would a history of volunteerism be the biggest indicator of moral courage? Helpfulness itself is not necessarily enough. What's more, being a member of the helping professions also turns out not to be enough. We will cover this in depth soon, after taking a detour to look at the biology of the human brain and see what light science can shed on these matters.

⋆   ⋆   ⋆

The new field of social neuroscience focuses on the brain structures involved in human interactions. Using such tools as fMRIs (Functional Magnetic Resonance Imaging), scientists have begun the hard work of teasing out the neural basis of complicated human emotion and response. One of the most intriguing findings demonstrates that when people interact with each other, the area of the their brains that activates contains a group of cells called mirror neurons, found in both hemispheres of the brain. When you see someone doing something that you have done yourself, the mirror neurons activate to stimulate a perception of their action within your own mind, allowing you to understand and feel for yourself what that person is doing.

Thus a baby, having figured out how to smile, and having learned to associate smiles with happy feelings, will see her mother smiling and intuitively understand that she is pleased. A child, having never fallen in love, will not understand his older brother's experience when he has his first heartbreak, but years later, after having similar experiences of his own, can relate to a friend who was dumped by his one true love. This happens because his mirror neurons were stimulated, allowing him to interpret someone else's experiences, a process which stimulates almost as much brain activity as it would if the same thing happened directly to him.

This phenomenon explains how we understand intuitively what others are going through. It extends beyond close friends and family to observations of total strangers, even indirect observations. Why do we get so involved watching basketball games or sad movies? A sports fan will watch two players collide, and he will wince or cry out, especially if he's ever played the game himself; the reader of a romantic novel may get excited or weep when the heroine flirts or gets her heart broken. Great actors instinctively move their bodies and faces, adding emotion as they play their parts in ways which evoke significant emotional responses from their audience.

Mirror neurons send messages to the emotional (limbic) center of the brain. Seeing someone be happy activates the same area of the brain that is active when we are happy; if we smile and identify with that person's happiness, it activates even more.

Similarly, if we see someone in distress, we feel some level of distress ourselves. Leading neuroscientist Dr. Vilayanur Ramachandran calls mirror neurons "Gandhi neurons," since they seem to "dissolve the barrier between you and me." Indeed, some of the most interesting research in the field of autism, whose victims lack the ability to read other people and empathize with them, seems to point to deficiencies in the mirror neuron system as the cause. When that system is provoked to stimulate reorganization in the brain, improvements in communication and sociability often occur.

⋆   ⋆   ⋆

Those of you who glaze over when science is discussed may wish to skip this next section, where we cover some of the emerging science behind these recent brain discoveries. For those of you with an intermediate level of tolerance, I promise that it shouldn't hurt too much.

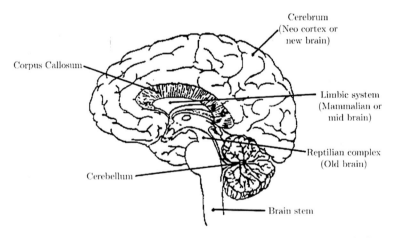

Figure 1.3: The main structures of the human brain. (Image from [11].)

The brain can be roughly divided into three sections. At the top of the spinal column, like the knob at the top of a walking stick, is a collection of neurons that is sometimes called the reptilian brain. We call it that because reptiles, and our reptile-like ancestors millions of years ago, have similar brain structures. In the picture above, these areas are labeled the brain stem through the Reptilian complex.

The reptilian brain controls such functions as:

- Breathing
- Swallowing
- Heartbeat
- An elementary visual tracking system
- The startle function

This part of the brain may continue functioning after a deeply injured person has been designated "brain dead." The higher parts of the brain may be severely damaged, but if the reptile brain functions continue, the body can remain alive for years.

Surrounding the reptilian brain is the limbic system, which seems to include what we think of as the subconscious mind. This section of the brain is centrally located, loosely capping the reptilian brain. The limbic system developed next, it seems, along with the new evolutionary branch of mammals, taking on those adaptations which our distant ancestors evolved as they split off from the reptiles and amphibians of the animal kingdom. The limbic system is primarily responsible for emotion and instinct, including such functions as:

- Nurturing behavior toward the young
- Non-verbal communications (cries of distress, singing)
- Dreaming
- The sense of smell
- Spatial memory
- Social interactions
- Leadership

Damage to the limbic system is not necessarily fatal. It can result, however, in the creature (human or other) completely losing their awareness of other beings, ignoring their young, or viewing members of their communities as no different than trees or rocks.

The third and largest region, the last to evolve, is the neocortex, from the Greek word *neo*, meaning "new," and the Latin word for "rind." This region surrounds and engulfs the limbic system and the reptilian brains. Earlier-evolving mammals, including the opossum, have only a thin rind of a neocortex.

More recent editions, including humans, have a veritable mushrooming of neurons sitting at the top of their brains. The cortex includes a number of areas which are responsible for higher level activities and thought, including:

- Spoken and written language
- Planning and problem-solving
- Sensations, awareness
- Conscious motor control
- Will
- Abstractions

The cortex is capable of much subtlety and nuance. It is also highly adaptive ("plastic," as the neuroscientists say), enough so that damage to any area will often result in other areas adjusting and compensating for much of the deficit.

Because the neocortex is verbal, its processes are significantly more obvious to the creature below than those of other areas of the brain which do not bother announcing their processes. This leads people to assume, too often, that thinking is what the brain is all about, and to think of their logical capacities as being in charge of the rest. They would often be wrong.

Thinking is a volitional process, and can to varying degrees be turned on and off. The lower portions of the brain are not in the realm of language or logic. They work largely on an involuntary basis: you cannot tell your limbic system who to love, when to be frightened, what to want, whether to be happy or not. This means that the outer brain ends up being the servant of the lower brain areas, facilitating what those other areas need or want, if it is a good servant, or failing to facilitate, if it is not. To the extent that it fails to facilitate these things, or tries to align the needs and desires of the lower regions with what it has decided it ought to want, there will be conflict.

Scientists have discovered a series of body maps within the brain, which match sensations from particular regions of the body to group of neurons that monitor and control reactions in those same regions of the body. One of the body maps is like a two-dimensional sheet of paper with different regions marked off for foot movements, hand movements, sensations of the face, etc. When you see a peanut lying on a counter, for example, and decide to pick it up, a group of cells in the body map of your pre-motor cortex are firing, directing the movements of your arm. The pre-motor cortex is in one of the frontal lobes of the cortex, where much planning of physical activity is accomplished. Yet under that body map is another small group of neurons in the same region which activate, not merely when you decide to pick up the peanut, but when you observe someone else picking up a peanut.

Mirror neurons are found in both the limbic system and the cortex. Some of them make up this second set of body maps lying underneath the body maps for our own bodies, which activate when we observe others doing things which we have done ourselves. Thus when your friend scratches a mosquito bite, your brain activates in the region immediately beneath the region that would activate if you were scratching your own mosquito bite; if your colleague at work grimaces at the inept response of a coworker, your brain fires, responding underneath the area which might have set off your own grimace. To the extent that we have experienced something, we have an innate sympathy based on our biology for others experiencing that same thing.

One of the scientists who first documented this phenomenon, Giocomo Rizzolatti, sums up the phenomenon this way:

> "When you see me doing something, you understand because you have a copy of the action in your brain... You become me. When I see you grasping an object, it is as if I, Giacomo, were grasping it.... We are exquisitely social creatures. Our survival depends on understanding the actions, intentions, and emotions of others. We simulate these automatically, without logic, thinking, analyzing."

But we do not experience it in full, nor do we act on it. The mirror neuron system cordons it off, just as you would cordon off the plan you are working on, or the statement you intend to make, until you are ready to act on them.

The actions of these mirror neurons do much to explain the easy identification we have with our friends and family, with the whooping and hollering of sports fans watching their favorite team win or lose on the screen or at the stadium, with how pornographic videos or pictures succeed in exciting people, and how a mother knows just how to soothe her distraught child. It explains how a good musician (or dancer or craftsman) picks up new techniques by watching others perform their art. In fact, for any kind of skill, someone with a fairly well developed sense of it can, if paying close attention, mirror their sequence of movements and expressions, develop an intuitive understanding that transcends any verbal attempt to describe, step by step, what is going on. And the more expert your own systems are in that domain, the deeper the understanding will be.

Mirror neurons may be the vehicle by which children learn language, culture, how to sort things, how to ride a bicycle, and so much more. Anything you can learn by observation may be at least partially facilitated by the mirror neuron system. The system kicks in shortly after birth. A newborn, seeing an adult stick out their tongue, may stick his or her tongue right back.

Mirror neurons don't simply define and interpret actions as they are being acted out by others; they also predict intentions. Brain scan studies indicate they are more active when it looks like someone is about to start something than when it looks like the action is complete. They also activate when people interact together in some joint capacity, creating a kind of bubble of perceived space in which your own and your partner's (or opponent's) actions are tightly monitored and rapid responses are called for. When you dress a child, carry furniture with another person, play ping pong or video games as a joint effort, shake hands with an acquaintance, or sing in a choir, your mirror neuron system is busy interpreting and helping coordinate your actions. Mirror neurons help people attune themselves to others, both physically and emotionally. Sharing a physical experience—even at the level of sharing a smile, or mimicking someone's posture.

In addition to the mirror neurons we have immediately below the action-oriented body map of the pre-motor and the parietal cortex, there are mirror neurons folded inside the superior temporal culcus, the area of the brain which processes facial and body movements and hand gestures. In other words, mirror neurons read and interpret other people's body language. They are also found in two areas deep within the cortex, the insula and the anterior cingulated cortex, parts of the brain which help read emotions and create a sense of empathy.

When you see a look of joy on someone else's face, or sadness, or disgust, the mirror neurons in your own *insula* activate, just as they are doing in your friend's brain. Both of you feel that particular emotion in your physiology, though they probably feel it stronger than you do, for you experience it in the underlying mirror mapping, while they experience it in the primary mapping area for emotions in the brain.

London neuroscientist Tanya Singer recruited pairs of lovers for an experiment. She placed the female of each pair in a brain scanning machine and took turns shocking both members of each pair. Each woman registered pain responses in the anterior cingulate, no matter whether it was herself being shocked or her partner. Unsurprisingly, women who were more empathetic in nature showed higher levels of response.

Singer's experiment underlines what other research has hinted at: when you observe another person, at some level you actually feel what they feel. Now it turns out that women tend to have a more active mirror response than men, just as women tend to score higher on measurements of empathy than men, but both men and women respond significantly by this "no man is an island" criterion.

One researcher found that people with a thicker right front insula, the control center for the body's efforts to regulate an even, homeostatic environment for itself, are better at at reading and tracking their own internal body feelings (heart rate, thirst, etc), and better at reading feelings in people other than themselves. There is an actual physical basis in these neural networks for the fact that some people are more emotionally aware than others.

The extent of these neurons is one of the ways that we differ from most animals, and even most other mammals. Rats, dogs and horses have insular mappings too, but theirs are simpler. Scientists are starting to accept that the higher animals have some degree of emotions and some level of self-awareness, albeit less defined and less well integrated with other areas of the brain. Many books have been sold celebrating the deeper, truer feelings of dogs, for example, and yet the range of emotions displayed by humans appears to be larger, including more complex feelings and a greater ability to catch the subtle distinctions of other people's experiences.

So the mirror neuron system seems like one fruitful place to explore the physiological mechanisms underlying bonds of love and community, empathy, and other deep forms of behavior. Researchers have started to do just that.

There is, additionally, a class of neurons we are only beginning to explore, called von Economo neurons, a type of cell which seems to be lacking in most species except for other great apes, elephants, and whales. These neurons are especially large, somewhat rare, and seem to be responsible for fast processing of intuitive judgments. They reside primarily in the anterior cingulated cortex and the frontal insula; more are found in the right hemisphere than the left.

They are particularly active during times of uncertainty, when you have to process vast amounts of information quickly and decide how to respond. Intuition neurons, you might call them; they also kick in when you first meet someone (allowing you to make quick judgments about how much to trust them, what their status is relative to yours, and so on), during emotionally-charged situations and in times of danger when you need to make split-second decisions about how to act. This class of neurons is still mysterious, but it too may be a fruitful area of research for those seeking to understand the physiological basis of courage.

⋆   ⋆   ⋆

Our default response, unless our underlying brain structures are inadequate or damaged, is to be empathetic, to feel other people's distress, at least at some low level of awareness. And feeling someone else's distress is a first step toward being motivated to work hard to alleviate it, if only to stop feeling that other person's pain.

Then why do we not spend more time helping those who are suffering? Why does the world continue to experience so much pain instead of taking strong measures to avoid or alleviate it?

Social psychologist Daniel Goleman speaks of distraction, the self-absorption we all feel when we focus on ourselves, our own problems, desires, and needs. Thus the perturbing results of a famous experiment at Princeton University, where a group of about 40 divinity students were told they had to give a sermon, not to a live audience, but for taping in front of a camera, for use at a later date.

Students of theology are people who are preparing, generally, to spend the rest of their adult lives as ministers, a career which is traditionally considered to be a profession devoted to helping people. You might assume that people training for such a life would be more likely to help a stranger in need than the average person. This should contrast with the more common reaction of people who might walk by a person in distress without stopping, or stand by on the sidelines without offering to lend a hand. As any emergency responder will note, by the time the police or the ambulances get to the scene of an accident, a small crowd of bystanders collects at the scene simply watching, doing nothing to help.

Sociologists call it the *bystander effect*: it's why people stand at the scene of any disaster without stepping in to help. Perhaps they are in a fog and cannot focus enough to help; perhaps they wash their hands of any responsibility because they don't know what to do, or fear that because they aren't trained, they are more likely to make a mess of things than to be helpful. Perhaps people are so used to the government stepping in and taking care of any emergency (via the police, fire, EMT, or other career responders) that the rest of the population has come to feel it is not their place to do anything. Often bystanders don't even call 911, everyone assuming someone else must have already called it in. Or they don't even stop to watch, being so busy with their own plans.

In the Princeton experiment, half the students were assigned to speak on the subject of the Good Samaritan, the other half assigned to other topics. One at a time the students were sent out to another building for the supposed appointment. Some of them were told that they were on time, others that they were already running late and the camera person was waiting for them. On the path between the two buildings, a man lay on the ground moaning, just off to the side. None of the students knew that this man was an actor paid to play the part.

What the experimenters were interested in was whether these ministers-in-training would be influenced by the topic they'd been focusing on. Surprisingly, most of the students completely ignored the man and hurried on to give their sermons. Some even stepped directly over him in their rush to get to their appointment. The students who sermonized, and presumably had been musing about, the generosity of the Good Samaritan, turned out to be no more likely to stop and offer help to the man on the ground than the students who'd been contemplating other sermon topics.

What did influence their likelihood of stopping to offer help was how hurried the students were, and how absorbed they were in their own thoughts. Those who were not in a rush were much more likely to volunteer help than those in a hurry; those who were in a thoughtful trance rarely stopped to offer any aid.

So even among divinity students, who are presumably more kind and helpful then most, self-absorption can be characteristic, and may lead to selfish, ungenerous, or cowardly behavior, even when the stakes are low.

⋆   ⋆   ⋆

In addition to routine self-absorption, there's the bystander effect mentioned above, and the related sense of *diffusion of responsibility*. These phenomena were the focus of much research beginning in the mid-1960s, when an incident in Queens, New York shocked the nation. A 28-year-old woman named Kitty Genovese was repeatedly stabbed over a half-hour period and died just a few feet from her own home. What was even more shocking than crime itself was the fact that a dozen people witnessed her murder, with many looking on from their safe apartment windows onto the street, and did nothing to stop it.

One neighbor did shout, scaring the attacker off. Ms. Genovese stumbled off, but she never made it to safety. And no one came to see if she needed any help. The attacker returned and resumed his attack after searching through a parking lot, a train station, and the apartment complex. He found her lying, having fainted, in the hallway near her door. There he stabbed her again, going on to rape her, stealing $49 from her purse, and left her to die. A second neighbor called the police, but not until after the attacker was gone. The young woman was taken by ambulance to a hospital, but died on the way.

Quizzed by reporters about their apparent indifference, one man said he didn't want to get involved. Others explained they only witnessed part of the attack, or they thought she was all right when they saw her staggering away. The seeming callousness from people who must have at least recognized their young neighbor, if not actually known her, spurred an outcry in the general public and some significant psychological research.

And yet, though the sad tale of Kitty Genovese has been widely publicized, similar incidents continue to happen. Ten years after her murder, another young woman was beaten to death on Christmas morning in the same neighborhood. Again neighbors reported hearing a fierce struggle and screams; again they did nothing to stop it. The 25-year-old model died from the attack. Her neighbors said they didn't want to get involved.

Over forty years of social psychology research since that time reveal the following:

- The more people who witness an emergency, the less likely that any one of them will take responsibility. People may feel no sense of responsibility, or they may sense a diffusion of responsibility, in some way seeming to release each individual from the need to act. Onlookers see others ignoring the situation, which gives them a sense that that's acceptable behavior. Witnesses justify ignoring it because they think that someone else must have the training, strength, or time to help. Some feel too self-conscious to help while other people watch—as if it is more important to avoid feeling embarrassed than to save another person's life. When the crisis is not immediate—the slow starvation of people in some far off foreign country, or a decline in the population of an endangered species—people feel they are exposed to so many calls for help that they are overloaded and begin to shut off the part of the mind that responds to emergencies. One small person can't fix the problem, so why should they even start?

- Diffusion of responsibility can also happen within hierarchical organizations—armies, government agencies, large companies, Boy Scout troops— where underlings can hide from responsibility by claiming they were following orders (or still waiting to be assigned the job). Supervisors may claim they were just issuing orders and didn't do anything bad themselves.

- Another way to understand the fallacy behind the diffusion of responsibility is to think about the Chinese saying that "No one raindrop thinks it caused the flood." Mother Teresa's dictum is an excellent response: "If you can't feed a hundred hungry people, feed just one."

One early experiment determined that when people think they are the only ones to witness a serious medical crisis, they almost always go for help. But the more people who seem to know about the problem, the less likely any one person is to pause and offer help. Additional experiments found that a serious illness was more likely to elicit help from bystanders than mere drunkenness, that men were much more likely to help victims in physical distress than women, and that people were somewhat more likely to help victims who were more like them, including being of the same race.

Do people have some internal calculation they go through before deciding to help? One psychological model proposes that bystanders decide whether to offer help based on a sort of cost-benefit approach: they subconsciously weigh the degree of discomfort they feel as they watch the crisis emerging, against the probable costs or rewards of reaching out to help. *Is this going to hurt, is this going to cost me, is this going to make me late for work? I'm not sure I remember all the steps for CPR. Will I be embarrassed, with me bending over, my shirt riding up, if I stop to help? Am I going to feel bad if I walk by? I wonder if there'll be some kind of reward?* These concerns are implicitly weighed against the familiar comforts and rewards of going about their business as normal, should they not stop and help.

One experiment was designed to tease out whether the bystander effect falls away during true emergencies, and if higher costs of ignoring a significant crisis increases the burden people are willing to bear. The psychologists found that the age and sex of the victims had little effect on bystanders' willingness to step in and intervene. In situations of high danger, over 40% of participants were willing to offer help, whether there were other people around or not. In less risky situations, when there were no other witnesses, half the participants were willing to help, whereas only 6% were willing if a lot of others were around.

Thus the bystander effect seems to impede volunteering when the outcome doesn't seem very bad. But there are times when people don't appear to be in great danger, yet they very well may be. When Kitty Genovese was attacked, many of her neighbors misconstrued the situation. It was 3:00 in the morning, after all, not the best time for making judgment calls. One neighbor thought it was a lover's quarrel. Many did not realize she was being stabbed; others saw her rise and leave the scene and so assumed she was okay. Poor Kitty, a victim not just of her assailant, but of her community's inability to recognize her suffering.

⋆　　⋆　　⋆

It seems that the more familiar the person in trouble is to us, the more likely their crisis will elicit our empathy, generosity, or courage to act; even more so if they are right in front of us. Verbal descriptions or statistics about the needy are more abstract and thus less likely to activate our mirror neurons, which trigger our senses of empathy or compassion. Having a crisis right in front of you may set off your limbic system's emotional response, whereas reading about it in the newspaper evokes only the thinking, abstract brain. Thus the ever-present pictures of children with cleft palates or malnourished faces in magazines; a visual image of a cute but bereft child puts the victim, physically on the other side of the world, within emotional reach. The pictures are much more likely to induce potential donors to reach for their wallets than an article about the same problem published in the same magazine.

The more distant the victim from us, the less likely our response. Distance may be a matter of being from a different place, time, culture, age, gender, class, or language group. The more of these distancing factors there are, the less likely it is that a person will feel compassion and be moved beyond their bystander daze enough to step forward and act, particularly if acting seems difficult, inconvenient, or requires courage.

The rare person who acts spontaneously, who readily leaps in, may be someone who doesn't stop to think, *Is this someone I feel sorry for?* They simply assume all people are worthy of their help, and they move into action by reflex. Over the course of their lives they may do this enough for it to become a long-standing habit.

Though Goleman points out that intelligence is separate from compassion or empathy; there is no statistical correlation between IQ and empathy. A writer once interviewed a high-IQ serial killer, the Santa Cruz Strangler, and asked whether he felt any pity as he committed his crimes.

"Oh, no!" the Strangler assured him. "If I'd felt their distress, I could not have done it. I had to turn that part of me off."

In order to act on the plan he embarked on in his thinking brain, he had to deny the emotional bond to others that he might have felt from the limbic system. This ties in with psychotherapist Dr. M. Scott Peck's experience working with evil—that it usually arises from well-entrenched narcissism, in a person so self-involved that they are completely oblivious and uncaring about their impacts on others. A similar finding comes from animal studies where certain monkeys' limbic systems were destroyed experimentally, who went on to step on their own offspring in order to climb a tree.

To feel empathy or compassion is to allow yourself to focus on another, which is at the opposite end of the spectrum from focusing only on yourself and your own preoccupations. "It is our empathy, our ability to tune in to others," says Goleman, "that separates us from the sociopaths."

Even generosity can reflect a variety of positions along the spectrum ranging from self-absorption to selflessness. Goleman reflects on his own feelings while going over his charitable deductions to prepare his tax return. His first response was a kind of glee that a friend of his would be happy to hear he'd donated to a particular charity. This he describes as a narcissistic joy, stemming the higher regard he'd earn when his friend heard of his good deed. Only then did he start to think about the people who would receive help because he donated money, in this case blind people in remote communities in

Asia. By moving his focus onto them, he reported the beginnings of a sense of compassionate joy, a feeling he felt much more proud of having than he did with his first reaction.

★   ★   ★

Besides a history of helping others, the second most common trait Tec found among the Holocaust saviors was that many of them had some status within the intellectual class of Polish society, including writers, artists, university professors, and so on. This would seem to contradict Goleman's dictum that intelligence and empathy are not correlated at all. Yet there may be a more roundabout connection.

Among the Polish peasant class, there was a long history of misinformation, including anti-Semitic prejudices passed down from priests and school teachers declaring that Jews were dirty or evil, and thus deserved their terrible fate. That the vast majority of peasants in Poland actively abetted the genocide of their Jewish neighbors is at least partly due to these widespread hate campaigns and many centuries of prejudice. Thus, in addition to the obvious dangers of helping the Jews, there were many long established barriers dividing Polish Jews from Polish Catholics, discouraging any impulse towards empathy or compassion. With such intensely constructed barriers, it was easy for people of the peasant class to turn their backs, to remain as bystanders to the Holocaust, even among those who were kind of heart and more prone to helping. A few bucked these prevailing traditions, but many more chose to benefit from others' misfortunes.

Among the middle classes, working in such occupations as storekeeper or salesman, many had some direct experience interacting with Jews, and yet there was a tendency to ignore their distress. Tec and others speculate that the Polish middle classes were largely happy to see the Jews rounded up and taken away. This left more customers for their own stores, less competition to worry about. The war brought many unexpected opportunities for middle class Poles. For example, when Jews were given 24 hours to liquidate their assets before being herded into the ghettos, they had to sell everything at fire-sale prices, usually to Polish business acquaintances; when they had to leave furniture and their homes behind, many Jews left them with people who promised to give them back when the war ended. The tiny minority of Jews who survived the concentration camps were frequently disappointed in the people they entrusted their belongings to. Having survived the Nazis, some of these returnees were turned away, even murdered by the Poles who'd taken over their property and didn't want to give it up.

The aristocrats, who were few in number and were often co-opted by the Germans, did not play a major role in leading any meaningful resistance. Thus the intellectual class, more likely to have ties with professional or artistic Jews, and often better educated out of the prejudices so common in their country, were the only group that was likely to reach out. They were the most likely to feel the empathy that should be natural, according to our neurobiological impulses, but was too often overridden by fear or prejudice in others.

Prejudice, as a barrier to the natural flow of interactions, has long been a focus of moral courage. Whether we are speaking of a lack of neighborly helpfulness, respect, or the hiring of qualified candidates for jobs regardless of sex or other categories, these barriers to fairness give rise to legitimate moral indignation. The civil rights movement, the equal rights movement, even the Revolutionary War required heroes with the moral outrage and courage to attack the numerous longstanding, unfair barriers. High intelligence is useful but not a necessary characteristic for someone to step outside of these prejudices and choose to challenge them. But it does take a certain kind of emotional or spiritual intelligence to see how much human potential such prejudices waste.

★   ★   ★

Forty years ago, a number of psychologists began asking the question, "Who can be evil?" And not only psychologists; coming on the heels of two world wars and continuing regional conflicts, but also philosophers, writers, politicians, and clergymen were wondering about the pervasiveness of evil. A series of experiments, including the infamous Milgram Experiment and the eye-opening Stanford Prison Experiment, led to the the unhappy conclusion that just about everybody was capable of some degree of evil towards others.

Partly as a result of tuning in to Nazi leader Adolph Eichmann's war trial in 1961, psychologist Stanley Milgram at Yale University became interested in the frequently-cited excuse for evil behavior that "I was only following orders." Was it legitimate to excuse people from responsibility for morally reprehensible actions if they were doing only what they were told?

Milgram set up an experiment with two actors and a series of students. One of the actors was dressed in a lab coat playing the role of a stern biology professor, as an authority figure. The second actor played "the learner," and spent most of the time in isolation. The experimental subjects, all students, were asked to participate in an experiment about learning conditions. They were given a list of word-pairs and told to ask the learner in the next room which words went with the word suggested by the student. If the learner chose the wrong word, the student was to administer an electric shock. Subsequent mistakes would be punished by stronger shocks. Before entering the isolation room, the learner informed the student he had a heart condition.

Unknown to the students, Milgram had set up a series of tape-recorded screams keyed to the increasing levels of shock the students thought they were administering (though in fact that too was faked). The learner's responses included reminders about his heart condition, banging on the walls, and simulated fainting spells. Uniformly the students kept administering shocks starting with an initial 45 volt shock. Some students began questioning the authority figure at around the 135 volt level, but the man prodded them to continue. Some hesitated, asking if they could check on the learner, or started exhibiting signs of stress themselves. Some quit, but many of the students continued all the way to the maximum of 450 volts, much more than a lethal shock.

Before the experiment, Milgram polled his graduate students and colleagues, who predicted that only one or two percent of students would complete the experiment. In fact, 65% of students gave shocks all the way up to the 450 volt level, a percentage that has since been replicated in similar experiments around the world. Even among the students who refused at an earlier point in the experiment, none of them insisted that the experiment itself be terminated; none of them actually went into the adjoining room to check on the condition of the "learner."

The sobering conclusion is that most people will follow orders, even if they violate common courtesy or any stricter standard of compassion. Faced with an authority figure urging them on, some will resist, but most are likely to keep going, even if they are uneasy about it.

In another experiment conducted in 1971, professor Philip Zimbardo recruited a group of 24 psychologically healthy, stable Stanford undergraduates.

Half were to play prison guards for two weeks, the others to play inmates in a mock prison set up in the basement of the psychology department building. After only six days, Zimbardo was forced to terminate the experiment. A third of the guards, previously carefree college students, had begun demonstrating genuine sadistic tendencies, resulting in many unfortunate incidents which left some of the faux prisoners with real and lasting psychological damage.

These experiments show that each of us, or at least most of us, are capable of inflicting harm on one another. This concept, which philosopher Hannah Arendt called "the banality of evil," indicates that even ordinary people can become evil under some circumstances.

The same Professor Zimbardo today postulates the parallel theory that any of us, similarly, can perform heroic deeds under some circumstance or another. Each person is a potential hero awaiting the right combination of need, circumstance, and mood to activate their bravery or courage.

This idea, that we are all nuanced creatures with the capacity to break out in the direction of either extreme, is an ancient idea in many cultures. There is an old story, said to be a Cherokee legend, about the boy who came to his grandfather, angry after a friend had wronged him. The grandfather suggests that he himself sometimes does things he isn't very proud of. "A fight is always going on inside me," he tells the boy.

> "It is a terrible fight, and it is between two wolves. One wolf is evil—he is anger, envy, sorrow, regret, greed, arrogance, self-pity, guilt, resentment, false pride. The other is good—he is joy, peace, love, hope, serenity, humility, kindness, benevolence, empathy, generosity, truth, compassion, and faith. The same fight is going on inside you—and inside every other person, too."

The grandson thinks about it for a minute and then asks his grandfather, "Which wolf will win?"

Grandfather takes a moment to answer. "The one that I feed," he concludes.

A similar theme runs through Jewish culture, of the twin angels sitting on each person's shoulders: the angel of the good inclination and the angel of the bad. These angels whisper from time to time, from the right shoulder or the left, urging the person to act for good or evil. It is considered the adult's responsibility to incline their head primarily toward the good angel and listen to his urgings, ignoring the temptation from the other side.

⋆   ⋆   ⋆

Some people worry that personality traits such as courage are fixed and cannot be changed. Psychologist Cynthia Pury has studied this idea and concluded that bravery can indeed be learned. Lack of bravery is a series of old, bad habits, and habits can be changed, though it takes intention and work to do so. People who behave bravely are often afraid, but their principles, values, or commitments to others leave them unable to sit back when a crisis hits, forcing them to take action. Pury's research with students revealed that the ones who act courageously usually do so because they feel strongly about the situation.

Many of Pury's research subjects followed a similar mental plan. Faced with a risky situation, they first took steps to calm themselves. They prepared for the situation, looking for a way to mitigate the danger, just as Donna Howard and Ken Pedeleose did when they carefully documented the abuses they saw. Then they focused on what they were trying to accomplish, reminding themselves how important it was. "I don't think any intervention about courage is going to go that far unless you help people decide what's important," Pury says.

There is a small group of people who may need no reflection about their own deeper values in order to act. Psychologist Frank Farley suggests that situational heroes, who act reflexively when they see immediate danger, are likely to be outgoing, Type-A personalities. Type As tend to be hard-working, achievement-oriented, higher stress people. Type-B personalities, in contrast, are more relaxed, quieter, more easy-going.

Not all Type-A people are prospects for turning into heroes. He defines a subset of Type A as risk-takers, calling them Type T (for thrill-seeking). Type Ts are more often male than female, and can often be identified as early as age two. Such people are exploratory, more independent of their parents. They show little fear. "They are the type of child that you find wandering off into the woods," Farley notes.

Type Ts tend to be outgoing, to put themselves forward for attention as well as in times of risk. But not all heroes are like that. Many are quieter people who act out of conviction, people striving to live up to their role models, people from all walks of life trying hard to listen to their better angels, trying to feed the good wolves within them.

It is in order to support these good angels, those good wolves within us, that we dedicate the second section of this book.

Part 2: Exercises and adventures

In the second part of this book, we look at some aspects of depth—courage, endurance and commitment—identified in the first section, and offer exercises to expand these capacities for anyone willing to spend time and energy doing so.

Some of the exercises provided may not seem like obvious paths leading to courage and commitment. Be patient and try them anyway. They will strengthen your foundation, help you understand yourself better, and help you identify the enduring values you hold and the things that motivate you. These are important steps to help you get where you want to go. Others are designed to deepen you, to strengthen your focus and your ability to withstand distraction; these will also help when you confront a crisis or a risky circumstance, increasing your effectiveness and ability to succeed.

Training to deepen courage is an old and honorable tradition. Many ancient cultures have used folklore and myths to offer indirect guidance to supplement the direct guidance coming from families, mentors, or religious leaders. Like reading any how-to book today, legends about the exploits of ordinary people who are suddenly confronted by extraordinary experiences can open people's eyes to the possibilities. Stories may offer logistical, moral, or psychological lessons about heroes, including when and how to be brave, when it might be foolish to act heroically and what kinds of rewards a hero might expect. They also offer vicarious experience, a safer way for a novice to learn than the real, hairy events themselves.

An ancient Greek wanting to make a name for himself could lean on his years of hearing elders regale people with tales of the siege of Troy, or Odysseus' long journey home. As he began preparing for his own manhood, he might imagine he took part in these adventures himself, dreaming about his interactions with the heroes and the challenges from the stories. Young people today may resonate more to *The Lord of the Rings*, graphic novels or the

Harry Potter series. There is a universal desire to be thrilled by heroic deeds, by the triumph of good over evil, and to some extent people are strengthened and inspired by these secondhand experiences.

Yet reading and listening may not be enough to create courage in each of us. Millions pay to watch an action-adventure movie, yet many will live their entire lives and have trouble recalling a single instance of personal heroics. Try surveying people and see for yourself. Most will hem and haw before offering a true tale of their friend's brother, something they saw on TV, or somebody they knew when they were kids. That is one reason most of us get so entranced reading about true heroism: it is rare, though it needn't be.

So, the passive methods of absorbing these possibilities are not enough to create heroes, though they may establish a certain amount of groundwork for depth. What about taking risks? Some risks do prepare you for taking others, while others don't. Taking risky dares as a youth is a common experience. When psychologists Mark Leary and Kathleen Martin interviewed 300 teenage boys, a quarter of them confessed to driving recklessly in order to impress people. A third admitted performing various reckless stunts in order to look cool. Some of these stunts were merely foolish, like juggling knives; others, like jumping off a bridge or riding on top of a car, were downright dangerous. Does such behavior train a person to take risks when the outcome is more important than merely impressing their friends? Not necessarily.

Such stunts may lead nowhere; they may also lead to a tendency towards recklessness without real reward. Some people become "adrenaline junkies" who love risk or adventure for its own sake. Sometimes such a focus is a way to avoid dealing with everyday life—avoidance in this case being its own form of cowardice. Yet some who follow these paths learn to channel their capacity to tolerate danger into work for the common good. So you shouldn't despair if you're the thrill-seeking type.

Still there is reason to believe that other, quieter steps maybe more effective ways to encourage bravery.

The following exercises and adventures aim at all aspects of you: mind, body, heart, and spirit. Because some people respond well to abstractions and others to experiential work, both are included. Do as many of these as appeal to you, and then a few more. Part of training yourself for courage involves pushing your own boundaries, even while still in the comfort of your own home.

Chapter 1: What kind of courage is for me?

Often the first step to strengthening the foundation for courage is to decide what kinds of commitment you are gearing up for. As the stories above demonstrate, different kinds of risks require different kinds of responses. People who are physically brave may not be ready for long-term acts of moral bravery, and those who take emotional or moral risks may not be physically daring. Nor need they be.

People who succeed in acts of **physical heroism** often demonstrate many of the following characteristics:

- strength
- training for emergencies
- experience with emergencies
- work smoothly as part of a team
- confidence going in
- clarity of their mission
- clear feeling for the community they serve
- a history of reaching out to help others
- faith or a strong commitment to a set of ethics they live by
- a lack of braggadocio, an appreciation of any allies, distant or direct
- willingness to take responsibility

People who repeatedly perform acts of physical heroism may additionally need the following:

- ongoing training
- acknowledgement from others that their efforts are necessary and appreciated
- respect from those around, below and above them

People who succeed in acts of **moral heroism** often display many of the following:

- a moral commitment or sense of responsibility for some larger purpose or community
- a willingness to bear the costs associated with that commitment
- a history of reaching out to help others
- faith or some other strong sense of ethics to live by
- a network of allies
- generosity of character, enabling them to extend their sense of connection or responsibility farther than their immediate circle
- a sense of urgency, that something needs to be done to right a wrong or the world will become a terrible place

People who continue over the long term with acts of moral heroism may additionally need the following:

- endurance
- allies around them affirming that the hardships and deprivations are indeed for a good cause
- people, habits, and circumstances to nurture and support them when they feel downhearted or depleted

Other kinds of heroes tend to exhibit the characteristics of one of the two categories covered above, or fall somewhere in between. So, noticing where you fit in, make a note of which areas you need additional (or ongoing) support or development in your life. Make this formal by using the chart below (Table 2.1). Then, as you go through your notes from the first section of the book, and as you continue through the rest of the chapters, add notes about the resources, ideas, and exercises that feel useful in maintaining or building up your readiness. Feel free to devise any variations or add additional exercises that support your own circumstances.

Table 2.1: Personal plan of action.

Areas I will generally need	Areas I need more of right now	Exercises to build this up (fill in as you read ahead)

Chapter 2: Who am I?

Most of us have an ever-present, free-form sense of who we are, floating around as an undercurrent of our everyday awareness. Yet there are times when we wander away from this assuredness, or when it becomes too diffuse to sense. We feel unmoored, uneasy, or uncertain where we are going or what we are doing here. These times can be confusing indeed. When we lose that sense of ourselves, it can feel like we are drifting along like a boat with nobody steering it, for those who should be steering have lost their grasp of the helm.

To refresh or deepen your sense of self can be a simple task. Take a pad of paper and pen (the old-fashioned implements work much better for this kind of thing than computers) or turn to the form at the end of this chapter. Sit somewhere with no interruption—a quiet room by yourself or a spot under a tree, the bathroom, whatever works best. Turn off your cell phone and isolate yourself from all distractions for the ten minutes or so that this assignment takes.

At the top of the page write the phrase "I Am." Following that, begin a list of all the positive things you are, all the things you enjoy in your life, all the things that affirm you. These characteristics and propensities are, to a great extent, who you are.

Write completely from the top of your head and don't be critical about whatever emerges. If it's embarrassing, don't worry; no one's looking over your shoulder. List at least ten things, then keep going as long as more keep coming to mind. Stop when you feel complete.

These are the things that represent you. Don't be shy; remember, only you will see this list. You can always burn it later, or fold it up and hide it in the back of a drawer. Or you can keep it in a notebook, and add updated versions from time to time.

Here's one person's list.

I am:

- tall
- funny

- bearded
- a good skier
- someone who loves every shade of blue
- a baker of cakes
- a gardener
- brother
- son
- mountain biker
- creative with my hands
- good at fixing things
- messy in the house
- an honest businessman

Here's another person's list:

- mother
- daughter
- sister
- good friend when people are in trouble
- chatty
- cheerful most of the time
- sad after Grandma died
- hiker
- lover of ferns and flowers
- knitter of sweaters and scarves
- caring
- swimmer and diver
- nurse
- good at managing others
- good at diverting people from pain
- good at reminding people to appreciate their families and friends
- lover of fine teas

Just looking at those lists, don't you feel like you kind of know the people who wrote them?

Now go ahead and do one for yourself. When you're done, read it over a few times and bask for a few moments in the *who*-ness of who you are.

Feel free to do this exercise again and again, weekly, monthly, or once in a blue moon. If you do, you may notice that some characteristics change while many stay the same. There is a coherent core to who you are, yet some things are ephemeral, and others change slowly, if at all.

Both the consistency and the changeability may be a comfort at different times.

Table 2.2: "I Am" Exercise.

I am

Chapter 3: Who and what do I stand for?

The deep life is a life devoted to meaningful work and relationships. In order to build a deeper approach for yourself, it helps to clarify who and what are meaningful to you, perhaps going so far as to prioritize these commitments and values. A firm, clear sense of your most important commitments will ground you when you need it most—when challenged, when tempted by opportunities that may not serve your best interests, or in times of trouble. Those who fail to develop this clarity are much more prone to letting the winds of circumstance blow them around. All of us gain from such preparation beforehand. Even those who say they know exactly what they stand for may benefit from this chapter.

Many people grow up with values handed down from above. Parents, teachers, and peers offer whole fistfuls of values, as do preachers, books, commercials, and so on. Some people accept these messages without thinking about whether they are right for them. But for most of us, one of the key tasks of adulthood is to decide, implicitly or explicitly, what our lives are going to be about.

People have to answer many questions which present themselves every day. Will she go to church this week? Will he join the police department, as his father and uncles did before him, or will he fulfill his dreams of opening his own store? Will she return the money she found on the street? Will he honestly report every source of income on his tax return? Will she send $20 a month to a starving child somewhere in Africa, or spend the money on hair care products? Will he help his wife get the kids to bed tonight or put his aching feet up and read the paper? Often these decisions are made on an ad hoc basis, but they are significantly easier to make when they are made in the context of a well-thought-out sense of ethics or a personal code of honor.

Values can be like the lighthouse shining through the darkness of a threatening storm. Through the violent rocking of the waves, through the loss of all other visible landmarks and the failure of your boat's compass, it is a blessing to have some faint reminder of how to steer and of where you want to end up. That doesn't mean there won't still be wild winds along the way, rocks or reefs to watch out for. But for all the tests and trials that come your way, you will never regret establishing these pinpricks of light to guide you from the shore.

Of course, there are many brave and courageous acts made without reference to a strong sense of what is important and where you are going. Skipping this step is certainly feasible. But keep in mind Yogi Berra's infamous warning: "You've got to be very careful if you don't know where you're going, because you might not get there."

Many cultures send their young people out on some version of a vision quest, fasting and meditating for days, praying for guidance, or traveling until they find a mentor or an oracle to give them guidance. Any of these are honorable routes and, if these appeal to you, bless your heart and go ahead. If you don't want to devote that amount of time, you can simply follow the exercises below. These have been designed to help you create a coherent sense of what you stand for. Use any or all of these; each comes from a different angle and will elicit slightly different, yet substantially similar, results.

I offer one warning. Sometimes the first few values that come to mind are not your truest values. They may be things you have long been told you should honor or value. Or they may be things that you genuinely believe in, but actually are not your deepest values. As they emerge, let yourself take a moment with each one and test the depth of your commitment to it. Do you feel lukewarm about it? Or do you feel enthusiasm, a kind of locking-in of puzzle pieces, an engaging of the gears when you start considering that person, group, place or cause? Does it get you moving, start your mind planning what to do, make you impatient to get going? If you do not feel this deeper connection, it may be someone else's value, not yours.

Find a quiet place where you will not have to respond to interruptions. Put aside cell phones, e-mail, and other distractions while you focus only on one or more of the following.

1. Consider a tall, well-established tree in a forest or a meadow, or even in your own yard. The tree is both a structure and a community unto itself. It supports nests, birds perch on it, and squirrels run over its branches. Animals and insects feed off its fruits, flowers, and sap; others burrow within its hollows for shelter; still others may find it easier to dig underground in the spaces it creates with its roots. The tree exists not only for itself but for a large community of others. When it sickens,

and finally dies, it is not the only life that flickers; many other creatures suffer too.

Visualize yourself as a tree. Sit in quiet for a few minutes. Close your eyes if you like, or stare blankly into space. As you begin to clear your mind, allow the image of a tree to fill it—any kind of tree you like (oak, willow, pine, whatever), as long as it is big and healthy. This tree represents you, in tree form. What creatures will you allow to climb on you, which ones will you feed and nourish? Your answers may include particular people, animals, causes. Add each of them into your image. Who or what will you welcome to sit under your sheltering branches? Add them into your image, too. Now just sit and enjoy letting this image fill your mind and heart, the image of you and the community you willingly and gladly support. And if there are a few gnats bothering you, it's a small price to pay for being a vibrant member of this community, growing in this fertile soil, letting the sun and the earth nourish you and yours.

2. At the very end of life, if a person has lived a life well led, it can be highly satisfying to look back and remember all they have done, all the people they loved, the allies they developed, and those they helped along the way.

Consider a deathbed scene which you might have at the end of your (hopefully) long and fruitful life. Envision yourself lying in that bed. Notice what it feels like to be in that setting, your body growing weary, your mind still active but beginning to accept that the end is near. See or sense your face, well-marked from the many meaningful years you lived, your body reduced to an older state. Perhaps you are surrounded by people who love and honor you, whom you once helped but are now taking care of you.

Look back and review the years you lived. Note the many big and small things you accomplished over that long span of time—professionally, personally, spiritually, emotionally—the successes you had, the ways you made a difference, creating change, making lives better, nurturing others or building things up. These many efforts took a lot of work and some sacrifice to get there, but weren't they worth it? Thank the universe for providing so many opportunities to learn, to grow, to reach out, and to help others. Forgive yourself for the few failures you had, for how else could you have known enough to succeed later? Notice also these things: Who are you glad to have with you at your bedside (either living or dead), comforting you, coming to make peace or say goodbye? What things are you happiest that your life was about?

3. What kinds of situations always seem to make you cringe? When someone in your family, or someone whom you've always respected, or even you yourself do or say something false which gives you a queasy feeling inside, that's something which violates your sense of what should be. These may be lies, hypocrisies, false or destructive behaviors that you never want to catch yourself doing; things you would hate if your friends, family, children, coworkers found you involved with, things that would embarrass you if you were associated with them in a headline of the local newspaper or in a popular blog. Let your awareness roam through the corners of your mind and note the things you've ever been involved in that make you feel a little sick. Keep asking yourself, "Is there anything else? Is there something more?" until nothing else comes to mind. These are values, people, situations which are NOT part of who you are and what you represent. You will want to minimize your involvement with these as much as possible.

4. If a fire breaks out in the house, you may have only a few minutes to rush about, saving the most important things. Similarly, if you found out you had only a few months to live, you would have only a short time to make or finalize a legacy for yourself. Pretend you have only a limited time left, though for the purposes of this exercise you can assume you have access to any reasonable resource needed in order to carry on or complete what you need to do (safes, trucks, moving vans, etc.). Think in terms of six to 18 months of time, whatever span makes sense, given your intended plan. How should you spend those last few months? Will you heal broken relationships, complete unfinished projects, write a book, travel the world, focus on family, friends, projects, causes, or take the time to relax and pamper yourself? Let your imagination flow and design a strategy for these final months in this body, on this planet.

Now, having done some or all these exercises, use the new perspective they bring to make a contract for yourself. What people, projects, causes, or values are critical to you? These are the core tenets of your being. Write them down—it will help firm them up as a kind of code of behavior for you. Use the form below, or come up with one that suits you better. You may find that these values change somewhat over time, but probably not by much. You are more likely to add a couple of new ones than to have any drop from the list.

Here's a sample of a few people's outcomes.

Andrew's Code of Ethics:

- I am a man of honor. I do not lie to myself or to others.
- When I make a promise, I keep it, or explain carefully why it cannot be kept.
- My family and close circle of friends are the most important thing to me. I would die for them if I had to.
- Beyond that, respect for life is my biggest priority. I will not desecrate people, trees, or the environment. I will advocate for all of those, and do my best to keep others from desecrating them too. This will be my life's work.

Sonia's Die-fors (in order of importance):

- My kids are first; no question about that. I would die for them if it would save them from harm.
- My little sister and my husband are next.
- My students
- Other kids in the area that need help
- Other kids anywhere
- The rest of my family
- Other people (I wouldn't die for them, but I will try to help when they're in trouble, as best I can)
- Kindness and compassion are important to me. I will keep those two values at the front of my mind in everything I do and say.

Justin's List:

- I work with animals. Representing those creatures that can't speak for themselves is what I am on this earth to do.
- I would die if it would save a lot of wild animals, or animals in our protective custody.

- I would risk harm, embarrassment, and shame if it would save a lot of animals from a life or death without dignity.
- I would risk harm, embarrassment, and shame if it would save my own family but I would not die for them.
- I will honor my mother and father
- I will not kill, commit adultery, steal, or bear false witness against others.
- This all sounds so earnest. I will interject a note of lightness, fun, or joy into situations even while pursuing serious things.

Write up your own covenant as you see it at this time. Feel free to amend it over the next few days. You might make a mental note to revisit this every few years to see if there are any changes you need to make.

Table 2.3: Covenant with myself.

My code/covenant

Chapter 4: Improving focus

"Life is just a bowl of cherries," as the old song goes, but sometimes it seems more like a long drive in the car. You know you're going somewhere, but there's a lot of ground to cover before you arrive at the final destination. Meanwhile there are distractions everywhere—places you can stop, people you can pick up along the way, long delays as you stop to fuel up. Some of these distractions are pleasant, while others are simply necessary. You may have your route plotted out fairly well, or you may prefer to figure things out as you go along. Even if you prefer to plan ahead, you might be forced to improvise unexpectedly if a bridge is out or someone bangs into you. Sometimes, mid-ride, your destination shifts altogether, either by timing, location, or a change in circumstance.

Even for short legs of the journey, distractions and temptations may arise, tempting you to leave your path for half an hour, a day, or the rest of your life.

Improving your focus is a way of ensuring you get where you intend to go. The man who promises to help a friend build a cabin on his next two weeks off might get distracted or sidetracked by an offer of a free vacation to Hawaii or a boss pressuring him to take on extra assignments. But if his focus is strong, he will honor the commitment to his friend, forgoing or postponing the other opportunities. The woman who decides to donate her kidney to a sick cousin may be overwhelmed when her fearful friends warn her about possible accidents or illnesses that could ruin her remaining kidney. She may be offered a new job starting in the week she would be recovering from the kidney operation, but if she has a deep commitment to helping her cousin, she will do it and accept the potential costs and consequences.

Keeping a clear sense of what matters most is helpful in order to maintain your focus on the scary or difficult tasks ahead of you. Take time to refresh your sense of values and commitments periodically by looking over the covenant you developed in the previous chapter. Amend it as necessary, but keep it as a touchstone. Refer to it by rereading during times of trouble, temptation, or chaos. You will find that many fears and temptations fade as you refresh your sense of who you are and what you intend to do while residing on this planet.

I offer a number of suggestions below that can strengthen your ability to focus on what is deep and true for you. Any of them may be helpful for some situations but not others. Feel free to browse through and choose what is most helpful at any given time, leaving the others for more appropriate occasions.

1. If you are embarking on a particular project—say, challenging a major industrial polluter that is dumping toxic waste in a river—it may help at some point early in the project to envision specifically the outcome you are hoping for. Take a few quiet moments with nothing else to distract you, in order to give this mini-project the attention it deserves. Make it visual and as ideal as can be for all parties concerned. In this case, a good image might include both parties shaking hands at a picnic along the river, the fish happily breaching in the water, or a spread in the newspapers with pictures and headlines announcing a generous settlement. Whatever your project, whatever outcome you envision, let that image remind you from time to time exactly what you're heading for. Let it be your lighthouse along the rocky coast at night, during times of fog and thunderstorms.

2. There will be times when distractions tempt you away from your stated purpose. Some people benefit from having a mental image that reminds them how to filter these things out. For some it is useful to envision a jar or a safe deposit box that they put such distractions in, to be sorted through later, when the project is complete. Take a moment to try out such an image, envisioning what the jar actually looks, feels, and smells like, where you might store it if it were real (under the bed, in a basement, tucked on a high shelf in a store room, in a safe deposit box), how big the safe deposit box is and where you would go to visit it. If these images seem useful, call them up whenever necessary. Alternatively, find someone to delegate these other matters to, or develop an actual list to be attended to later, so that they are taken care of without distracting you in the present.

3. There may be times when you want to say goodbye to your mentors or loved ones, and get their blessing for the work ahead, but you cannot actually do it for one reason or another—illness, death, distractions, distance, or misunderstandings. Still you can do this in your own mind, envisioning them standing behind you and receiving some sense of the

moral support they would offer, if they only could. Sit or lie down in a quiet place somewhere and free your mind to dwell for as long as you wish on a scene where you say your farewells and/or receive their blessings. You may create some variation on the following: "Bye, honey, I'm going off to do a job now!" "I love you all. See you when I get back." "I wouldn't leave if I didn't have to. Wait for me until I get back." complete with them kissing or hugging you (and you doing the same back), clapping a hand on your shoulder, reminding you what an outstanding job you'll do, and wishing you luck.

4. During most long and difficult efforts, disappointments arise, support erodes, supplies fall short, people take wounds to the body or the spirit, or allies drop away. As these trials arise, it may be helpful to adapt a kind of warrior mentality. Use the image of the graceful warrior, stepping through a battlefield, still moving forward even when sustaining small hits to the shoulders or arms, even as comrades fall, even as they run through one clip of ammunition (or quiver of arrows), adjusting their tactics as needed, still gracefully and effectively moving closer to the objective ahead.

5. Drummer Dan Gorlin writes that, in the West African tradition, leading as well as following, in ways that benefit everybody, are taught through shared musical performances. "In a remarkable way," he says, "these disciplines teach a state of mind which can overcome great obstacles, which can turn ordinary people into heroes." To a lesser extent, the ability to work together harmoniously can be found in other musical collectives, and to some extent on sports teams. Volunteer efforts may also draw on nascent teamwork abilities, though they may not train specifically for those ends. Groups of parents frequently work together to raise funds for schools and other good causes; church groups, fraternal organizations and others may collect money or provide days of community service work. Find a venue where you can participate on a regular basis, and pick up through osmosis whatever leadership and follower-ship skills you can. These will be useful and satisfying for all your deep endeavors.

6. Lamaze training for childbirth and many forms of yoga teach people to use particular breathing patterns in order to stay focused. Lamaze

childbirth specifically uses the breath to withstand the pain of childbirth (a major distraction for sure!) so that the hard work of birthing the baby can proceed in the healthiest possible way. There are many useful patterns that can be adopted to keep calm and focused, to stave off panic, or to keep moving forward during tough times. One easy pattern to practice now, and to repeatedly practice on a regular basis so you will be able to adopt it to help you get through any form of crisis is this: Take a deep breath in, all the way into the center of your belly, while counting slowly to six. Hold your breath for a count of four, then slowly exhale, completely emptying your belly, for another count of six. Repeat this cycle twenty times for the practice of it. Use it as long as necessary during an actual crisis.

7. Mentally rehearse the feeling of working with your allies to overcome some hardship. A good example comes from Jim Lawson's training for civil rights activists. Lawson taught his students that nonviolence was not merely a tactic, but a principle to live by. The activists would need complete inner certainty, enough to be able to withstand an enemy flinging rocks at them, grinding a burning cigarette into their necks, whatever evil they might do to try and break them. All the while, the activists would have to keep love in their hearts for that enemy, regardless of the enemy's fear and hate toward them. You can visualize as they were taught to do. Start by figuring out what you want to place in your heart—love for mankind, the cause you are connected to, the team of buddies you work with. Place an image of them in your heart. Treat this image tenderly and tuck it safely inside. Then, picture walking away from the safe zone into the inferno, with that glowing little image warming your heart every step of the way.

Chapter 5: Who will support my work?

"No man is an island entire of itself; every man
is a piece of the continent, a part of the main..."—John Donne

Sometimes people get an idea that gives them the energy to go charging forward on their own. It may seem like too much work to convince others to help pull the load with you. But the man who pulls a heavy load on his own will soon tire, while the one who finds an ally to spell him, or a confederate with a van or truck, is that much more powerful than one man alone.

So take this time to figure out who you can enlist to help. It may be one, it may be many, but no one needs to struggle alone.

Below here is an exercise to help you find your allies. Take ten minutes to fill in Table 2.4 (or another form that works for you) for whichever project you plan to embark on. Fill it in even if you use it only to figure out who will bring you water, who will welcome you back, or who would be proud when you set the load onto the ground somewhere further down the road. When you're done, begin the task of enlisting their help by filling them in on what you're up to, inviting them to participate in whatever limited way you had in mind, and remembering to be grateful for whatever help is offered. And if any one potential ally will not offer help at this time, keep them updated regularly, because you may be able to enlist their help in the future if they see how sincere you are, as they come to recognize the merits of the work involved.

Table 2.4: Who are my allies?

Kind of ally	What he or she can provide	How to maintain our connection
From my immediate circle of people		
From my business or professional circle		
From training, experiences		
Equipment, structures, organizations		
Other		

Chapter 6: Closing the distance

Closing the distance between a plan and the actions required to carry it out is sometimes an onerous task itself. You know what you want to do—the overall plan—and yet somehow you can't bring yourself to dive in. The water looks cold, murky and deep. Monsters may be lurking in the depths.

This may be a problem of the difference between strategy and tactics. As a friend of mine used to say, there is a big difference between knowing what the forest looks like when you're on the mountain above it, and knowing what path to take, step by step, as you walk through that same forest.

If you take time to translate from the big picture to the smaller one, allowing you to see what step to take next, and the step or two after that, the project looks much more doable. As Mother Teresa might have suggested, if you can't feed 100 people, focus for now on figuring out how to feed just one. Then the next, and the one after that.

Break the overall plan into bite-sized pieces. Or break it down into whole meals, and then break each meal down into bite-sized pieces. If it suits you better, break the overall project down into meals, break the first meal into bite-sized pieces, and trust that as you get toward the end of that first meal, you'll already be starting to figure out how to break down the next one.

Trust in your own growing competence, because as you continue to do this work, your experience will grow, your confidence will increase, and your fears and anxieties will diminish. Use the following tables or devise your own:

Table 2.5: Break the plan into meals.

Task group	Task	Allies

Table 2.6: Break the meals into bite-sized pieces.

Task group	Task	Allies

You may find that as you go along, the original tactical plan needs to be changed. That's fine. Go ahead and change it, using the above tables again if that helps. You may need to revamp your tactics again and again, but that's normal for any big, complicated project. Just keep checking back to make sure you are still serving the overall purpose, and that the overall purpose continues to serve the values and communities you hold dear.

Chapter 7: Managing fear

"Fear arises from separation, alienation or disconnection. Courage, unconditional love and serenity are different faces of the same thing. They arise from the same place—a place where you feel connected and unified with your own deeper self as well as with others, nature and the cosmos."—psychologist Edmund Bourne

Fear, or its close cousin anxiety, can creep in silently and mug a person in an instant. Either way, it tends to take over, hijacking them from their intended destinations, creating mid-course hesitations, deflating their tires or creating leaks in their fuel lines. One worrisome comment, a wrong glance, a lurking shadow, or a sudden noise and adrenaline fills the heart, ice fills the veins, and the person stops in their tracks. A drop of rain at a vulnerable moment and, like Chicken Little, they begin to worry that the entire sky is falling. They imagine the worst—their project in flames, fiery walls toppling down, enemies circling, and the entire world turning against them.

Fear may be justified or not, but either way it does no good to be immobilized by it, much less panicking and blindly pursuing a foolish and risky withdrawal.

If you seem to be bogged down in darkness, sit down in a quiet place and take a look at the situation. It probably is nowhere near as bleak as you think. Use this four-part process as a reality check to shake yourself out of the mire. You can practice now with a hypothetical situation, so that you will be ready to use it when a real situation hits.

1. Identify the emotion. Your body will be a good indicator, if you stop to pay attention. Some of the clearest indicators of emotion are physical. Fear, for example, presents itself through these reactions: sweating, feeling nervous in the belly, feeling jittery or jumpy, shaking, trembling, breathing fast and shallowly, feeling breathless, muscles tensing, stomach cramping. Noticing a number of these symptoms is a strong clue that you are scared. There is nothing wrong with these feelings. Our bodies are wise to send up a flare, because the conscious mind can sometimes be blind to the overall picture, focusing too hard on plans and pathways

through the immediate circumstance. "Danger," our nervous stomachs are telling us; "watch out, tread carefully." It is true wisdom to pay attention to such things. The next time you feel this way, you will be quicker to recognize that you are afraid.

2. Figure out what message the emotion is sending. The fear or anxiety you feel tells you to be prepared for anything. Ask yourself, in order to clarify what is going on: is it a physical danger? A moral or psychological one? Who is the immediate threat, and who is actually being threatened? Take several deep breaths as you stop to consider the situation. Our bodies often tense up in the face of danger and we forget to breathe, thus depriving our brains and muscles of the very oxygen which is essential for figuring things out.

3. Acknowledge your fear or anxiety and let yourself be aware of it. Take as long as you need to fully experience it in your imagination or meditation now, while we are practicing, and the stakes are so low. If you can give yourself permission to fully experience it now, to learn what these feelings have to teach you, you will make them allies instead of enemies. Then, when the real thing comes, you will be that much more prepared. Breathe into this uncomfortable emotion, in and out, as if you could hold the fear in your hands like a paper bag. If you resist feeling it, it will grow bigger and bigger until you are overwhelmed. If you allow yourself to feel it, to be aware and fully tolerate it, it will begin to diminish until it is bearable or even disappears altogether. Don't fret that there's no time for all this airy-fairy stuff; there are always enough moments to breathe. If you don't let yourself have these moments, you are likely to find yourself panicking, which almost always leads to disaster. So take a preventive ten minutes to feel and breathe. That's what we call "coping." You can actually add it to your list of things you have to do throughout the crisis.

4. Ask yourself if it makes sense to be afraid in this particular situation, with this particular enemy or threat. If yes, all the more reason to go carefully, revisiting your reasons and motivations, collecting allies, devising strategies and otherwise preparing yourself before going into battle. If you decide the answer is no, all the better, knowing you are fully up to the task of righting these wrongs without fear. Often the answer

is no, either because your fear is overblown or because there are many things you can do to diminish the threat. If the latter, look around for allies, wisdom, or useful suggestions. If you arm yourself appropriately, you'll be better able to handle the circumstances, whatever they are.

For now, at a time when there is no danger, take the time to practice this. Find a quiet place to think or meditate. When you are ready, imagine a daunting incident you might have to face someday. Or call to mind a time in the past when something frightened you, which you might now re-imagine facing in some new, better way. Perhaps it is a social or emotional confrontation, or a physically dangerous circumstance. Imagine or recall as many details as you can—what the room or the setting looks like, if it is warm or cold, what sounds you hear in the background, what you are holding or wearing, who is there with you, who is there against you. As you begin to fully imagine the situation, ask yourself: what is the first thing that alerts you to danger?

Now take a few moments to notice what your body feels in this time of hyper-alertness. What is your skin's response? What do you feel in your belly? What other parts of your body are reacting to stress? Notice all the ways your body alerts you to danger. Notice these messages and thank your body for communicating so clearly with you, using the only language it knows how to speak.

When you are done with that, return to the second question: What message is the fear sending? What kind of danger is this? Who is threatening to do what, and why? Who is at risk? Why does the situation throw you into a state of fear instead of your dealing with it as just another challenge?

As you consider these things, remember to keep breathing, slowly and intentionally. You may find it useful to adopt the deliberate pattern of breathing suggested above.

Depending on how this exercise goes, you may want to repeat it several more times with related or differing incidents in mind. You may find that your fears are usually overblown. Or you may find that an unwavering sense of caution is the best course for you. Whatever you find will be a valuable lesson. Cherish it; use it wisely and well.

Here are some other techniques to decrease fear:

- Getting training for dangerous events

- Reminding yourself that you've been trained for such an event

- Forcing yourself to take a deliberate reality check. We've covered one way to do this above, but you may prefer Pury's more elaborate version, especially if you are a person who tends to be anxious. Anxious people tend to see a dire outlook where a more confident person would see there's a good chance of accomplishing their goals. So, deliberately set the situation in a more optimistic perspective. For example, instead of obsessing that you'll probably get caught sending that whistle-blowing letter to the Department of Health, focus on the more likely reality that nobody is around to see you mailing the letter and you'll probably get through unobserved.

- Secure the image in your mind of the successful course of events. For example, slipping into the post office to mail that whistle-blowing letter, and getting away without being seen. Keep going back to this image of success whenever you feel a twinge of fear or anxiety.

- Remind yourself that fear does not have to mean "STOP." It can, instead, mean "Listen," or "Prepare," or "Proceed with Caution."

- Eating (especially comfort foods) is a common technique to alleviate anxiety. However the calming effect is very short-term: it wears off, leaving people to resort to additional stress-reduction eating. And the side effects of high caloric stress-reduction are not necessarily good for your overall well-being. There are better techniques for coping with fear and anxiety; use one or more of the others listed in this section instead.

- Smoking, drinking, and drugs are also easy short-term solutions with probable bad side effects. Again, choose one or more of the more effective strategies in this section instead.

- Relaxation techniques can provide a much-needed break from anxiety:
  - Focus on a soothing, calming piece of music or art. Breathe in the experience. Enjoy for at least three minutes, maybe even up to twenty.
  - Breathing exercises of various kinds, including the one described in Chapter four, step six.
  - Picture yourself at the beach, a lake, or other calm, beautiful scene of your choosing. Meditate on that for 5 minutes, letting your mind wander into a daydream about it if you prefer.

- Progressive relaxation techniques (described in the following chapter)

- Change fear into anger. People have long sensed that fear or anxiety can be turned into anger, which jazzes them up and can be channeled into action, for better or for worse. The rise of Hitler, in the wake of Germany's hyper-inflationary economic collapse, can be at least partially ascribed to his manipulation of this very phenomenon. Similarly, many terrorist organizations recruit from the ranks of the unemployed, poorly educated young men and women with few prospects for betterment. By turning their anxiety about their future into hatred of some external enemy, they create a large supply of dedicated people willing to fight the wrongs they perceive. Unfortunately, anger rarely chooses its methods or targets wisely. We recognize the limits and dangers for channeling anxiety into anger; still, it can create a lot of momentum on a short-term basis.

Social scientists and psychologists, generally turn to thought-oriented approaches, such as the reality check described above, but these are not the only options. Prayer, for example, is an age-old technique for alleviating fear, used by people throughout time and in cultures all around the world. Compare this prayer of St. Francis of Assisi, born in 12th century Italy:

Dear Lord
Make me an instrument of Your peace:
Where there is hatred, let me sow love;
Where there is injury, forgiveness;
Where there is doubt, faith;
Where there is despair, hope;
Where there is darkness, light;
And where there is sadness, joy.

Divine Master, grant that I may not so much seek to be consoled
as to console;
To be understood as to understand;
To be loved as to love;
For it is in giving that we receive;

In forgiving that we are forgiven;
And it is in dying that we are born to eternal life.

with this one from the Lakota tradition:

O Great Spirit,
Whose voice I hear in the winds
and whose breath gives life to all the world,
Hear me.
I am small and weak.
I need your strength and wisdom.
Let me walk in beauty
Let my eyes ever behold the red and purple sunset.
Make my hands respect the things you have made
and my ears grow sharp to hear your voice.
Make me wise so that I may understand the things
You have taught my people.
Let me learn the lessons you have hidden
In every leaf and rock.
I seek strength not to be greater than my brother or sister,
but to fight my greatest enemy, myself.
Make me always ready
To come to you with clean hands and straight eyes
So when life fades as the fading sunset,
my spirit may come to you without shame.

Both prayers are inspirational and calming, reminding the worried soul of the much greater perspective available to them. Try these yourself and you will see. Or choose another prayer or meditation that you like better; mark it and read it whenever you need sustaining.

Alternatively you may devise prayers more suited to your personality and circumstance. Here's one that a therapist friend uses before seeing her most troubled clients:

Dear Lord,
Please help me find the strength, energy, wisdom, and courage to
say and do the things needed to help this person. Amen.

While she says these words, she visualizes the energy centers for each of those traits in turn, each growing brighter when she names them in her prayer. Should you feel hesitant about devising an effective prayer of your own, keep these general guidelines in mind:

- Keep it short and focused
- Don't bother asking to win at the expense of others; if there is a contest between two sides, then surely people on the other side are also asking to overcome. Obviously both sets of prayers can't be honored.
- Instead, ask for the qualities that will help, no matter the outcome: Ask for courage, clarity, strength, insight, wisdom, for help adjusting to whatever comes up, or for help for others.
- You can always ask for guidance.
- You can always ask for the best possible outcome for everyone involved that would be in accordance with divine will.

Sometimes it is useful to meditate or contemplate the subject of what is holding you back. Whichever you prefer, take a few minutes in a quiet place to visit this important question. Let your body get comfortable; let your mind quiet down, then ask yourself, "What is holding me back?" or "What is holding us back?"

Allow for a wide variety of possible responses: words, images or feelings, including old fears, current logistical difficulties, competing responsibilities, rivalries or resentments. Let your ideas emerge unscathed and uncriticized; they will most likely be trustworthy and useful, though maybe indirect. Let each possible roadblock come to the forefront of your mind and let it take as much time to inform you about itself as it needs. You could, if you like, ask what you can do about it, and allow the answer to emerge without judging. Then ask what else is holding you back, and allow that to emerge as well. Keep asking that question, one after the next, until nothing else emerges.

When the process is complete, record everything you remember in the form below, or take notes in some other form of your own devising. Only after you've recorded all the objections should you begin to fill in the second column of possible solutions for overcoming them.

One woman's list:

- My mother always worries
- I barely have time to do my ordinary work

- My husband would never let me
- Fear—when I was a kid I tried something like this, but I got hurt pretty bad

One man's list:

- Who will feed and clothe my kids if I die?
- I don't think I have the guts to go through with it (fear)
- What if I make a mistake and more people get hurt? (fear)
- What if I blow it, and everyone remembers what a doofus I was? (fear)
- What if people laugh at me for caring about stuff like that? (fear)

Table 2.7: Obstacles and their elimination.

What is holding me back?	What can I do to ease this?

Chapter 8: Additional breathing and relaxation techniques

"If I am not for myself, who will be for me?
If I am only for myself, what am I?
And if not now, when?"—Rabbi Hillel of Jerusalem, circa 2000 years ago

Once you've used the fear-defeating exercises from the previous chapter a few times, repeating the process will become simpler and quicker. It may become almost automatic. But there will be other times when something even simpler is called for.

Not every situation needs to be thought through every time. Sometimes you know what you are facing, and whether caution or boldness is appropriate, yet you still need something to diminish the ongoing tension. Use one or more of the following breathing exercises as soon as you notice the fear or anxiety overtaking you. Simple and effective, they do as much good in their own way as the lengthier procedures above.

Deliberate relaxation through deep breathing: Fear and anxiety cause the body to tense up. Over millions of years our species has evolved to react quickly by fleeing or fighting whatever threatens us.

Thus the human being, like most creatures, responds to danger both quickly and at times when it turns out not to be warranted. Faced with a lesser threat, you may not feel the cold rush of adrenaline but you may notice after a while that your shoulders ache, your jaw or muscles are tight, or your stomach hurts. Your body prepared itself to flee or fight, and you're still holding that tense readiness, just in case. Your body may not have noticed that the danger was not very immediate; it simply noticed the danger and prepared to respond.

Whenever the adrenaline rushes through your body and you feel foolish about it, or when you notice your muscles or jaw tensing and your stomach hurts, stop for a moment to calm yourself down. There is a quick and effective antidote to tension that you can learn, a response which brings immediate relaxation to your body and mind. By activating the relaxation response, your body will begin to recover within a few short minutes. All you have to do to set off this response is breathe.

But not any old kind of breathing. When people are tense they tend to take short, shallow breaths, or even sometimes hold their breath, starving the muscles and brain of much needed oxygen. The type of breathing that counters this is deep, abdominal breathing. Try this:

1. Inhale slowly, through your nose unless it is blocked, letting the air fill your lungs from the very bottom to their tops, counting silently to six. Pause for a count of four, then exhale through nose or mouth, counting again to six.

2. Repeat this cycle for twenty breaths.

3. Notice how much more calm you feel. Taking this time for yourself has allowed you to shed the fear or anxiety that interfered with everything else.

4. You are ready to return to your activities, refreshed and better able to respond appropriately. The first time you try this, sit in a comfortable chair. With practice you will be able to do this sitting, standing, lying down, standing in line at the grocery store, driving in rush hour traffic, wherever you find yourself growing tense. Done often enough, it will sometimes come on automatically, without your having to think about it.

A variation: As you inhale, breathing in, let your mind fill up with the syllable "Re." On the exhale, breathe out with the syllable "lax." Thus you are reminding your conscious mind to relax while letting your subconscious relax with the mere cessation of tension. You might choose a different phrase reflecting other concerns such as "peace... now" or "you're... safe," the first word for the inhale, the second one for the exhale. You might try inhaling for the same count through the nose, exhaling through the mouth, a tension-cleansing practice which many yoga instructors recommend.

Countering statements: If you find yourself worrying about specific fears or obstacles, you can counter the mental fearfulness with statements devised to run counter to the fears, neutralizing them. The physical symptoms of fear and panic may come at you unexpectedly, but you can establish an attitude of taking control over them. This allows you to be the master instead of the slave to your own inner attitudes, to be more of an optimist than a pessimist, to enjoy a frame of mind which supports you in your work instead of getting in the way. Combining such statements as the following, along with the deep breathing, is a very powerful combination:

"I've been through stuff like this before and came through fine."

"I trained for this and am good at it."

"I can deal with whatever comes up."

"All I have to do is my part and the others will do the rest."

"I survived worse than this, this time I'll be fine too."

"I can be anxious and still deal with this situation."

A client of mine was working on a driving phobia that required her to walk more than she would have liked, or else take a complicated set of bus connections if she couldn't get a ride. Going for her weekly grocery run was a nightmare whenever her husband was out of town. Finally she came to me for help. Among other techniques we developed to help was this statement she created for herself: "My 17-year-old daughter can drive this friggin' car; so can I."

A rescue worker, suffering from post-traumatic stress, returned to work, aided by using the phrase, "I can handle this, I move through it like water."

People choose countering statements to suit their particular needs and circumstances. What particularly helps is to make a positive statement about what you can do, instead of making a negative statement. This is because the subconscious mind handles actions much better than abstractions like the words "not," "no" and "none," or worse yet, contractions including them. Rather than saying "I won't let it get to me," which the subconscious sometimes hears as "I let it get to me," a more powerful positive statement like "I move through it easily" gives the subconscious mind a useful direction to follow.

Someone facing physical risks might create a statement about those situations, such as "I am part of a great team and we work well together," or "I can take as much time as I need to set it up right," or "I am strong and trained for just this kind of thing."

Someone facing moral risks might create a statement like "I am doing the right thing for these people," or "It's OK that people resist it for now. I am teaching them something new."

Someone facing psychological risks might say, "I am ready for this," or "This is just fear; I will move through it," or "I am going to do it differently this time no matter what!" or "This fear will pass and I will be OK."

Try constructing your own statement for whatever situation you are likely to face. Next, imagine yourself using it at just the right time.

Then, when the right time comes, use it as often as necessary.

Affirmations: Positive statements like the above are great for dealing with particular fears or worries. Affirmations are a more general way to cheer yourself on, even build yourself up, shoring up confidence and firming up a new direction.

Affirmations, like countering statements, are best chosen or created by the person for themselves. They are positive statements that can be said when rising in the morning, getting ready for bed, and at random moments throughout the day. As a therapist I told my clients to choose an affirmation and say it on rising and another 20 times during the day. Of course they didn't count the number of times they said it; the important thing, especially at first, was to keep reinforcing the intention built into the affirmation. You can assign yourself certain periodic times to say it to yourself, in addition to when you rise in the morning and when you get ready for sleep. Use it whenever you stop for a stop sign or a red light. Use it before eating a meal or taking the first sip of a drink. Use it every time you go into or pass by a bathroom.

Affirmations are short, positive statements about the kind of person you want to become, or the kind of intention or impact you want to have. Affirmations help counter old self-images or conditioning to create a stronger, more intentional way of living. Such statements as these might give you some ideas for your own use:

I am strong, bold, and free.

I am a light in the darkness.

Every day I help somebody climb higher.

I love my strong arms and shoulders. They carry people out of danger.

I am healthy, happy, and loved. I have so much to give others.

I am getting wiser and better at _____ every day.

I am a _____. (Insert whatever you are working on becoming—terrific pilot, skillful firefighter, accomplished musician, etc.)

Take a moment now to construct an affirmation that represents you at your best. Start by using it five times in the next five minutes, and then several times every day for at least the next month.

Deep relaxation techniques: There are a variety of names for the following simple exercise: meditation, self-hypnosis, and progressive relaxation.

Whatever name you prefer, use this for times of ongoing stress and tension. It works better than tranquilizers for many people, along with the additional benefits of costing less and having no negative side effects.

1. Find a room or place (couch, bed, sofa, restroom) where no one will disturb you for at least 10 minutes. Turn off your cell phone, pager, and anything else that might disrupt the silence. If the ticking of a watch or clock is distracting, put it in a drawer, pocket or another room to mute the sound.

2. Take a few moments to stretch, wiggle, do a couple of pushups or jumping jacks, whatever it takes to get the kinks out of your body. You will be more ready to relax afterwards.

3. Lie down in a comfortable position on a sofa, mat or bed. Kick off your shoes, loosen your tie or belt, take off your glasses, do whatever is necessary to get comfortable. If you need something to cushion your head, find it and resume your position.

4. Close your eyes and take a couple of deep, relaxing breaths. You might use one of the breathing techniques described above. Sigh when releasing the breath if you like. Keep breathing, slowly and evenly, filling your lungs and emptying them. You should start to feel calmer and steadier already.

5. Clench the toes of both feet tightly, holding them tight for a couple of seconds, then let them relax. Clench them a second time and then relax.

6. Now clench the muscles of your feet and ankles, holding them that way for a couple of seconds before letting them relax. Clench them a second time and relax them again.

7. You will continue tightening and releasing various muscle groups in turn, progressing upwards through the body in this same way: Tightening and holding, then relaxing, tightening and holding them a second time and relaxing them again. Do this, one area at a time, first with your feet and ankles, then the calf muscles, then your knees, next the muscles of the thigh, then the groin and buttocks area followed by the stomach region and then the upper chest.

8. Now, branch off to relax each area of the fingers, the hands, then the forearms, next the upper arms and shoulders. Finally, clench and relax the muscles of the neck, then the jaw, the face and the forehead in turn.

9. Once this is done, take a moment to imagine smoothing the muscles of the entire face and body. You might even imagine fluffing them like you'd fluff a pillow, or petting them appreciatively, stroking them as you'd stroke a cat, for all the good work they do for you.

10. Lie there for a few minutes enjoying the sensations, whatever they are: emptiness, serenity, relaxation, the feeling of the blood flowing through your body, the contented humming of the nerves. From this state of greater contentment you will be more ready to cope with whatever comes your way. If you have trouble falling asleep, use this exercise in your bed at night, allowing yourself to drift into a contented state of relaxation afterwards.

11. Take as long as you like to bask in this relaxation. When you are ready, slowly open your eyes and stretch. Bend the knees and roll on your side before slowly getting up and resuming your activities for the day.

In addition to these, we should never forget the ancient wisdom of taking care of yourself before taking care of the world. Many people forget this most basic bit of wisdom. I used to remind my clients that if they were sprinters, they could spring up and run their short lengths, but most people need to be marathoners to get through a long life, so they need to learn how to marshal their energies for the long run. They need to take care of themselves in order to go the distance.

Other clients responded well to another metaphor, comparing their physical selves to a house. I would remind them that every house needs a strong foundation before the roof and walls can be built to shelter a family, and if they neglect to keep their foundations strong, shore up any cracks, etc., they won't be sheltering their families safely for long.

So, in order to keep your own foundation strong, letting you function in good times and bad, you need to do certain things on a regular basis. Eat good nutritious foods, get decent amounts of sleep every night, find enough time to exercise your body several times a week. Let yourself enjoy a day of rest, relaxation, and restoration every week, whether you call it the Sabbath day or something else. There is wisdom in those ancient practices that even non-believers can appreciate. Relax and spend time with friends and family whenever you can. Pray, if you are a praying person; dance, sing or laugh if you find joy that way. Then, when you have committed to your own well being, look around to see what else you can commit to.

Life is a precious gift from the universe. Do not waste the opportunity. Go ahead and make the best darned use of it that you can possibly imagine.

Chapter 9: Make friends with your endgame

"Is he lonesome
Or just blind,
That guy who drives
So close behind?"
—Burma Shave sign on the highway

A lot of energy gets wasted by people who are either oblivious or afraid of death. Death can come at any time, and so it is useless to waste a lifetime worrying about it. At the same time it's a bit silly to live in denial that it will come to any one of us just as it comes to everyone else. With certain facts of life such as this, the wise person ultimately finds it more helpful to find some way to embrace them, to turn their lemon-ness into lemonade.

One of the best ways to do this is to make friends with your end. Death becomes your friend just like anyone or anything else, when you accept that it brings good things as well as challenges into your life.

Okay, you may be saying to yourself, the challenge it brings is obvious, but what good can Death possibly bring? Well, a lot of things, actually. If there were no death, the world would be vastly overpopulated and everyone would starve. States everywhere offer hunting licenses to keep the deer population from the same misery in a world with few predators; without something to keep their numbers in check they would not thrive.

Death brings an end to the game of Life, and thus makes it both finite and precious. Even believers in eternal life or reincarnation are usually reluctant to let go of this life they are in now. Death reminds us that this place where we are, here and now, is only ours for a short time, and we should find a way to enjoy it, to make it meaningful, to make a difference, and be remembered somehow, hopefully in a good way. The knowledge that Death is imminent, as in having a terminal illness, only makes this understanding more real.

The person who accepts that Death will come for them usually has a greater sense of perspective than the person who denies it. They are more likely to find the courage to do something worthwhile, more likely to build and maintain healthy relationships, to figure out clean and sustainable ways to live. They are much less likely to waste precious time on destructive or frivolous pursuits that do little good for anyone.

If you have even the least tinge of discomfort dwelling on this issue, I encourage you to try the following:

Find some quiet, out of the way place where no one will disturb you for at least ten minutes. Turn off your cell phone, pager, and anything else that might disturb you. If the ticking of a watch or clock is distracting, put it in a drawer or pocket to mute the sound. Sit in a comfortable chair or lie down, whichever you prefer.

Close your eyes and let your mind drift like a child carried on the tail of a kite to a far and distant place—in this case to the very end of your lifetime. Doing this exercise, you get a chance to peek in and see this older self—maybe a bit older or maybe a lot older. Take a few moments just to notice—the tone of your skin, the color of your hair (is it white, streaked, or some other color?), and the tone of your muscles. Are you lying in a hospital bed or somewhere else? Are you surrounded by loved ones, or alone?

You are the creator of your life, so envision this ending in a way that seems right to you, as wholesome and homey as you could want it to be.

Now enter your awareness into the body of this older self, just enough to notice: Does this older you feel content with the life you have lived? Do you feel comfortable with the legacy you are leaving behind, the family and friends, the projects? Just notice and be aware of whatever comes up.

Take a few moments now to let your mind drift around, imagining the people whose lives you've touched over the course of your long and full life. Let them come through, one at a time, and say their goodbyes. Some might be younger, some might be older, the living and the dead; let them each come through to say what they need to say in order to complete their relationship with you. They might want to say thanks for what you have taught them, what you have done together, anything you gave them or built; they might want to hear thanks or acknowledgements or apologies from you as well. Allow this to happen with as much fullness as needed for each person in your life.

Then take a few moments to do the same with each project, each process you have been involved with, completed, or left incomplete. Let each one in turn come through and complain, thank you or acknowledge what you have done together. You may do the same for each of them in turn.

When these are done, take a moment to ask, is there anything else I need to do or say or see to, before I complete my time here on Earth? Let any answers come to you without judgment. Note whatever comes up, and if you can use this time to complete this, go ahead.

When all these are done, when you feel ready, thank your older self for letting you be part of this scene. Make note of anything you can learn for the present time from this scene, unfinished business for example, and then allow yourself to grab the tail of the kite and let it pull you slowly across the sky and back to the present time.

When this is complete, take a few moments to secure what you have learned and whatever else you need to do between now and the end of your time here.

Most people come back from this experience more grounded and accepting of both Death and Life.

Chapter 10: Increasing bravery

"Now that my storehouse
has burned down, nothing
conceals the moon."
—Masahide, Japanese doctor, 1688

There is some evidence that bravery in one area can extend into others. Someone skilled at navigating boatloads of people through white water rapids may also be capable of leading people safely down the stairs through a burning building. Some of those who risked their lives smuggling food into the Warsaw Ghetto later taught themselves to shoot and set explosive charges during the Ghetto uprising against the much better trained and armed forces of the Third Reich. Nelson Mandella, who risked his life while incarcerated in prison by choosing a courtroom defense strategy which had capital punishment as an option so that he could make a political point about the plight of his people, later had the courage to accept the presidency of his country, and in retirement continues fighting for AIDS relief and to uplift poverty throughout the African continent.

Training to handle physical risks may help some brave both physically and emotionally risky challenges as well. There is anecdotal evidence that people who study martial arts, for example, are better able to endure tough social situations. Not all, of course; some physically brave people are not courageous in emotional confrontations, for example, but a great percentage may be. Even without resorting to physical action, their increased confidence and awareness, their greater experience with stilling the heart and focusing only on the immediate circumstance is helpful in difficult situations of many kinds.

Training for risky endeavors, whether it be through white water rafting, martial arts, learning to fly an airplane, rock climbing, scuba diving, downhill skiing or other activities, can bring many rewards, several of which may indirectly or directly help increase the ability to be brave under all kinds of circumstances. First, there's a heightened awareness in any tricky situation, and those who have experienced it before may feel more comfortable operating within it again. Second, being in the middle of danger helps a person focus on whatever is important to the situation and ignore whatever is not. By practicing a variety of risky activities, you develop a greater ability to instinctively weed out what's unimportant in times of high stress.

Third, by succeeding in other risky areas, you increase your self-confidence and your ability to trust yourself in new situations. You learn to get yourself out of tough situations and are likely to be able to do so again.

Fourth, if you've practiced working through theoretical difficulties, when the real thing comes up, your instinct should kick in, shortcutting any planning or figuring out that needs to be done before you can act effectively. Pilots-in-training practice emergency maneuvers, including slips, stalls, spins, and the loss of an engine so that if the real thing ever comes up, they don't have to grab for an instruction manual; they automatically put the plane through the appropriate emergency maneuvers. Firefighters and Delta Rangers similarly practice all manner of challenges so that they have instincts to fall back on as needed.

If you've ever been in danger and had to swallow your fears in order to find your way to safety, there's still a chance you will freeze up, facing some future danger. But there is a greater chance that it will be easier to set aside your fears the second time, and more so the third or fourth time. For some it eventually becomes routine.

Indeed, confronting your fears can have the effect of reminding you during smaller crises how much smaller they are on the scale of things. Whatever doesn't kill you makes you stronger, the old saying advises. Now, that does not mean you should go skiing close to the edge of a mountain or seeking other life-threatening experiences. But pushing your personal envelope can widen your set of capabilities, your confidence, and your ability to perform in a crisis.

At the other extreme, those who expose themselves to frequent danger may become "adrenaline junkies" who may get jaded and flirt too much with danger. Even Stephen Knight, the twice-decorated Canadian policeman, decided that he might be putting his wife and family at too much risk of losing him, and is considering toning down his heroic tendencies, even at the expense of who he feels he truly is.

The burst of pride you feel after surviving a brush with danger could make you a little smug in the company of those who have not done what you have. Remember, true heroes tend to be grateful for the opportunity to help;

they acknowledge the contributions of others besides themselves and typically decline the opportunity to boast.

Physical risk-taking offers the immediate gratification of success, where emotional or moral risk-taking may take years to achieve a satisfactory end-result. Any success can lead to greater self-confidence, more patience and persistence, and more achievements as a whole. Risk-taking in the physical domain may also help those who have lived more limited, sheltered or proscribed lives, thus stretching their sense of identity. Returning to their everyday lives, they may see more clearly what has been limiting them and lend the courage to break free.

Finally, taking physical risks is an ongoing reminder that life is uncertain, and we are all subject to unexpected danger or change. Those who live with the illusion of safety are less likely to be able to make necessary, life-saving adjustments, more likely to react to threats with unhelpful strategies like denial, wishful thinking, or a stubborn sticking to old assumptions and patterns which are dysfunctional under the new circumstances, possibly even threatening to their well-being.

University of New Hampshire Professor Michael Gass, who studies the benefits of physical risk-taking, suggests that there are three kinds of people, each of which should pursue different strategies if they decide to incorporate a higher level of risk-taking into their lives:

- People who habitually avoid risks altogether are better off beginning by merely stepping out of their normal daily routines. Taking up a mildly risky hobby such as indoor rock climbing, canoeing in a river with a small run of white water, snowshoeing, or cross-country skiing might be good first steps for them.

- People who take risks but habitually work to reduce the risks they face might start by pushing themselves just a bit further. Taking themselves on a strenuous high-altitude hike sometime, especially if they already hike in less strenuous areas, learning to scuba dive, or going solo on a vision quest or night camping in a nearby woods or desert might be good next steps for them.

- People more willing to take risks can increase their edge by making physical training or risk-taking a life-long pursuit and challenging themselves from time to time in new ways. Tough pursuits like hang gliding or helicopter skiing might appeal to them, or simply venturing out in ways they've never done before, whenever they feel it's the right time to try something new.

Here are some additional techniques for increasing your level of bravery or willingness to take risks:

- Increase your capacity for courage through increasing confidence in your own background and training. Review your background, especially your past successes:

  - especially where they helped you overcome obstacles

  - especially if they were similar to the risky situation in front of you

  - especially where they can be attributed to your abilities (intelligence, fortitude, etc) and not to random luck

- Glass half-full or empty. People who look optimistically at past successes as due to their own personal abilities are more likely to take credit for them, take ownership of them as we sometimes say, feel optimistic about their ability to act effectively in future situations, and thus become more effective in general. People who look pessimistically at their past successes and regard themselves generally as failures are less likely to take credit and less likely to feel they might succeed in the future, thus becoming less effective, less confident, and less courageous. So, consider some of the events where you were successful in the past. Find at least three things you did or three characteristics of yours which contributed to each success. Take credit for the good deeds you have accomplished, and go on to accomplish more. That's an order!

- Decide to regard yourself as someone who is always improving; that attitude leads to more confidence about the future and your ability to succeed in the future.

- Clarity about your goals, strategies and tactics leads to clearer vision about how to proceed, thus increasing the effectiveness of your work and the likelihood of its success.

- Good role models help. The effects of those models are stronger and more likely to be called on if:

- They seem similar to you in some way or another

- You notice or recall your role model(s) while planning or going ahead with the project

- You understand what steps the role model took and try to follow them where appropriate

- Your role model got rewarded for their efforts. Rewards could be financial, honors, or some other change in status. If you stand up to bullies, you rise in stature, and the chances that others who saw or heard about it will emulate you.

• Make the situation seem less risky through training, practice, or simulation, through planning (think it through, sketch it out, diagram, or role-play it), bring in better safety equipment and conditions, pursue preventative activities (removing obstacles beforehand, taking care of part of the problem in advance so that what's left is simpler)

• Highlight the noble or valuable nature of the goal, thus increasing motivation

• Create a personal book of role models. Draw on family stories, book or movie characters you identify with, even your own past history of courage.

• Think of a situation where you'd like to be more courageous. Identify the goal. Analyze the risks. Is there a way to reduce the risks? Is there a way to increase the chance of success? What steps can you take to do these? Is fear in the way, and of what? How can you diminish the fear? How can you increase your sense of confidence or train for it? What can you do right now to address these obstacles?

Chapter 11: Practice taking moral or social risks

The previous chapter primarily addressed increasing bravery in the face of physical danger. This chapter focuses more on increasing bravery in other tough situations.

Courage can be learned by practicing small doses of it in everyday situations. Speaking up when you get cut off in line, for example, or making sure a bully does not get his way. You can train yourself to be courageous by noticing and acting on such opportunities. Each of us has times when they get uncomfortable about a situation but let it go by without reacting. The next time this happens, take a few moments afterwards to consider what you could have done instead. "Excuse me," you might say to the person who shoved in front of you. "I was here first. I've been waiting for five minutes already; you can wait right there behind me." Chances are they will; they may not have noticed there was a line.

Standing up to bullies may be scarier for some, but using your other skills might help. Looking around for allies, for example, and including them in the interaction, either through pulling them in to help if you can, or at least by making eye contact with them while confronting the bully and keeping him or her from getting their way.

Some situations might allow you turn to your own values and ethics as your ally. "It's not fair to take advantage of someone younger and smaller than you," you might tell the line-cutter or the bully, reminding them of the ordinary sense of fair play. Even if they lack that sense themselves, they may be ashamed to have others see they lack this basic form of civility; they may still back down.

Setting up small behavioral experiments for yourself can be a fruitful approach. People often experiment with foods, clothing, with different ways to arrange their furniture, and many of these experiments move them toward a better use of resources, a better fit for their needs. Similarly people can experiment with different behavior, trying something new to develop an expanded sense of what works for them. Flexibility is a hallmark of psychological health.

It can be energizing, even thrilling, to step out of long-established habits and try on a newer, larger persona.

Taking small daily risks can prepare us for the unexpected time when courage is needed on a larger scale. The person who has stood up to bullies on a playground will be better equipped to stand up to a bully in a neighborhood, such as a developer trying to force the elderly to sell their homes so the he can raze them and build more upscale housing.

In a society which is increasingly risk averse and fearful of lawsuits, we are too often prone to letting things slip by. The more chances we take to test ourselves and the wrongs around us, the more likely we will see justice done.

Chapter 12: It's OK if they think you're weird

Cultivate loneliness. Sometimes you'll be out of tune with the rest of your friends, family, or society in general. You may be the only one who believes in whatever your cause is. That's okay.

If you know in your heart that you are right, you have several options. You can pretend to believe like everyone else, and do nothing about your true beliefs. You can quietly sneak around and act on your beliefs. Or you can hold you head high and act directly on them. Often the progression is from the first of those to the last, as people gain the courage of their beliefs. It may be lonely at times but that's okay too. Someday more of the people you care about will discover the courage to join you in the deeper end of the pool. They may discover it because you showed them the way.

Practice loneliness for little bits of time. Practice believing something new for two minutes—maybe that giraffes are the secret masters of the universe, or that Zoroastrianism is the only route to heaven. Take a moment to imagine what you'd do if you just found that out, but no one else understood it yet. Would you read everything you could about it, start clueing in your friends and family, post pictures of giraffes or Zoroastrian religious practices on your Facebook page?

If other people looked at you funny for doing that, how would you feel? Especially knowing you understood more about it than they did?

If people complained about you doing that, how would you respond? Would it bother you? Can you do it if you believe it's important, in spite of others thinking you're crazy?

After all, who stays contentedly in the shallow end of the community pool?

The answer is, only small children and their caretakers. Ultimately, to be fully adult, you have to learn to swim in the deep end or you'll always be looking at the grownups from the wistful edge of the pool.

Chapter 13: Once you've assessed the risks, go for it!

Daniel Kahneman, winner of the 2002 Nobel Prize in Economics for his work on decision-making under uncertain conditions, proclaimed that

> "It's a wonderful thing to be optimistic. It keeps you healthy and resilient. But I personally would not want my financial adviser to be optimistic; I'd like him to be as realistic as possible. There are contexts where optimism helps. Generally where it helps is in executing plans. It keeps you on track. It gives you energy to overcome obstacles.

> "When you are making a decision whether or not to go for something, my guess is that knowing the odds won't hurt you, if you're brave. But when you are executing, not to be asking yourself at every moment in time whether you will succeed or not is certainly a good thing. In many cases, what looks like risk-taking is not courage at all, it's just unrealistic optimism. Courage is willingness to take the risk once you know the odds. Optimistic overconfidence means you are taking the risk because you don't know the odds. It's a big difference."

In other words, once you've looked at the risks and decided it's worth it, adopt a positive attitude, then put your foot down at the start of the path and start walking.

Chapter 14: What to do right now?

We've spent plenty of time looking at the idea of depth as a personal dimension, at what courage is and what conditions support heroic and enduring behavior, and how to encourage courage, either in yourself or in others.

Now look back at your notes for the personal plan of action you began devising at the start of this book. Revise it while these ideas are still fresh in your mind. Highlight the areas that you still feel need more attention. Go through the chapters in the last section of the book, picking out which activities or exercises to repeat. Feel free to devise variations to shore up any the areas where you feel something is lacking. Then go back and redo your personal plan of action once again.

If you still feel unready, ask yourself what is holding you back. Then ask whether it is a legitimate hesitation or one which is based on groundless fears. The answer may be either, but either way it will be helpful in deciding what to do next.

I wish you the best of luck.

Acknowledgements

Thanks to the many heroes whose stories inspired me, many of whom have found their way into this book. Thanks to several unnamed former clients of mine, whose bravery often astounded me, and whose stories are told here, though their details have been deliberately obscured or changed to render them unidentifiable.

Thanks to Scott Gorlin for scientific skepticism and referral to several sources on the neuroscience of behavior.

Thanks to Joe Aronson, storyteller and friend, for reading the manuscript in an early stage and offering encouragement and punctuation alike.

Thanks to Dan Gorlin for information on tribal African cultures and music.

Thank you to Richard Crandall, and to all the folks at PSI, whose efforts resulted in getting this book to work out.

Thanks to Joel Levitt, who generously offered me sanctuary, encouragement, and enthusiasm about the stories herein.

Personal notes

(The reader might wish to use these pages for private musings.)

References

[1] J.M. Allman, K.K. Watson, N.A. Tetreault, and A.Y. Hakeem, *Intuition and autism: a possible role for Von Economo neurons*, TRENDS in Cognitive Sciences **9** (2005), no. 8.

[2] Chris Myers Asch, *The senator and the sharecropper: The freedom struggles of James O. Eastland and Fannie Lou Hamer*, New Press, 2008.

[3] Red Auerbach and John Feinstein, *Let me tell you a story: A lifetime in the game*, Little, Brown and Company, 2004.

[4] Allen Barra, *Yogi berra: Eternal yankee*, W. W. Norton and Company, 2009.

[5] John M. Barry, *The great influenza: The epic story of the deadliest plague in history*, Viking Adult, 2004.

[6] Alison Bass, *Side effects: A prosecutor, a whistleblower, and a bestselling antidepressant on trial*, Algonquin Books, 2008.

[7] Marc Bekoff, *The emotional lives of animals: A leading scientist explores animal joy, sorrow, and empathy - and why they matter*, New World Library, 2007.

[8] Sandra Blakeslee and Matthew Blakeslee, *The body has a mind of its own: How body maps in your brain help you do (almost) everything better*, Random House, 2007.

[9] Sarah H. Bradford, *Scenes in the life of harriet tubman (the black heritage library collection)*, Beaufort Books, 1869.

[10] Gordon Brown, *Courage: Eight portraits*, Bloomsbury Publishing, 2007.

[11] Renate Nummela Caine and Geoffrey Caine, *Making connections: Teaching and the human brain*, Dale Seymour Publications, 1994.

[12] John Colapinto, *Brain games: The marco polo of neuroscience*, The New Yorker, May 2009.

[13] John M. Darley and C. Daniel Batson, *"From Jerusalem to Jericho": A study of situational and dispositional variables in helping behavior*, Journal of Personality and Social Psychology **27** (1973), no. 1.

[14] Devra Lee Davis, *When smoke ran like water: Tales of environmental deception and the battle against pollution*, Basic Books, 2002.

[15] Lucy S. Dawidowicz, Lucy S. Dawidowicz, and Lucy S. Dawidowicz, *The war against the jews: 1933-1945*, Bantam, 1986.

[16] Kevin Dockery, *Navy seals: The complete history*, Berkley Books, 2004.

[17] James Farmer, *Lay bare the heart: An autobiography of the civil rights movement*, Arbor House, 1985.

[18] John P. Forsyth and Georg H. Eifert, *The mindfulness and acceptance workbook for anxiety: A guide to breaking free from anxiety, phobias, and worry using acceptance and commitment therapy*, New Harbinger Publications, 2008.

[19] Gregory A. Freeman, *The forgotten 500: The untold story of the men who risked all for the greatest rescue mission of world war ii*, New American Library, 2007.

[20] V. Gallese, C. Keysers, and G. Rizzolatti, *A unifying view of the basis of social cognition*, Trends Cogn Sci. **8** (2004), no. 9, 396–403.

[21] Mohandas Karamchand Gandhi, *Gandhi an autobiography: The story of my experiments with truth*, Beacon Press, 1993.

[22] Marcia Garcia, *Guide to indian country: Windspeaker's aboriginal tourism supplement*, Wind Speaker, June 2002.

[23] Maria Garcia, *Dance honors courage of the steelworkers*.

[24] Shakti Gawain, *Creative visualization: Use the power of your imagination to create what you want in your life*, Bantam, 1997.

[25] Louise I. Gerdes (ed.), *Contemporary issues companion: Battered women*, Greenhaven Press, 1998.

[26] Sir Martin Gilbert, *The righteous: Unsung heroes of the holocaust*, Henry Holt and Co., 1993.

[27] Sidney Goldstein, *The basketball coach's bible: A comprehensive and systematic guide to coaching*, Golden Aura Publishing, 1994.

[28] Daniel Goleman, *Social intelligence: The new science of human relationships*, Bantam, 1996.

[29] ———, *Emotional intelligence: Why it can matter more than IQ*, Bantam, 1997.

[30] Dan Gorlin, *Songs of west africa: A collection of over 80 traditional west african folk songs and chants in 6 languages with translations, annotations*, Aloki Press, 2000.

[31] Israel Gutman, *Resistance: The warsaw ghetto uprising*, Houghton Mifflin, 1994.

[32] David Halberstam, *The children*, Random House, 1998.

[33] Caroline Kennedy, *Profiles in courage for our time*, Hyperion, 2002.

[34] Frances Moore Lappe, *You have the power: Choosing courage in a culture of fear*, Penguin, 2004.

[35] Thomas Lewis, Fari Amini, and Richard Lannon, *A general theory of love*, Random House, 2000.

[36] Shane J. Lopez (ed.), *Positive psychology: Exploring the best in people*, vol. 1, Praeger Publishers, 2008.

[37] Marcus Luttrell, *Lone survivor: The eyewitness account of operation redwing and the lost heroes of seal team 10*, Little, Brown and Company, 2007.

[38] Richard Marcinko, *Rogue warrior*, Pocket, 1993.

[39] Jeffrey Moussaieff Masson and Susan McCarthy, *When elephants weep: the emotional lives of animals*, Delta, 1996.

[40] Greg Mortenson and David Oliver Relin, *Three cups of tea: One man's mission to promote peace... one school at a time*, Penguin Books, 2007.

[41] Davia Nelson, Nikki Silva, and et al., *Sonic memorial project*, Recorded interviews, 2006.

[42] M. Scott Peck, *People of the lie: The hope for healing human evil*, Touchstone, 1998.

[43] Jayne Pettit, *A time to fight back*, Houghton Mifflin, 1996.

[44] Richard Picciotto and Daniel Palsner, *Last man down: A firefighter's story of survival and escape from the world trade center*, Berkley Hardcover, 2002.

[45] Colin L. Powell and Joseph E. Persico, *My american journey*, Ballantine Books, 1996.

[46] C. L. S. Pury and R. Kowalski, *Distinctions between general and personal courage*, Journal of Positive Psychology **2** (2007), 99–114.

[47] ———, *Human strengths, courageous actions, and general and personal courage*, Journal of Positive Psychology **2** (2007), 120–128.

[48] Stanley Rachman, *Fear and courage*, W.H. Freeman & Company, 1989.

[49] Richard L. Rashke, *Escape from sobibor*, Houghton Mifflin, 1982.

[50] Kathleen K. Reardon, *Courage as a skill*, Harvard Business Review (2007).

[51] Hans A. Schmitt, *Quakers and nazis: Inner light in outer darkness*, University of Missouri Press (1997).

[52] James B. Stewart, *Heart of a soldier: A story of love, heroism, and september 11th*, Simon and Schuster, 2002.

[53] Nehama Tec, *When light pierced the darkness: Christian rescue of jews in nazi-occupied poland*, Oxford University Press, 1986.

[54] Harriet Tubman, *Harriet tubman: The moses of her people*, Citadel, 2000.

[55] Susan Ware, *Forgotten heroes: Inspiring american portraits from our leading historians*, Free Press, 1998.

[56] Susan Weitzman, *"not to people like us": Hidden abuse in upscale marriages*, Basic Books, 2001.

[57] Phillip Zimbardo, *Stanford prison experiment*, 1971.